The *Treasury* of Newfoundland Dishes

BOULDER
PUBLICATIONS

Library and Archives Canada Cataloguing in Publication

The treasury of Newfoundland dishes / Jill Whitaker, editor.

First ed. published 1958 under title A treasury of Newfoundland dishes.
ISBN 978-0-9809144-0-5

1. Cookery, Canadian–Newfoundland style. I. Whitaker, Jill

TX715.6.T7355 2008   641.59718   C2008-905822-4

Layout: John Andrews

Printed in Canada

boulderpublications.ca

Newfoundland
Labrador

We acknowledge the financial support of the Government of Newfoundland and Labrador through the Department of Tourism, Culture and Recreation.

INTRODUCTION

Welcome to the 50th-anniversary edition of *The Treasury of Newfoundland Dishes*, first published in 1958 and reprinted eleven times. Despite being out of print since 1983, the Treasury has maintained its reputation as one of the best collections of authentic local recipes ever published.

The cookbook was a joint project of the Newfoundland Home Economics Association and Maple Leaf Milling Company. Homemakers across Newfoundland submitted thousands of recipes as well as local sayings and lore; from this collection, The Treasury was created.

The public face of Maple Leaf, which produced Cream of the West flour, was Sally West, a home economist originally from Ontario, whose actual name was Ethel Whitham. She and many of the home economists who selected and tested the recipes have since died. Maple Leaf has sold its flour business to Smucker Foods, and Cream of the West flour is no longer produced.

But the Treasury itself remains alive in kitchens and cupboards of countless homes. Copies have been handed down from mothers to their children, given as gifts, used until they have fallen apart, and their absence mourned when replacement copies were no longer available. With this new edition, another generation can enjoy dishes which have long been celebrated at the tables of families throughout Newfoundland.

Christine Macdonald, a home economist on the original committee, noted that some recipes lack ingredients that are considered standard today (e.g., eggs) because they weren't always available. Today, these recipes are especially appreciated by people with specific food allergies.

Since the publication of the first edition of *The Treasury of Newfoundland Dishes*, Canada has adopted the metric system; a conversion chart has been included for the reader's convenience.

A sincere thank you to those who participated in this project, especially the contributing homemakers of Newfoundland and the original committee members who created the book.

Jill Whitaker, B.Sc. (H.Ec.)

A Message from the

NEWFOUNDLAND
HOME ECONOMICS ASSOCIATION

We, the members of the Newfoundland Home Economics Association, have enjoyed making the final selection of Newfoundland recipes from those sent in as a result of the radio programme sponsored by the Maple Leaf Milling Company. In approving the recipes to be included in this "Treasury of Newfoundland Dishes", we have endeavoured to choose those that will preserve the distinctive cooking art of our Island along with good standard recipes used in any home. We sincerely hope that you will find them tasty.

We invite you to join us in a Newfoundland toast:—

"I bows toward you."

"I nods accordin'."

"I catches your eye and I smiles!"

Yours sincerely

Newfoundland Home Economics Association

TABLE OF CONTENTS

YEAST BREADS AND ROLLS

Everybody likes home-baked bread and rolls—the golden, crusty goodness and the grand fragrance they bring to your kitchen.

BREADS:

FAMILY WHITE BREAD
WHITE BREAD
NEWFOUNDLAND WHITE BREAD
BROWN BREAD
MOLASSES WHOLE WHEAT BREAD
WHOLE WHEAT BREAD
ROLLED OATS AND WHOLE
   WHEAT BREAD

OATMEAL BREAD
CORN OAT BREAD
HEALTH LOAF
BROWN SUGAR RAISIN BREAD
DATE AND NUT BREAD
CHRISTMAS STOLLEN
OLD FASHIONED CHRISTMAS
   SWEET BREAD

ROLLS:

ROLLS
ROLLS—OVERNIGHT
LUNCH ROLLS
SPOON ROLLS

EVERLASTING ROLLS
PARKER HOUSE ROLLS
BOWKNOTS
FRENCH ROLLS

SWEET DOUGHS:

HONEY TWIST
BRAIDED ORANGE ROLL

CINNAMON ROLLS
HOT CROSS BUNS

FAMILY WHITE BREAD

2   packages or cakes of yeast
½ cup lukewarm water
1   teaspoon granulated sugar
4   cups liquid (milk or powdered milk and water)
1   tablespoon granulated sugar
1   tablespoon salt
2   tablespoons shortening or margarine
15 cups (approximately) sifted CREAM OF THE WEST Flour

Dissolve yeast in lukewarm water to which sugar has been added. Let stand for 10 minutes.

Heat liquid, sugar, salt and shortening. Cool to lukewarm. Add dissolved yeast.

Add 6 cups of flour and beat until it bubbles. Add more flour to make a dough which is just stiff enough to be handled.

Knead for about 10 minutes on a lightly floured board.

Let rise, covered, until doubled in bulk. Then, break down the air bubbles and divide into loaf size pieces. Shape and put into greased bread pans. Cover lightly and let rise until doubled in bulk.

Bake at 350° F. for one hour.

Note: If a soft crust is desired, grease the top of bread after taking from the oven.

> *Grounds—sediment of spruce beer or hops used as yeast or barm in making bread.*

WHITE BREAD

1   package yeast
½ cup lukewarm water
1   teaspoon granulated sugar
½ cup milk
½ cup water
1   tablespoon granulated sugar
2   teaspoons salt
2   tablespoons shortening
4½ cups sifted CREAM OF THE WEST Flour

Dissolve sugar in warm water; sprinkle yeast over it and let stand for 10 minutes.

Combine milk, water, sugar, salt and shortening; heat to scalding point. Cool to lukewarm.

Stir yeast mixture; add to lukewarm liquids.

Place sifted flour in a large bowl; make a well in centre of the dry ingredients. Add the liquids and blend to form a fairly stiff dough. (½ cup more flour may be added, if necessary.)

Knead for 7 to 8 minutes on a lightly floured board.

Place dough in a greased bowl; grease the top, cover and let rise in a warm place until doubled in bulk (about 1½ hours).

Punch down, form into 2 balls and let stand for 15 minutes. Shape into loaves; place in greased pans. Let rise until doubled (about 1 hour).

Bake at 400° F. for 30 to 35 minutes.

NEWFOUNDLAND WHITE BREAD

2   packages yeast
1   cup lukewarm water
2   teaspoons granulated sugar
2   cups scalded milk
1   cup lukewarm water
1   tablespoon salt
2   teaspoons granulated sugar
½ cup butter
12 cups sifted CREAM OF THE WEST Flour

Add yeast to 1 cup lukewarm water in which 2 teaspoons sugar have been dissolved. Let stand in a warm place for 10 minutes.

Scald milk; add water, salt, sugar and butter to it; cool to lukewarm. Stir dissolved yeast and add it to the lukewarm milk mixture. Then add half of the flour and beat until smooth. Gradually add remaining flour, blending in last of it with your hand.

Knead dough for 10 minutes or until smooth and elastic. Place in a greased bowl; grease top of the dough; cover and let rise in a warm place until doubled in bulk (about 1½ hours).

Punch down the dough, form in 4 balls and let rest for 15 minutes. Then shape into loaves; place in greased pans and let rise until doubled (about 1 hour). Bake at 400° F. for 35 to 40 minutes.

> *Toutons—bread which had been made the day before and hastily baked in the morning without a second 'rising'. Sometimes done in round pans on top of the stove.*

BROWN BREAD

1   package dry or compressed yeast
1/4 cup lukewarm water
1   teaspoon granulated sugar
1½   cups rolled oats
3   cups boiling water
1   tablespoon salt
4   tablespoons shortening
½   cup molasses
1   cup graham flour
About 5 cups sifted
     CREAM OF THE WEST Flour

Soak yeast in lukewarm water and sugar for 10 minutes. In the meantime, pour boiling water over the rolled oats; add salt and shortening. Stir and allow to cool until lukewarm.

Add yeast mixture to cooled rolled oats; then blend in molasses, graham flour and enough white flour to make it easy to handle. Knead until smooth and let rise in a greased bowl until double in bulk. (About 1 hour). Punch down, shape into three loaves and let rise in pans.

Bake at 375° F. for 45 to 50 minutes.

Whole Wheat Flour may be used instead of graham flour.

MOLASSES WHOLE WHEAT BREAD

2   packages dry yeast
4   teaspoons granulated sugar
1   cup lukewarm water
1½   cups scalded milk
2   cups water
½   cup margarine
½   cup molasses
2   tablespoons salt
6   cups whole wheat flour
5   cups sifted
     CREAM OF THE WEST Flour
1   tablespoon finely grated orange rind, if desired

Add yeast and sugar to lukewarm water; stir well. Let stand in a warm place for 10 minutes.

Meanwhile scald milk; add water, margarine, molasses and salt. Cool to lukewarm. Add dissolved yeast to the lukewarm milk mixture. Add flour cup by cup until dough is stiff enough to handle. Sprinkle with finely grated orange rind.

Knead until smooth. Place in a greased bowl; brush with a little melted butter. Let rise in a warm place about 1¼ hours (until almost doubled in bulk). Then knead enough to release gas bubbles and cut into four equal parts. Form into balls and let rise for 15 minutes.

Shape into four loaves and place in greased pans. Let rise about 1 hour. Bake in a 400° F. oven for 30 to 35 minutes.

WHOLE WHEAT BREAD

1/4 cup lukewarm water
1   teaspoon granulated sugar
1   package yeast
4   cups whole wheat flour
2   cups sifted
     CREAM OF THE WEST Flour
1   tablespoon salt
½   cup dark brown sugar
4   tablespoons butter
1¾   cups lukewarm water

Add 1 teaspoon granulated sugar to the lukewarm water and sprinkle yeast over the top. Let stand for 10 minutes.

Combine flours, salt and brown sugar in large bowl; rub in the butter. Make a well in the centre of the dry ingredients; add dissolved yeast which has been well stirred and the lukewarm water. Mix well.

Knead on a lightly floured board until dough is soft and elastic (from 8 to 10 minutes). Place in a greased bowl, cover and let rise for 1½ hours or until doubled in bulk. Knead dough down and form into two balls; let stand for 10 minutes. Shape into loaves; place in greased pans and let rise for 1½ hours.

Bake at 400° F. for 30 to 35 minutes.

Note: Some of the dough may be shaped into roles; allowed to rise for about one hour and baked at 375° F. for 20 minutes.

ROLLED OAT AND WHOLE WHEAT BREAD

2   cups boiling water
2   cups quick cooking rolled oats
½   cup molasses
1/4 cup brown sugar
½   cup shortening
1   package dry or compressed yeast
½   cup lukewarm water
1   teaspoon granulated sugar
4   cups warm water
2   cups sifted whole wheat flour

6 cups sifted
 CREAM OF THE WEST Flour
2 tablespoons salt

Add rolled oats to the boiling water and cook for 3 minutes. Pour into a bowl and add the molasses, brown sugar and shortening. Set aside and cool to lukewarm.

Dissolve the yeast in lukewarm water to which you have added 1 teaspoon granulated sugar.

Add 4 cups warm water to the lukewarm porridge mixture; then add the dissolved yeast and sifted flours and salt. Knead to a smooth and elastic dough (about 10 minutes). Grease the surface of the dough and let rise, covered, in a greased bowl until doubled in bulk. Knead for 2 minutes and let rise again until doubled.

Divide into loaves; place in greased pans and let rise until loaves are doubled in size. (Keep covered with a damp cloth.)

Bake at 350° F. for 50 to 60 minutes. When done, grease or glaze the crust.

Note: This dough makes excellent rolls if 2 packages yeast used. Raisins, candied fruit, peel or nuts may be added for variety.

A spurt—active work of short duration—

"He was up in the States for a spurt."

OATMEAL BREAD

2 packages yeast
1 cup lukewarm water
2 teaspoons granulated sugar

Add yeast to the lukewarm water in which the sugar has been dissolved. Let stand for 10 minutes and then stir to blend.

Combine in a large bowl:
1 cup scalded milk
⅔ cup melted shortening
½ cup granulated sugar
2 teaspoons salt

Blend and then stir in:
1 cup sifted
 CREAM OF THE WEST Flour
2 eggs, well beaten
 dissolved yeast
1½ cups uncooked rolled oats

Add additional CREAM OF THE WEST Flour to make a dough which is stiff enough to knead (about 5 cups sifted flour).

Knead dough for 8 to 10 minutes. Place in a greased bowl, cover and let rise for 1 hour. Punch down.

Place flattened dough on a lightly greased board; sprinkle with a mixture of 1 tablespoon granulated sugar and ½ to 1 teaspoon cinnamon. Knead a few times to work this into the dough.

Cut dough in 3 equal parts; form into smooth balls and cover. After 15 minutes form each ball of dough into a loaf. Place in greased loaf pans, pressing dough against the sides so it will rise more evenly.

Cover and let rise until doubled in bulk (45 to 60 minutes). Bake at 375° F. for 40 to 45 minutes.

CORN OAT BREAD

1 cup rolled oats
⅓ cup cornmeal
2 teaspoons salt
1 tablespoon shortening
½ cup molasses
½ cup brown sugar
2½ cups boiling water
1 package yeast
½ cup lukewarm water
1 teaspoon granulated sugar
6 to 6½ cups sifted
 CREAM OF THE WEST Flour

Combine first six ingredients; add boiling water and mix well. Set aside to cool.

Add yeast to lukewarm water in which 1 teaspoon sugar has been dissolved. Let stand for 10 minutes. Then stir briskly and add it to the lukewarm cereal mixture.

Add flour gradually, beating with a spoon. Work in last of flour by hand. Knead for about 5 minutes and then let rise until doubled in bulk (about 1½ hours).

Divide dough into 3 balls; let rest for 15 minutes, then shape into loaves. Place in greased loaf pans and let rise until doubled (about one hour).

Bake at 350° F. for 50 to 60 minutes. Rub with butter while hot.

HEALTH LOAF

1   package or cake of yeast
1   cup lukewarm water
1   teaspoon granulated sugar
1   cup scalded milk
4   tablespoons light brown sugar
2   tablespoons butter
2   teaspoons salt
1½ cups graham flour
3 to 3½ cups sifted
    CREAM OF THE WEST Flour

Dissolve yeast in lukewarm water to which 1 teaspoon sugar has been added. Let stand for 10 minutes.

Scald milk; dissolve sugar, butter and salt in it. Cool to lukewarm. Add the yeast.

Add flours gradually, until dough can be handled. Knead thoroughly. Cover and set to rise for about 2 hours.

When doubled in bulk, mould into loaves, place in greased pans, cover and let rise again for one hour.

Bake at 350° F. for 45 minutes.

Note: This may be fortified by the addition of 3 tablespoons each of wheat germ and powdered milk.

BROWN SUGAR RAISIN BREAD

2   packages dry or compressed yeast
½ cup lukewarm water
2   teaspoons granulated sugar
3   cups raisins
    Enough boiling water to cover raisins
2½ cups brown sugar
5   teaspoons salt
½ cup margarine
2   cups boiling water
2   cups evaporated milk
2   eggs (optional)
1   teaspoon baking soda
12 cups sifted
    CREAM OF THE WEST Flour

Soak yeast in lukewarm water to which 2 teaspoons granulated sugar have been added. Pour enough boiling water over raisins to cover; let stand for 5 minutes and then pour off water and dredge raisins with flour.

Combine brown sugar, salt and margarine; add 2 cups boiling water. Stir until margarine melts. Add milk and cool to lukewarm. Add beaten eggs, if desired.

Add yeast to cooled milk mixture; add soda and half of the flour. Beat until smooth. Now add remaining flour and dredged raisins. Knead to make an elastic dough. Let rise, covered, in a greased bowl until double in bulk.

Shape into 5 large loaf pans; let rise. Bake at 425° F. for 35 to 40 minutes.

Note: Let bread stand until a day old, as it will then slice more easily.

DATE AND NUT BREAD

½ cup lukewarm water
2   teaspoons granulated sugar
2   packages yeast
1½ cups scalded milk
1   cup brown sugar
2   teaspoons salt
½ cup shortening
2   eggs, well beaten
1   cup chopped dates
½ cup chopped walnuts
6 to 6½ cups sifted
    CREAM OF THE WEST Flour

Dissolve sugar and yeast in lukewarm water. Let stand for 10 minutes. Meanwhile scald milk and add sugar, salt and shortening to it. Stir until shortening melts and cool to lukewarm. Add yeast mixture which has been stirred briskly with a fork and the beaten eggs. Flour the dates and walnuts. Add half of the flour; beat until smooth and then add the floured dates and walnuts. Add remaining flour.

Knead for 8 to 10 minutes on a lightly floured board. Place in a greased bowl; cover and let rise for 1½ hours or until doubled in bulk. Punch down and shape into 2 balls; let stand for 10 minutes. Shape into loaves and place in greased pans. Let rise until doubled (about one hour).

Bake at 400° F. for 35 to 40 minutes.

> "Let's have a boil-up on the bogie."
> Bogie—a very small stove with no oven and used for heat only.

CHRISTMAS STOLLEN

1   package dry or compressed yeast
¼ cup lukewarm water
1   teaspoon granulated sugar
1   cup milk
1   cup granulated sugar

¾ cup butter or shortening
1 tablespoon salt
2 eggs, well beaten
4½ to 5 cups sifted
   CREAM OF THE WEST Flour
2 teaspoons grated lemon rind
½ teaspoon nutmeg
1 cup seeded raisins
½ cup mixed candied peel
½ cup halved candied cherries

Dissolve yeast in lukewarm water to which 1 teaspoon sugar has been added.

Scald milk; add sugar, shortening and salt. Stir until shortening melts. Cool to lukewarm.

Add dissolved yeast to the lukewarm milk mixture; stir in well beaten eggs. Add flour, lemon rind and nutmeg. Knead until smooth and elastic (about 10 minutes).

Place dough in a greased bowl; cover and let rise in a warm place until doubled in bulk. Punch down. Work floured fruit into the dough. Shape into 2 long oval loaves. Brush with melted butter; let rise again.

Bake at 400° F. for 15 minutes; lower temperature to 350° F. and bake for an additional 30 to 40 minutes.

When done, brush with this mixture:

2 tablespoons milk
2 teaspoons granulated sugar
½ teaspoon vanilla

OLD FASHIONED CHRISTMAS SWEET BREAD

2 packages dry or compressed yeast
1 cup lukewarm water
2 teaspoons granulated sugar
3 cups lukewarm water
1 cup molasses
3 tablespoons melted butter
12 cups sifted
   CREAM OF THE WEST Flour
6 tablespoons granulated sugar
4 teaspoons salt
3 cups raisins
2 to 3 teaspoons caraway seed
   (if desired)

Dissolve yeast in 1 cup lukewarm water to which 2 teaspoons sugar have been added.

Combine 3 cups lukewarm water, molasses and the melted butter. Sift dry ingredients; add the raisins and caraway seed. Stir dissolved yeast into the molasses mixture;

stir in flour mixture. Knead for about 10 minutes.

Place in a greased bowl and turn dough over 2 or 3 times to grease the top and thus prevent a crust from forming. Cover, and let rise until doubled (about 2 hours). Divide dough into 4 or 5 pieces and form into loaves. Place in greased pans and let rise until doubled in bulk (about 1 hour).

Bake at 375° F. until loaves give a hollow sound when tapped (about 1 hour).
Brush tops with melted butter while hot, if a soft crust is desired.

The old custom is that Christmas celebrations begin on Christmas Eve with a Thanksgiving meal of salt fish followed by sweet raisin bread called "Christmas Fruit Loaf." Fishing was the means of livelihood and so fish had its place in thanksgiving before the day of feasting.

ROLLS

1 cup scalded milk
¼ cup margarine
¼ cup granulated sugar
4 teaspoons salt
1 package dry or compressed yeast
1 cup lukewarm water
1 teaspoon granulated sugar
2 eggs, beaten
7 to 8 cups sifted
   CREAM OF THE WEST Flour

Scald milk; add margarine, sugar and salt; stir until margarine melts. Cool to lukewarm.

Dissolve yeast in the lukewarm water to which you have added 1 teaspoon sugar.

Add dissolved yeast and beaten eggs to the lukewarm milk mixture.

Stir in the flour to make a soft dough.

Knead until smooth and satiny. Place in a lightly greased bowl and let rise until doubled in bulk. Punch down and mould into rolls; place in a greased pan. Let rise until doubled in size.

Bake at 350° F. for 20 to 25 minutes.

ROLLS—OVERNIGHT

1   pint milk
2   tablespoons granulated sugar
2   tablespoons butter
1   yeast cake
 ½   cup warm water
1   teaspoon granulated sugar
5½   cups sifted
     CREAM OF THE WEST Flour
1   tablespoon salt
1   egg
 ½   cup sifted
     CREAM OF THE WEST Flour

Scald milk in saucepan. Add 2 tablespoons sugar and butter. Pour into mixing bowl and cool to lukewarm. Dissolve yeast in warm water to which 1 teaspoon sugar has been added. Let stand 10 minutes, then stir well with a fork. Add to cooled milk mixture and stir well. Sift flour and salt together. Add one-half of the dry ingredients to the liquid mixture and stir well. Add the rest of the flour, working the last in by using your hands. Knead 8 to 10 minutes. Place in greased bowl and grease the top of the dough. Cover with a clean tea towel and set to rise until doubled in bulk (approximately 1½ hours). Punch down. Add egg and work it in by using your hands; then add ½ cup flour to knead the dough. Set dough to rise in a greased bowl overnight. Grease top of dough and cover with clean tea towel. In the morning, punch dough down and let rise again in bowl (approximately 1 hour). Punch down, shape dough into balls and place in greased pans. Cover and let rise in pans (approximately 1 hour). Bake in a 400° F. oven for 20 minutes.

LUNCH ROLLS

 ½   cup lukewarm water
1   teaspoon granulated sugar
1   package yeast
1¼   cups scalded milk
2   tablespoons granulated sugar
1   teaspoon salt
2   tablespoons shortening
1   egg, well beaten
4½   cups sifted
     CREAM OF THE WEST Flour

Dissolve 1 teaspoon sugar in lukewarm water; add the yeast and let stand in a warm place for 10 minutes.

Scald milk; add sugar, salt and shortening; cool to lukewarm. Stir yeast well; add it to the lukewarm milk mixture. Add beaten egg. Beat in half of the flour; then work in remaining flour and knead for 5 minutes. Place in a greased bowl; cover and let rise until doubled in bulk (about 1½ hours).

Punch down and shape dough into small round balls. Place 1 inch apart in a greased pan and allow to rise for about ½ hour. Brush with melted shortening and bake at 425° F. for 20 minutes.
Makes 3 dozen rolls.

SPOON ROLLS

1   package dry or compressed yeast
 ¼   cup lukewarm water
1   teaspoon granulated sugar
 ¾   cup scalded milk
 ⅓   cup shortening
1   teaspoon salt
 ¼   cup granulated sugar
 ½   cup cold water
1   egg, beaten
3½   cups sifted
     CREAM OF THE WEST Flour

Dissolve yeast in lukewarm water to which 1 teaspoon sugar has been added. Let stand for 10 minutes.
Scald the milk; add shortening, salt and sugar; stir until shortening is melted. Add cold water.
Add dissolved yeast to cooled milk mixture. Blend in beaten egg and sifted flour.
Place in a greased bowl and let rise in a warm place until double in bulk (40 to 60 minutes). Then, stir down dough and spoon into well greased muffin tins until half full.

Let rise again until dough has reached edge of the muffin cups and is nicely rounded (about 45 minutes). Bake in a 400° F. oven for 15 to 20 minutes.

EVERLASTING ROLLS

1   package dry or compressed yeast
 ½   cup lukewarm water
1   teaspoon granulated sugar
 ½   cup shortening
 ½   cup granulated sugar
1   egg, beaten
1½   teaspoons salt
2   cups warm water
8   cups sifted
     CREAM OF THE WEST Flour

Dissolve yeast in ½ cup lukewarm water to which 1 teaspoon granulated sugar has been added; let stand for 10 minutes.

Cream shortening well with the sugar; add the beaten egg, salt, warm water and dissolved yeast. Then add sifted flour and knead to an elastic dough. Let rise in a warm place until doubled in bulk.

Shape into rolls; place in greased pans and let rise again until doubled in bulk (about one hour).

Bake at 400° F. for 20 minutes.

Note: This dough may be kept in the refrigerator to be used at some later time. When it is used, knead down, shape rolls and let them rise in pans until doubled in bulk.

PARKER HOUSE ROLLS

2 cups scalded milk
4 tablespoons granulated sugar
1 package dry or compressed yeast
2 tablespoons melted lard or butter
6 cups sifted
CREAM OF THE WEST Flour
1 tablespoon salt

Scald milk; add sugar and cool to lukewarm. Dissolve yeast in the lukewarm milk. Add melted fat and ½ of the flour. Beat until perfectly smooth.

Cover and let rise in a warm place until light (about 45 minutes). Add remaining flour and the salt. Knead well. Place in a greased bowl and let rise until doubled in bulk.

Roll out dough until it is ¼ inch thick; brush lightly with melted butter; cut with biscuit cutter. Grease through the centre with a dull edged knife and fold over.

Place in a well greased pan (1 inch apart). Cover and let rise until light.

Bake for 15 to 20 minutes at 400° F.

BOWKNOTS

½ cup scalded milk
¾ cup water
1   teaspoon granulated sugar
1   package dry yeast
2   tablespoons soft shortening
3   tablespoons granulated sugar
1½ teaspoon salt
1   egg, well beaten
5   cups sifted
CREAM OF THE WEST Flour

Scald milk; add water and remove ½ cup. Dissolve 1 teaspoon sugar in this ½ cup warm liquid and sprinkle with yeast. Let stand for 10 minutes.

Meanwhile, add shortening, 3 tablespoons sugar, salt and well beaten egg to remaining liquid. Sift flour into a large bowl.

Add the bubbly yeast to the egg mixture. Pour over the flour and mix until blended. Knead on a lightly floured board until smooth (about 5 minutes). Place in a greased bowl; cover and let rise until doubled in bulk (about 1 hour). Punch down and let rise again.

Press dough into a rectangle; cut into 24 pieces and roll into pieces which are 6 inches long and ½ inch thick. Tie each in a knot; place on greased baking sheets. Cover and let rise (about 30 minutes).

Bake at 375° F. for 25 minutes. Place on a rack; brush with melted butter.

FRENCH ROLLS

1   tablespoon granulated sugar
1   teaspoon salt
1   tablespoon shortening
1   tablespoon margarine
1   cup boiling water
1   package of yeast
4½ cups sifted
CREAM OF THE WEST Flour
2   egg whites

Combine sugar, salt, fat and boiling water; cool to lukewarm. Add the yeast and let stand for 10 minutes. Then add 1 cup of flour and beat for 3 minutes. Fold in the stiffly beaten egg whites. Add remaining flour to make a dough. Knead for 10 minutes.

Place in a bowl; cover and let rise for 1½ hours or until doubled in bulk. Punch down and let rise until again doubled in size. Knead for one minute.

Cut into about 24 pieces; shape into rolls. Place on greased baking sheets which have been sprinkled with cornmeal. Let rise until doubled.

Bake at 450° F. for 20 minutes.

Note: A large pan of boiling water under the rolls during the baking helps to increase the crustiness.

HONEY TWIST

2 packages dry yeast or 2 yeast
   cakes
1 cup lukewarm water
2 teaspoons granulated sugar
1 cup scalded milk
¼ cup butter
½ cup granulated sugar
2 teaspoons salt
2 eggs, beaten
7 cups sifted
   CREAM OF THE WEST Flour

Sprinkle yeast over warm water in which 2 teaspoons sugar have been dissolved. Let stand for 10 minutes.

Scald milk; pour it over the butter, sugar and salt. Cool to lukewarm. Add yeast and well beaten eggs to the lukewarm milk mixture.

Beat in flour to form a soft dough. Knead for 5 to 7 minutes on a lightly floured board. Let rise in a covered, greased bowl until doubled in bulk (about 1 hour).

Punch down the dough and divide in two. Shape each into a long roll 1-inch in diameter. Coil rolls into 2 greased baking pans (about 12-inch x 9-inch) beginning at the outside and covering the bottoms. Brush with honey topping.

HONEY TOPPING

¼ cup butter
⅔ cup confectioner's sugar
1 egg white
2 tablespoons honey

Cream all ingredients together and brush on the twisted dough. Let rise in a warm place until doubled (about 45 minutes). Bake at 375° F. for 25 to 30 minutes.

BRAIDED ORANGE ROLL

1 package yeast
1 teaspoon granulated sugar
¼ cup lukewarm water
1¼ cups scalded milk
½ cup shortening
⅓ cup granulated sugar
2 teaspoons salt
¼ cup orange juice
2 teaspoons grated orange rind
2 eggs, well beaten
5½ to 6 cups sifted
   CREAM OF THE WEST Flour

Sprinkle yeast over ¼ cup lukewarm water in which 1 teaspoon sugar has been dissolved. Let stand for 10 minutes.

Scald milk; add shortening, sugar and salt. Cool to lukewarm and add orange juice and rind, beaten eggs and yeast which has been stirred. Add the flour and work into a dough. Knead for about 5 minutes on a lightly floured board. Let rise in a covered greased bowl until doubled in bulk (about 1½ hours).

Punch down dough; roll into a rectangle which is about 18 inches x 8 inches. Cut into six long strips. Braid these dough strips into two loaves; place on greased cookie sheets and let rise for about 30 minutes.

Bake at 400° F. for 30 to 35 minutes. Remove from the oven and spread with topping made from these ingredients:

1½ cups sifted icing sugar
2 teaspoons grated orange rind
3 tablespoons orange juice

CINNAMON ROLLS

1 package dry or compressed yeast
¼ cup lukewarm water
1 teaspoon granulated sugar
1 cup scalded milk
¼ cup granulated sugar
1 teaspoon salt
2 tablespoons shortening
4 cups sifted
   CREAM OF THE WEST Flour
1 egg, beaten

Soften yeast in lukewarm water to which you have added 1 teaspoon sugar.

Scald the milk; add ¼ cup sugar, salt and shortening. Mix and cool to lukewarm.

Add yeast mixture to the cooled milk mixture; stir in 1½ cups sifted flour. Add the beaten egg and mix until smooth. Add remaining flour; knead. Place dough in a greased bowl and let rise until doubled in bulk. Punch down and let rise again until almost doubled.

Knead and roll dough into an 18-inch x 9-inch rectangle. Brush with ¼ cup melted butter.

Combine:

½ cup granulated sugar
2 teaspoons cinnamon
⅓ cup raisins

Sprinkle this mixture over the dough. Roll up like a jelly roll. Cut in 1-inch slices.

Combine:

½ cup melted butter
¾ cup brown sugar

Spread this mixture over bottom of two 8-inch x 8-inch x 2-inch pans. Dot with walnut halves.

Place rolls in pans. Let rise until double. Bake at 375° F. for 25 minutes.

HOT CROSS BUNS

1   **cup scalded milk**
1   **tablespoon granulated sugar**
1   **package dry or compressed yeast**
3¼ **cups sifted**
     CREAM OF THE WEST Flour
 ¼ **cup butter**
 ⅓ **cup granulated sugar**
1   **egg, well beaten**
 ¼ **teaspoon salt**
 ¼ **cup raisins**

Dissolve yeast and 1 tablespoon sugar in milk, which has been scalded and cooled to lukewarm. Add 1½ cups flour and beat until smooth. Cover and let rise in a warm place until light (about 1 hour).

Cream butter and sugar; add well beaten egg and salt. Add these to the sponge and then blend in floured raisins and the remaining flour to form a soft dough.

Knead lightly on a board; place in a greased bowl. Cover and let rise in a warm place until double in bulk (about 2 hours). Then shape with hands into medium-sized round buns; place in well greased pans about 2 inches apart. Cover and let rise about 1 hour.

Glaze top with egg diluted with water. Use a sharp knife to cut a cross in the top of each bun.

Bake at 400° F. for 15 to 20 minutes.

Just before removing from the oven, brush the tops with sugar moistened with water. While hot, fill the cross with plain frosting.

NOTES:

QUICK BREADS

You can serve delicious quick breads all day long...pancakes for breakfast, fruit loaf with lunch, and tender, flaky biscuits at dinner.

BISCUITS AND BUNS:

DELICATE TEA BUNS

CREAM BISCUITS

SCONES

SCONES

SALT PORK BUNS

ROLLED OAT BUNS

RAISIN BUNS

ORANGE DATE ROLLS

PINWHEEL ONION ROLLS

LOCHLEVEN (POTATO) BISCUITS

PANCAKES:

PANCAKES

BLUEBERRY PANCAKES

MUFFINS:

PLAIN MUFFINS

OATMEAL MUFFINS

BRAN MUFFINS

BLUEBERRY MUFFINS

CRANBERRY MUFFINS

ENGLISH MUFFINS

COFFEE KUCHEN

LOAF BREADS, Etc.:

NUT BREAD

DATE BREAD

DATE LOAF

BLUEBERRY NUT BREAD

NUT AND RAISIN BREAD

CRANBERRY BREAD

BANANA QUICK BREAD

PARTRIDGEBERRY—ORANGE BREAD

APRICOT BREAD

PINEAPPLE NUT BREAD

CINNAMON BREAD

APPLE RAISIN COFFEE CAKE

DELICATE TEA BUNS

2 cups sifted
  CREAM OF THE WEST Flour
4 teaspoons baking powder
½ teaspoon salt
1 tablespoon granulated sugar
¼ cup shortening
⅔ cup milk and water

Sift dry ingredients; cut in shortening. Add liquid to make a soft dough. Toss on floured board; knead lightly, 8 or 10 times. Roll to ½ inch thickness; cut out with round cutter. Bake on a greased cookie sheet for 10 to 12 minutes at 450° F.

CREAM BISCUITS

1 cup sifted
  CREAM OF THE WEST Flour
2 teaspoons baking powder
½ teaspoon salt
½ cup heavy cream

Sift together the flour, baking powder and salt. Make a well in the centre of these dry ingredients. Add cream and stir quickly until ingredients are moistened. With lightly floured hands, pat dough into a rectangle ½ inch thick on a greased cookie sheet. Cut into 6 squares but do not separate. Brush top with melted butter. Bake at 450° F. for 12 to 15 minutes.

SCONES

2 cups sifted
  CREAM OF THE WEST Flour
½ teaspoon baking soda
1 teaspoon cream of tartar
½ teaspoon salt
3 tablespoons margarine
3 tablespoons shortening
¼ cup granulated sugar
⅓ cup currants
⅓ cup sultanas
1 egg yolk (beaten)
½ cup milk

Sift flour, baking soda, cream of tartar and salt. Work in margarine and shortening; add sugar and floured fruit. Combine beaten egg yolk and milk; mix into dry ingredients.

Knead lightly on a floured board. Roll to ½" thickness, cut into 2" rounds. Place on greased baking sheets and bake at 425° F. for 12 to 15 minutes.

The scones may be brushed over with a little egg yolk or milk before baking, or with melted butter as soon as cooked.

SCONES

2 cups sifted
  CREAM OF THE WEST Flour
4 teaspoons baking powder
2 teaspoons granulated sugar
½ teaspoon salt
4 tablespoons butter
2 eggs, beaten (set aside a little of the egg whites)
⅓ cup milk or cream

Mix and sift dry ingredients. Cut in butter with pastry blender. Add beaten eggs (small amount of egg white reserved) then add milk or cream. Remove to floured board. Pat or roll to ¾-inch thickness. Cut into rounds, squares or triangles. Brush the tops with the reserved egg white and sprinkle with sugar. Bake in hot oven 425° F. for 15 minutes.

SALT PORK BUNS

1 cup finely chopped salt pork
4 cups sifted
  CREAM OF THE WEST Flour
8 teaspoons baking powder
½ teaspoon salt
¼ cup margarine
½ cup molasses
1½ cups water

Fry out salt pork; drain well. Sift dry ingredients into a bowl. Cut in margarine. Add scrunchions and mix with a fork until the pork is well scattered. Combine molasses and water, add them to the flour mixture and stir lightly. Roll out on a floured board to ½ inch thickness, cut into desired shapes; place on floured baking sheet. Bake at 400° F. for 15 minutes.

ROLLED OAT BUNS

2 cups rolled oats
2½ cups sifted
  CREAM OF THE WEST Flour
5 teaspoons baking powder
¾ teaspoon salt
1 cup brown sugar
1 cup butter
1 cup milk

Combine the dry ingredients until thoroughly mixed. Cut in butter. Add milk to make a soft dough.

Roll out on lightly floured board to ½" thickness; cut out and place on a greased cookie sheet. Bake at 400° F. for 12 to 15 minutes.

Makes 3 dozens 2 inch buns.

RAISIN BUNS

2½ cups sifted
   CREAM OF THE WEST Flour
5   teaspoons baking powder
1   teaspoon salt
 ½ cup sugar
 ½ cup margarine
1   cup raisins
About ¾ cup cold milk or water

Sift dry ingredients into a bowl. Cut in margarine. Add raisins and enough liquid to make a soft dough.

Place on a lightly floured board and roll to ½-inch thickness. Cut with a small cutter and place on a greased cookie sheet. Bake at 425° F. for about 15 minutes.

ORANGE DATE ROLLS

2   cups sifted
   CREAM OF THE WEST Flour
4   teaspoons baking powder
1   teaspoon salt
 ⅓ cup shortening
 ½ to ⅔ cup milk

Sift dry ingredients together. Cut in shortening to make a fine, even crumb.

Add enough milk to form a soft dough. Roll to ¼ inch thickness.

Brush surface with melted butter and then spread with:

 ½ cup chopped dates
1   teaspoon grated lemon rind

Roll up like a jelly roll. Cut in 9 pieces and place cut side down in a 8" or 9" square baking pan.

For the syrup, boil together for 5 minutes:

1   cup sugar
1   cup water
 ¼ cup orange juice
1   teaspoon grated orange rind
2   teaspoons lemon juice

Pour hot syrup over the date rolls. Bake at 400° F. for 30 minutes or until nicely browned.

PINWHEEL ONION ROLLS

4   medium onions (sliced)
2   tablespoons butter
 ¾ teaspoon salt
   Few grains pepper
2   cups sifted
   CREAM OF THE WEST Flour
1½ tablespoons baking powder
 ½ teaspoon salt
 ¼ cup shortening
 ⅔ cup milk
1   egg
 ⅓ cup milk
   Few grains salt

Cook onions in butter until golden brown, add salt and pepper; allow to cool.

Sift dry ingredients, cut in shortening. Add milk and mix lightly to form a dough. Roll dough into a rectangular shape, about ¼-inch thick. Spread with cooled onion mixture, roll up like a jelly roll. Cut into slices about 1-inch thick, arrange cut side down on a greased 8-inch baking dish.

Beat egg, add milk and salt. Pour this mixture over the rolls.

Bake at 400° F. for 25 minutes. Serve with a hot dinner.

LOCHLEVEN (POTATO) BISCUITS

1½ cups sifted
   CREAM OF THE WEST Flour
4   teaspoons baking powder
 ½ teaspoon salt
3   tablespoons shortening
1   cup riced potato
 ½ cup cold milk

Sift together dry ingredients; cut in shortening.

Lightly mix in cooled riced potatoes. Add cold milk to make a soft dough. Turn on a floured board, lightly roll out and cut into required shapes.

Bake on a greased sheet at 400° F. for 20 minutes.

"Our contributor says: 'My grandmother used to make such lovely things with potatoes I thought I should send her recipe for Potato Biscuits. I make them often, and my family can't get enough. My mother and I have enjoyed them down through the years'." SALLY WEST.

PANCAKES

1⅔ cups sifted
    CREAM OF THE WEST Flour
3   teaspoons baking powder
½ teaspoons salt
2   tablespoons granulated sugar
1   egg
1½ cups milk
3   tablespoons melted shortening

Put griddle or heavy frying pan on low heat to prewarm.

Sift dry ingredients into a bowl. Beat egg until foamy, add milk and melted shortening. Make a well in the centre of dry ingredients; add liquid ingredients all at once. Mix with an egg beater only until smooth. Test griddle for temperature. Grease lightly for first cakes. Drop batter from tablespoon onto hot griddle and spread gently until four inches in diameter. Cook on one side and then turn over.

Serve at once with butter and syrup.

Yield: 14—4-inch pancakes.

> *Flacoons or damper dogs—pan-cakes. Pan-cakes made of a flour and water mixture and cooked on top of the stove.*

BLUEBERRY PANCAKES

1½ cups sifted
    CREAM OF THE WEST Flour
3   teaspoons baking powder
½ teaspoon salt
⅓ cup granulated sugar
1   egg, beaten
1   cup milk
3   tablespoons melted butter
¼ teaspoon vanilla
1   cup floured blueberries

Sift dry ingredients, add beaten egg and milk, beat well. Blend in melted butter and vanilla and then gently fold in floured berries.

Bake on a griddle which is not too hot.

Serve with melted butter and brown sugar between the layers of pancakes.

PLAIN MUFFINS

2 cups sifted
    CREAM OF THE WEST Flour
4 teaspoons baking powder
1 teaspoon salt
2 tablespoons granulated sugar
1 egg, well beaten
1 cup milk
4 tablespoons melted fat

Sift dry ingredients and make a well in the centre. Add milk and melted fat to the beaten egg. Pour liquids into the well in centre of dry ingredients. Stir only until flour is dampened.

Fill greased muffin pans about two-thirds full. Bake at 400° F. for 20 to 22 minutes.

OATMEAL MUFFINS

1 cup sifted
    CREAM OF THE WEST Flour
3 teaspoons baking powder
2 tablespoons sugar
1 teaspoon salt
2 cups quick cooking rolled oats
1 cup milk
1 egg, slightly beaten
2 tablespoons melted shortening

Sift dry ingredients into a bowl; stir in rolled oats. Combine milk and slightly beaten egg and melted shortening. Quickly stir liquids into the dry mixture until just blended. Let stand for a minute or two.

Spoon into greased muffin pans. Bake at 400° F. for 20 to 25 minutes.

Serve hot.

BRAN MUFFINS

¾ cup bran
1¼ cups sifted
    CREAM OF THE WEST Flour
½ cup graham flour
4   teaspoons baking powder
3   tablespoons sugar
½ teaspoon salt
1   egg, beaten
¾ cup milk
¼ cup melted shortening

Mix dry ingredients together in a bowl. Combine beaten egg, milk and melted shortening. Add the wet ingredients to the dry mixture; stir only until blended.

Fill greased muffin pans ½ full. Bake at 425° F. for 15 to 20 minutes.

Makes 12 large muffins.

BLUEBERRY MUFFINS

2 cups sifted
    CREAM OF THE WEST Flour
3 tablespoons sugar
4 teaspoons baking powder
1 teaspoon salt
1 cup fresh blueberries
1 egg, well beaten
1 cup milk
2 tablespoons melted shortening or
    butter

Sift dry ingredients into a bowl; add fresh blueberries. Make a well in the centre of the dry ingredients. Combine beaten egg, milk and melted butter. Add them to the dry ingredients and stir until just blended.

Fill greased muffin tins about 2/3 full. Bake for 20 minutes at 400° F.

Yield: 16 medium size muffins.

CRANBERRY MUFFINS

1   cup cooked cranberries, drained
1/4 cup sugar
1/4 cup sifted
    CREAM OF THE WEST Flour
1/4 cup butter
1/4 cup sugar
1   egg
1 3/4 cups sifted
    CREAM OF THE WEST Flour
4   teaspoons baking powder
1/2 teaspoon salt
1/2 cup milk

Combine cranberries, 1/4 cup sugar and 1/4 cup of flour; let stand one hour.

Cream butter and sugar; add egg and beat. Add sifted dry ingredients alternately with the milk.

Stir in cranberries. Fill greased muffin tins half full.

Bake at 400° F. for 20 to 25 minutes.

ENGLISH MUFFINS

1   package dry or compressed yeast
1/4 cup lukewarm water
1   teaspoon granulated sugar
1   cup scalded milk
3   tablespoons butter
1 1/4 teaspoons salt
2   tablespoons granulated sugar
1   egg, beaten
3 1/2 cups sifted
    CREAM OF THE WEST Flour
1/4 cup cornmeal

Dissolve yeast in lukewarm water to which 1 teaspoon sugar has been added; let stand 10 minutes.

Pour scalded milk over butter, salt and sugar. Cool to lukewarm. Then add yeast, a well beaten egg and 2 cups sifted flour. Blend well. Knead in remaining flour until dough is thick and elastic. Let rise, covered, in a greased bowl until double in bulk (about 1 hour).

Sprinkle cornmeal on a lightly floured pastry board or cloth. Roll dough to 1/4-inch thickness. Cut with English Muffin rings or a 3 1/2-inch cookie cutter. Let muffins rise until doubled in bulk (keep them warm and covered).

Bake on a lightly greased griddle or heavy aluminum frying pan, over a moderate heat. Bake for about 15 minutes on the first side and 7 minutes on the other.

COFFEE KUCHEN

3   cups sifted
    CREAM OF THE WEST Flour
3   teaspoons baking powder
1/2 teaspoon salt
2   cups brown sugar, firmly packed
1   cup margarine
1/2 cup cold strong coffee
1/2 cup evaporated milk
1/4 teaspoon baking soda
2   eggs, beaten
1   teaspoon cinnamon

Sift together the flour, baking powder and salt; mix in the brown sugar. Cut in margarine with two knives or a pastry blender. Reserve one cup of this mixture to use for topping.

Combine strong coffee, evaporated milk and baking soda. Add to dry ingredients and mix well. Add beaten eggs and stir.

Spoon batter into large greased muffin tins until half full.

Add 1 teaspoon cinnamon to the reserved topping mixture. Sprinkle it over the muffins.

Bake at 375° F. for 25 minutes.

Makes 1 1/2 dozen.

NUT BREAD

1 1/2 cups sifted
    CREAM OF THE WEST Flour
1   teaspoon baking powder
1   teaspoon baking soda

½ teaspoon salt
½ cup whole wheat flour
1 cup brown sugar
1 cup raisins
½ cup chopped walnuts
1 egg
1 cup sour milk
2 tablespoons melted fat

Sift the flour, baking powder, soda and salt. Add whole wheat flour, brown sugar, raisins and walnuts.

Beat the egg; add sour milk and melted fat to it. Add liquids to the flour mixture and stir until just mixed.

Turn into a greased 8½-inch x 4½-inch loaf pan and allow to stand in a warm place for 20 minutes before baking.

Bake in a 350° F. oven for one hour.

Cool before slicing.

DATE BREAD

1 cup chopped dates
1 teaspoon baking soda
1 cup hot water
2 tablespoons butter
1 cup brown sugar
1 egg, beaten
1 teaspoon vanilla
2 cups sifted
    CREAM OF THE WEST Flour
1 teaspoon baking powder
½ teaspoon salt

Place chopped dates in a bowl. Dissolve soda in hot water and pour over the dates. Let stand for 5 minutes.

Add butter to above mixture while still hot. Then add sugar, beaten egg, vanilla and sifted dry ingredients. Stir only until combined.

Pour into a greased loaf pan (8½-inch x 4½-inch). Bake at 350° F. for 50 to 60 minutes.

Note: ½ cup finely chopped nuts may be added, if desired.

DATE LOAF

3 tablespoons butter
¾ cup brown sugar
¼ cup molasses
1 egg
1 teaspoon baking soda
1 tablespoon hot water
2 cups sifted
    CREAM OF THE WEST Flour

1 cup whole wheat or graham flour
½ teaspoon salt
1 cup chopped dates, floured
½ cup chopped nuts
1 cup cold strong tea

Cream butter and brown sugar; add molasses and egg; beat well. Stir in soda dissolved in hot water. Add dry ingredients, floured dates and nuts. Stir in cold tea.

Put batter into a large greased loaf pan (about 11 x 4½ inches). Bake at 350° F. for one hour.

BLUEBERRY NUT BREAD

2 eggs, well beaten
1 cup granulated sugar
1 cup milk
3 tablespoons melted butter
3 cups sifted
    CREAM OF THE WEST Flour
4 teaspoons baking powder
1 teaspoon salt
1 cup fresh blueberries
½ cup chopped nuts

Beat eggs well; gradually add sugar and mix thoroughly. Add milk and melted butter. Sift dry ingredients into the liquids; stir only until blended. Carefully fold in blueberries and nuts.

Pour into a large greased loaf pan (about 11 x 4½ inches). Bake at 350° F. for 50 to 60 minutes.

NUT AND RAISIN BREAD

1½ cups sifted
    CREAM OF THE WEST Flour
4 teaspoons baking powder
1 teaspoon salt
2 cups graham flour
½ cup corn meal
½ cup brown sugar
¾ cup chopped nuts
1 cup ground raisins
2 cups milk
½ cup molasses
¼ teaspoon baking soda

Sift flour, baking powder and salt; stir in the graham flour, corn meal and brown sugar. Add the nuts and raisins. Add the milk and mix well. Combine the molasses and soda; blend into the batter.

Pour into a greased 11-inch x 4½-inch loaf pan. Bake at 350° F. for 60 to 70 minutes. (If you prefer, use two small loaf pans and bake at 350° F. for 40 to 45 minutes.)

CRANBERRY BREAD

2   cups sifted
      CREAM OF THE WEST Flour
1   cup sugar
1½   teaspoons double-acting baking
      powder
½   teaspoon baking soda
1   teaspoon salt
1   egg, well beaten
      Juice and rind of one orange
2   tablespoons shortening
      Hot water
1   cup chopped nuts
1   cup sliced cranberries (raw)

Sift dry ingredients into a large bowl. Combine well beaten egg, orange juice and grated rind. Put shortening in a cup and add enough hot water to make ¾ cup. Add liquid ingredients to the flour mixture. Stir only until the flour is dampened. Blend in nuts and cranberries.

Pour into a greased 8½-inch x 4½-inch loaf pan. Let stand for 10 minutes before baking.

Bake at 350° F. for 55 to 60 minutes. Cool thoroughly before slicing.

BANANA QUICK BREAD

⅓   cup shortening
⅔   cup sugar
2   eggs, slightly beaten
1   cup mashed banana
1¾   cups sifted
      CREAM OF THE WEST Flour
2¾   teaspoons double-acting baking
      powder
½   teaspoon salt
½   cup chopped nuts
1   cup mixed candied fruit and peel
¼   cup raisins

Cream shortening and sugar until fluffy. Add eggs and beat thoroughly. Blend in mashed banana.

Add sifted flour, baking powder and salt. Then, stir in nuts, fruit and raisins.

Pour into a greased 8½-inch x 4½-inch loaf pan. Bake at 350° F. for 60 to 70 minutes.

PARTRIDGEBERRY ORANGE BREAD

2   cups sifted
      CREAM OF THE WEST Flour
½   teaspoon salt
1½   teaspoons baking powder
⅓   teaspoon baking soda
1   cup granulated sugar
1   orange
2   tablespoons butter
      Boiling water
1   egg, beaten
1   cup chopped nuts
1   cup partridgeberries

Sift together dry ingredients. Grate orange rind and extract juice from the orange; put in a cup; to these add the butter and enough boiling water to make three-quarters of a cup; cool.

Add the beaten egg to cooled butter mixture; then blend in dry ingredients. Add chopped nuts and partridgeberries to the batter.

Using a greased loaf pan (8½ x 4½ inches), bake at 350° F. for one hour.

Allow to stand for 24 hours before cutting.

> *Note re Margarine*
> In *Newfoundland fortified Margarine with colour added is generally used in all recipes which call for butter or shortening. In fact Margarine is often referred to as 'butter' and fresh or dairy butter is called 'good butter' or 'table butter'.*

APRICOT BREAD

1   cup apricots
1   orange
      Boiling water
½   cup raisins
2   cups sifted
      CREAM OF THE WEST Flour
1   cup sugar
2   teaspoons baking powder
½   teaspoon baking soda
½   teaspoon salt
1   egg, beaten
2   tablespoons melted butter

Soak apricots in warm water for ½ hour. Squeeze the orange and pour the juice into a measuring cup; add boiling water to make one cup; cool.

Grind the drained apricots, orange skins and raisins.

Sift dry ingredients; add ground fruit. Make a well in the centre, add the cooled orange juice and water, beaten egg and melted butter.

Pour into a greased 11-inch x 4½-inch loaf pan. Bake at 350° F. for 50 to 60 minutes.

PINEAPPLE NUT BREAD

2¼ cups sifted
      CREAM OF THE WEST Flour
¾ cup sugar
3   teaspoons baking powder
½ teaspoon baking soda
1½ teaspoons salt
1   cup bran
¾ cup chopped walnuts
1   egg, well beaten
1½ cups crushed pineapple (not drained)
1   tablespoon melted butter

Sift measured flour with sugar, baking powder, baking soda and salt. Add bran and walnuts. Combine beaten egg, crushed pineapple and melted butter. Add to the dry ingredients and stir until flour disappears.

Bake in a greased loaf pan (8½ x 4½ inches) at 350° F. for 60 to 70 minutes.

CINNAMON BREAD

2½ cups sifted
      CREAM OF THE WEST Flour
2   cups brown sugar (firmly packed)
2   teaspoons cinnamon
2½ teaspoons baking powder
½ teaspoon salt
½ cup shortening
2   eggs, slightly beaten
¾ cup buttermilk

Combine flour, sugar, cinnamon, baking powder and salt. Add shortening and mix together with the hands. Put aside ½ cup of this mixture to use as the topping. Add beaten eggs and buttermilk to remaining flour mixture; mix well with a spoon.

Grease 2 eight-inch pie plates and divide batter between them. Sprinkle topping over these.

Bake at 350° F. for 35 to 40 minutes.

Note: Evaporated milk may be used if buttermilk is not available.

APPLE RAISIN COFFEE CAKE

¼ cup soft shortening
¾ cup sugar
1   egg
½ cup milk

1½ cups sifted
      CREAM OF THE WEST Flour
2   teaspoons baking powder
½ teaspoon salt
½ cup seedless raisins, floured
1   large apple
1   teaspoon cinnamon
2   teaspoons sugar

Cream shortening and ¾ cup sugar; beat in the egg. Add milk and stir. Sift the flour, baking powder and salt; flour the raisins. Add the dry ingredients and raisins, blend well.

Pour batter into a 9-inch square pan which has been greased. Arrange thinly sliced apple in an attractive design on the top; press apples into the batter slightly. Combine cinnamon and 2 teaspoons sugar; sprinkle over the top.

Bake for 35 minutes at 350° F.

NOTES:

_____

_____

_____

_____

_____

_____

_____

_____

_____

_____

_____

_____

_____

_____

_____

CAKES

Here's where imagination can really go to work, since we all have our own baking or trimming tricks which make a recipe "our very own"

BUTTER TYPE:

WHITE CAKE
NEVER FAIL CAKE
GOLD CAKE
BUTTERSCOTCH CAKE
COCOANUT CUP CAKES
PRIZE ORANGE CAKE
CHOCOLATE CAKE
PARTY CHOCOLATE CAKE

EGGLESS CHOCOLATE CAKE
CHOCOLATE COCOANUT CAKE
CRUMB CAKE
WHOLE WHEAT SPICE CAKE
GREAT-GRANDMOTHER'S
 GINGER BREAD
RAISIN GINGERBREAD—
 NEWFOUNDLAND STYLE
MARMALADE GINGERBREAD

SPONGE, Etc.:

SPONGE CAKE
VINEGAR SPONGE CAKE
FEATHER SPONGE CAKE
SPICY SPONGE CAKE
POTATO-FLOUR SPONGE CAKE

JELLY ROLL
CHOCOLATE ROLL
PINEAPPLE FLUFF CAKE
ORANGE CHIFFON CAKE

SPECIAL FRUIT:

BROWN SUGAR FRUIT CAKE
LIGHT FRUIT CAKE
DARK FRUIT CAKE
BOILED DARK FRUIT CAKE
GRAPE JUICE CAKE
STRAWBERRY SPICE CAKE

PEACH FRUIT CAKE
MOLASSES FRUIT CAKE
EGGLESS FRUIT CAKE
YOU ARE A CHRISTMAS CAKE
OLD TIME PORK CAKE FOR CHRISTMAS
ECONOMY CHRISTMAS CAKE

FRUIT:

CHERRY CAKE
BAKED POT CAKE
HOT MILK POUND CAKE
JAM CAKE
BLUEBERRY CAKE

BLUEBERRY SPICE CAKE
EGGLESS, MILKLESS, BUTTERLESS CAKE
MOM'S DANDY CAKE
TOMATO SOUP CAKE

WHITE CAKE

1   cup granulated sugar
3/4 cup sweet cream
1½   cups sifted
     CREAM OF THE WEST Flour
2½   teaspoons baking powder
¼   teaspoon salt
1   teaspoon lemon extract
3   egg whites

Combine sugar and cream. Blend in sifted dry ingredients and lemon extract. Beat egg whites until stiff. Fold them into batter. Bake in a greased 8-inch or 9-inch pan at 350° F. for 30 to 35 minutes.

ICING

½   cup whipping cream
1   egg white
1   teaspoon granulated sugar
½   teaspoon lemon extract

Whip cream and egg white. Combine with sugar and lemon extract.

> *A spell—a rest*
> *When creaming butter and sugar for a cake 'take a spell.'*

NEVER FAIL CAKE

Break 2 eggs into a measuring cup, then add sweet milk to make 1 cup.

Sift together:

1¾   cups sifted
     CREAM OF THE WEST Flour
1   cup granulated sugar
3   teaspoons baking powder
¼   teaspoon salt

Add egg and milk mixture, 3 tablespoons melted butter or margarine and 1 teaspoon vanilla to the sifted dry ingredients. Beat together until smooth. Pour into greased 8-inch or 9-inch layer pans or one 9-inch shallow pan and bake at 350° F. for 30 to 35 minutes.

GOLD CAKE

3   tablespoons butter
3/4 cup granulated sugar
1   teaspoon vanilla
3   egg yolks
1½   cups sifted
     CREAM OF THE WEST Flour
3   teaspoons baking powder
¼   teaspoon salt
½   cup milk

Cream butter and sugar well. Add vanilla and the egg yolks which have been beaten until thick. Sift flour, baking powder and salt. Add them to the first mixture, alternately with the milk.

Bake in a greased loaf pan (about 9 x 5 inches), for 30 to 40 minutes at 350° F.

Cover with icing when cool.

BUTTERSCOTCH CAKE

½   cup shortening
1⅓   cups brown sugar
2   eggs
1   teaspoon vanilla
1¾   cups sifted
     CREAM OF THE WEST Flour
2½   teaspoons baking powder
¼   teaspoon soda
⅓   teaspoon salt
½   cup cold strong coffee

Cream shortening, add sugar slowly; cream well. Add unbeaten eggs one at a time, beating well after each addition. Add vanilla. Add sifted dry ingredients alternately with the coffee. Blend well.

Pour into a 9-inch square pan which has been greased and floured. Bake at 350° F. for 50 minutes. Cut in squares to serve.

"This recipe was handed down to our contributor from her grandmother and mother and she finds it to be very delicious. So did we." SALLY WEST

COCOANUT CUP CAKES

1   cup butter
1   cup granulated sugar
2   cups sifted
     CREAM OF THE WEST Flour
3   teaspoons baking powder
¼   teaspoon salt
½   cup milk
2   cups cocoanut
1   teaspoon flavouring
3   egg whites

Cream butter; gradually blend in sugar. Add sifted dry ingredients alternately with the milk. Blend in cocoanut and flavouring and fold in stiffly beaten egg whites.

Fill cup cake tins about ⅔ full.

Bake in a 350° F. oven until brown (about 20 minutes).

Decorate as desired.

PRIZE ORANGE CAKE

½ cup butter
1 cup granulated sugar
1 whole egg
2 eggs, separated
½ cup sour milk
  Juice from 1 large orange
2 cups sifted
  CREAM OF THE WEST Flour
1½ teaspoons baking powder
¼ teaspoon salt
½ teaspoon baking soda dissolved in
  a teaspoon of hot water
1 cup seedless raisins (minced)
  Pulp and peel from one large
  orange (minced)

Cream butter until light; gradually add sugar, beating constantly. Add one whole egg and 2 egg yolks. Beat well. Stir in milk and orange juice.

Sift flour, baking powder and salt together 3 or 4 times. Add them to the butter mixture. Stir in soda dissolved in hot water. Add raisins, orange rind and pulp which have been put through a food chopper. Fold in stiffly beaten egg whites.

Bake in two greased 8-inch layer pans at 350° F. for 30 to 35 minutes.

Put layers together with orange filling and frost with orange frosting.

CHOCOLATE CAKE

½ cup milk
2 squares unsweetened chocolate
½ cup granulated sugar
1 egg
½ cup butter
1 cup granulated sugar
1 egg and 1 egg yolk
2 teaspoons vanilla
1 cup milk
½ teaspoon baking soda
2 cups sifted
  CREAM OF THE WEST Flour
½ teaspoon salt

Put ½ cup milk in a double boiler to scald. Melt the chocolate and add ½ cup granulated sugar and 1 well beaten egg. When the milk is hot add it to the chocolate mixture and then put back in double boiler and cook for 5 minutes. Remove from heat and cool.

Cream together the butter and 1 cup granulated sugar; add 1 egg and yolk of

another and heat for 5 minutes. Add vanilla and 1 cup of milk in which the soda has been dissolved. Then add the sifted flour and salt; beat well.

Now combine the chocolate mixture and the batter and mix thoroughly. Bake in greased 8-inch or 9-inch layer pans at 350° F. for 35 to 40 minutes.

PARTY CHOCOLATE CAKE

1 cup butter
1⅓ cups firmly packed brown sugar
3 eggs
2 squares unsweetened chocolate
  (melted over hot water)
2¼ cups sifted
  CREAM OF THE WEST Flour
1 teaspoon baking soda
¼ teaspoon salt
1 teaspoon vanilla
¾ cup cold water

Cream butter thoroughly. Add sugar gradually. Cream together until light. Add eggs very well beaten or (if desired add well beaten yolks, reserving whites to be beaten stiffly and folded in at the last). Sift together flour, soda and salt. Add alternately with the water to the creamed mixture. Add the chocolate and vanilla. Bake in greased 12-inch x 8-inch x 2-inch pan at 350° F. for 45 to 50 minutes.

EGGLESS CHOCOLATE CAKE

⅔ cup butter
2 cups brown sugar
½ cup cocoa
2½ cups sifted
  CREAM OF THE WEST Flour
¾ teaspoon salt
1 cup milk
1 teaspoon baking soda
½ cup hot water

Cream butter. Mix sugar and cocoa; then add gradually to creamed butter; combine well. Add sifted flour and salt alternately with the milk. Dissolve soda in hot water and stir into the batter.

Pour into a greased 9-inch square pan. Bake at 350° F. for 50 minutes.

"This is the favourite recipe of a contributor in Northern Newfoundland, where in the winter months eggs are a scarce commodity. They are connected to the railway only by boat and cannot import eggs." SALLY WEST

CHOCOLATE COCOANUT CAKE

¼ cup margarine or other shortening
1 cup granulated sugar
1 egg, well beaten
1½ cups sifted
 CREAM OF THE WEST Flour
1 teaspoon baking powder
½ teaspoon baking soda
½ teaspoon salt
½ cup sour milk
2 squares unsweetened chocolate, melted
½ cup boiling water
1 cup cocoanut

Cream margarine and sugar; add well beaten egg. Mix and sift the dry ingredients and add them alternately with the sour milk to the creamed mixture. Stir in the melted chocolate, boiling water and cocoanut; mix well.

Bake in a greased 9-inch square pan for 35 to 40 minutes at 350° F.

CRUMB CAKE

¾ cup butter
1 cup granulated sugar
2 cups sifted
 CREAM OF THE WEST Flour
2 teaspoons baking powder
½ teaspoon baking soda
1 teaspoon cloves
1 teaspoon cinnamon
1 cup raisins, floured
1 egg, beaten
1 cup sour milk

Cream butter and sugar until light and fluffy. Add sifted flour and cut in with a pastry blender or 2 knives until mixture resembles coarse cornmeal. Remove 1 cup of this crumb mixture and set it aside. Add the baking powder, soda, spices and floured raisins to remaining butter mixture. Beat egg; add sour milk to it. Add this to the butter mixture and mix well. Pour into a greased pan (about 9 inches square). Sprinkle crumbs evenly over top of the batter.

Bake at 350° F. for 40 minutes.
Serve warm.

WHOLE WHEAT SPICE CAKE

¾ cup margarine
1 cup granulated sugar
2 eggs
¼ teaspoon vanilla
1 cup whole wheat flour
1 cup sifted
 CREAM OF THE WEST Flour
4 teaspoons baking powder
¼ teaspoon salt
2 teaspoons allspice
1 cup milk

Cream margarine and sugar; add eggs and vanilla; beat well. Add whole wheat flour. Then add other sifted dry ingredients, alternately with the milk.

Bake in a greased 9-inch square pan for 50 minutes at 350° F.

Ice with Coffee Icing.

GREAT-GRANDMOTHER'S GINGER BREAD

½ cup butter or lard
½ cup granulated sugar
1 egg, beaten
1 cup molasses
2½ cups sifted
 CREAM OF THE WEST Flour
1½ teaspoons baking soda
½ teaspoon salt
1 teaspoon cinnamon
1 teaspoon ginger
½ teaspoon cloves
1 cup hot water

Cream butter and sugar. Add beaten egg and molasses; beat well. Blend in sifted dry ingredients. Add hot water last and beat until smooth.

Bake in a greased 9-inch square pan for 45 minutes. Use a 350° F. oven.

"This recipe is well over 100 years old."
SALLY WEST.

RAISIN GINGERBREAD
(Newfoundland Style)

1 cup raisins
½ cup shortening
⅓ cup granulated sugar
6 tablespoons dark molasses
2 eggs, beaten
2½ cups sifted
 CREAM OF THE WEST Flour
½ teaspoon salt
2 teaspoons ginger
2 teaspoons cinnamon
¾ cup buttermilk
1 teaspoon baking soda

Rinse raisins in hot water, drain and dry on a towel.

Cream shortening and sugar; stir in molasses. Add beaten eggs and beat well. Add flour sifted with salt and spices, alternately with buttermilk in which soda has been dissolved. Beat well; stir in raisins.

Pour into a greased 8-inch x 12-inch baking pan.

Bake at 350° F. for 40 minutes.

Serve hot with butter.

"This is an old Newfoundland recipe for Raisin Gingerbread and was given to our contributor by her grandmother years ago." SALLY WEST.

MARMALADE GINGERBREAD

3 tablespoons butter
1 cup orange marmalade
1 egg
1/2 cup molasses
1¾ cups sifted
   CREAM OF THE WEST Flour
1 teaspoon baking powder
1/2 teaspoon baking soda
1/2 teaspoon salt
1 teaspoon ginger
1 teaspoon cinnamon
4 tablespoons boiling water

Cream butter; blend in marmalade. Then add the egg and molasses; beat well. Sift all the dry ingredients together and add them to the marmalade mixture. Stir in boiling water.

Use a greased 9-inch square pan and bake at 350° F. for 35 minutes.

SPONGE CAKE

1 cup granulated sugar
1/4 teaspoon salt
1 cup sifted
   CREAM OF THE WEST Flour
1 teaspoon baking powder
3 eggs
1 teaspoon flavouring
3 tablespoons evaporated milk
3 tablespoons hot water

Sift sugar and salt together.

Sift flour and baking powder together three times. Beat eggs until thick and lemon coloured. Add sugar 1/3 at a time and beat well after each addition. Add flavouring.

Next, add flour 1/3 at a time and beat after each addition.

Combine milk and hot water. Quickly stir into the batter.

Pour into two ungreased 8-inch or 9-inch layer pans. Bake at 400° F. for 15 to 20 minutes.

When baked, invert with edges of pans resting on tea cups. Allow to cool thoroughly and then remove from the pan.

VINEGAR SPONGE CAKE

6 eggs, separated
1 cup granulated sugar
1 tablespoon vinegar
1/2 teaspoon vanilla or lemon extract
7/8 cup sifted
   CREAM OF THE WEST Flour
1/4 teaspoon salt

Beat egg yolks until thick and lemon coloured. Add sugar gradually, and continue beating while adding the vinegar and flavouring. Sift flour four times with the salt; add to the egg mixture. Then fold in stiffly beaten egg whites.

Bake in an ungreased tube pan at 325° F. for 50 to 60 minutes. When baked, invert and allow to cool thoroughly before removing from the pan.

FEATHER SPONGE CAKE

6 egg yolks
1/2 cup cold water
1½ cups granulated sugar
1/2 teaspoon vanilla
1/2 teaspoon orange or lemon extract
1¼ cups sifted
   CREAM OF THE WEST Flour
1/4 teaspoon salt
6 egg whites
3/4 teaspoon cream of tartar

Beat egg yolks until very thick and lemon coloured. Add water and continue beating until very thick. Gradually beat in sugar, then flavourings. Fold in flour sifted with salt, a little at a time. Beat egg whites until foamy; add cream of tartar, and beat until they form moist glossy peaks. Fold in egg yolk mixture. Bake in 10-inch tube pan, ungreased, at 325° F. for 1 hour. Invert pan to cool.

Threaten—intend
"I threaten to make a cake."

SPICY SPONGE CAKE

3   egg yolks
½ cup granulated sugar
½ cup brown sugar
½ teaspoon vanilla
1 cup plus 2 tablespoons
    CREAM OF THE WEST Flour
¼ teaspoon salt
1   teaspoon baking powder
¼ teaspoon cinnamon
¼ teaspoon nutmeg
⅛ teaspoon cloves
6   tablespoons hot milk
3   stiffly-beaten egg whites

Beat egg yolks until thick and lemon coloured. Gradually beat in the sugars. Add vanilla. Add sifted dry ingredients. Add milk, stir quickly until batter is smooth. Fold in egg whites. Bake in an ungreased 8-inch square pan in a moderate oven, 350° F., 35 to 40 minutes. Invert to cool.

POTATO-FLOUR SPONGE CAKE

4   egg whites
4   egg yolks
¾ cup granulated sugar
½ tablespoon lemon juice
½ cup potato flour
1   teaspoon baking powder
¼ teaspoon salt

Beat egg whites until stiff but not dry and beat in gradually 1 tablespoon sugar for each egg white (out of sugar called for in recipe) and set aside. Add lemon juice to egg yolks and beat until lemon coloured and so thick that the beaters turn with difficulty. Beat in remaining sugar. Combine yolks and whites and fold together with spoon until mixture is even. Add sifted dry ingredients, cutting and folding into egg mixture. Pour into ungreased 10-inch tube pan. Bake in a moderate oven 350° F. for 30 minutes. Invert pan to cool.

JELLY ROLL

3   eggs, separated
1   cup granulated sugar
1   tablespoon cold water
½ teaspoon vanilla or lemon extract
1   cup sifted
    CREAM OF THE WEST Flour
1   teaspoon baking powder
¼ teaspoon salt

Beat egg whites until soft peaks start to form; gradually add sugar and beat until stiff but not dry.
Beat egg yolks until thick; add cold water and flavouring. Fold the beaten yolks into the egg whites; then fold in sifted dry ingredients.
Line bottom of a shallow pan (about 10 x 15 inches) with waxed paper. Pour in batter; spread evenly. Bake at 400° F. for 12 to 15 minutes.
Turn out on a towel which has been dusted with confectioner's sugar.
Remove waxed paper and trim the edges. Spread with jam, jelly or cream filling. Roll up.
Wrap in waxed paper until serving time.

CHOCOLATE ROLL

5   egg yolks
1   cup confectioner's sugar
⅓ cup sifted
    CREAM OF THE WEST Flour
½ teaspoon salt
3   tablespoons cocoa
1   teaspoon vanilla
5   stiffly-beaten egg whites

Beat egg yolks until thick and lemon coloured. Add sifted dry ingredients and beat until well blended. Add vanilla and fold in egg whites. Turn into a greased and lined 15-inch x 10-inch pan. Bake in moderately hot oven, 375° F., for 15 to 20 minutes. Turn into a clean tea towel sprinkled with icing sugar. Remove paper; cut off crisp edges. Spread with sweetened whipped cream. Roll up like jelly roll; dust with icing sugar.

> "He smokes like a winter tilt."
> —a temporary shelter built in the woods and occupied only when the men go inland to cut wood.

PINEAPPLE FLUFF CAKE

6   egg whites
¼ teaspoon salt
¾ cup granulated sugar
6   egg yolks
¾ cup granulated sugar
1   tablespoon lemon juice
½ cup unsweetened pineapple juice
1¾ cups sifted
    CREAM OF THE WEST Flour
1   teaspoon baking powder

Beat egg whites with salt to form moist, glossy peaks. Gradually beat in 3/4 cup sugar. Beat egg yolks with remaining 3/4 cup sugar until very thick. Add fruit juices; beat until sugar dissolves. Add sifted dry ingredients. Fold in egg white mixture. Bake in 10-inch ungreased tube pan at 325° F. for 80 to 85 minutes. Invert pan to cool.

ORANGE CHIFFON CAKE

1¼ cups sifted
   CREAM OF THE WEST Flour
1½ teaspoons double-acting baking powder
¾ cup granulated sugar
¼ cup salad oil
3 unbeaten egg yolks
6 tablespoons cold water
   Grated rind of one orange
1 teaspoon lemon extract
4 egg whites
½ teaspoon salt
¼ teaspoon cream of tartar

Sift together flour, baking powder and sugar. Lightly mix together the salad oil, egg yolks, water, orange rind and lemon extract. Beat first and second mixture together until well blended. Beat egg whites with salt and cream of tartar until stiff peaks form. Add egg white mixture to other ingredients, cutting and folding until well blended. Bake in an ungreased 10-inch tube pan at 350° F. for 35 to 40 minutes. Invert pan until cake is cool. Ice with orange icing or whipped cream.

BROWN SUGAR FRUIT CAKE

1 cup butter
2 cups brown sugar
3 eggs, beaten
3 cups sifted
   CREAM OF THE WEST Flour
3 teaspoons baking powder
1 teaspoon salt
   Juice and rind of one large orange
6 cups raisins
3 cups currants
2 cups peel
1½ cups red cherries
1½ cups green cherries

Cream butter and sugar thoroughly. Add beaten eggs and continue beating until the mixture is very light. Sift flour, baking powder and salt together and reserve a little to use for flouring the fruit. Add sifted dry ingredients to the egg mixture; then add orange juice and rind. Finally, fold in floured fruit.

Use a large 10-inch pan which has been well lined.

Bake at 275° F. for 3 hours.

LIGHT FRUIT CAKE

1 cup butter
1½ cups granulated sugar
5 eggs, separated
3 cups sifted
   CREAM OF THE WEST Flour
1 teaspoon baking powder
¼ teaspoon salt
1 cup milk
1 teaspoon lemon extract
1½ cups almonds, blanched
2 cups mixed peel
1½ cups candied cherries
1 cup white sultana raisins

Cream butter and sugar; add 5 well beaten egg yolks. Sift ½ cup flour over the prepared fruit. Sift together remaining flour, baking powder and salt. Add dry ingredients to creamed mixture, alternately with the milk to which the lemon extract has been added.

Stir floured fruit into the batter. Beat egg whites until stiff but not dry; fold into the cake.

Use a lined bake pan (9 or 10 inches in diameter and 3 to 4 inches high).

Bake at 325° F. for 2½ to 3 hours.

DARK FRUIT CAKE

1 cup molasses
1 tablespoon cinnamon
1 tablespoon allspice
1 tablespoon cloves
1 cup butter
1 cup granulated sugar
5 eggs, well beaten
3½ cups sifted
   CREAM OF THE WEST Flour
½ teaspoon salt
3 cups currants
3 cups raisins
2 cups citron peel
2 cups lemon peel
1¼ cups dates (if desired)
1 teaspoon soda
2 tablespoons hot water

A wine glass of whiskey or rum (if desired). Our contributor reports that, to add flavour, she brushes the top of the cake with rum before icing. Spirits tend to evaporate in the oven heat.

Steep spices in molasses over a low heat. (Do not let boil, but the longer it is allowed to steep, the darker your cake will be.)

Cream butter and sugar, then add the well beaten eggs and cooled molasses mixture. Dust fruit with ¼ cup of the flour.

Add remaining flour and the salt to the butter mixture and blend well. Stir in floured fruit.

Last of all, mix in soda dissolved in hot water.

Use a large baking pan lined with three layers of brown paper. (An iron bake pot is best and it should be at least 10 inches wide and 3 inches deep.)

Bake at 275° F. for 3 to 3½ hours.

Of course in the old days they cut their own fruit, but now you can used mixed cut peel instead of the lemon and citron if desired.

"Our contributor says: 'My friends have urged me to send you an old family recipe for a really dark fruit cake, which makes a beautiful cutting cake for Christmas or other occasions and will keep for years (if you can save it that long). It has been handed down for generations and originally came with my ancestors from England in the 1700's. They settled in Calvert (then Caplin Bay) on the Southern Shore. My mother remembers her grandmother making it and she got the recipe from her mother. Mother is now 76 and her grandmother is dead over 53 years, and she was 98 when she died." SALLY WEST.

"Stun-a-bull"—dunchy or heavy cake. At a scoff a lad when offered cake which looked heavy, said:

"Yes I s'pose, thou I 'lows 'twould stun-a-bull."

BOILED DARK FRUIT CAKE

3   **cups raisins**
2   **cups brown sugar**
1   **teaspoon salt**

¼ **teaspoon each of cinnamon, all-spice, nutmeg and cloves**
½ **cup butter**
2   **cups hot water**
3   **cups sifted**
     CREAM OF THE WEST Flour
1   **teaspoon baking powder**
1   **tablespoon cocoa**
1   **cup chopped walnuts**
1   **cup citron peel**
½ **cup orange peel**
¾ **cup candied cherries**

Combine raisins, sugar, salt, spices, butter and hot water; boil for five minutes. Cool.

Sift together the flour, baking powder and cocoa. Add to the cooled raisin mixture; blend well. Add nuts and fruit.

Pour into a lined bake pan (9 or 10 inches in diameter and 3 to 4 inches high).

Bake in a 325° F. oven for 2 hours.

Top with a creamy icing.

GRAPE JUICE CAKE

3   **cups sultana raisins**
4   **cups shredded cocoanut**
1   **cup mixed peel**
1   **small bottle cherries and juice**
¾ **cup blanched almonds**
1   **small bottle grape juice (12 oz.)**
¾ **cup butter**
1½ **cups granulated sugar**
6   **eggs**
4   **cups sifted**
     CREAM OF THE WEST Flour
½ **teaspoon baking powder**
1   **teaspoon salt**
½ **cup milk**
2   **teaspoons vanilla**
2   **teaspoons almond extract**

Cut up fruit and nuts as desired; mix together and add grape juice and liquid from the cherries. Soak overnight.

Next morning cream butter and sugar well. Add eggs, one at a time; beat after each addition. Blend in the soaked fruit and juice. Add the sifted dry ingredients alternately with the milk and flavouring extracts.

Pour batter into two greased and lined pans (each about 8 inches square). Bake at 275° F. for 2½ to 3 hours.

Suent—smooth
"a nice suent batter."

STRAWBERRY SPICE CAKE

½ cup shortening
1 cup granulated sugar
2 eggs
1 cup strawberry jam
2 cups sifted
    CREAM OF THE WEST Flour
2 teaspoons baking powder
½ teaspoon salt
1 teaspoon cinnamon
1 teaspoon ginger
½ teaspoon cloves
½ cup milk
½ cup chopped nuts
⅔ cup raisins, floured

Beat shortening until creamy; add sugar and beat well. Add the eggs one at a time and beat after each one. Stir in the strawberry jam. Sift the flour, baking powder, salt, cinnamon, ginger and cloves. Add them alternately with the milk to the creamed mixture. Stir in nuts and floured raisins.

Use a 9-inch square pan which has been well greased. Bake at 350° F. for 45 to 50 minutes.

PEACH FRUIT CAKE

1 cup butter
1½ cups granulated sugar
3 eggs, well beaten
1 tin peaches (20 oz.)
3 cups sultana raisins
1½ cups cherries
1 cup cocoanut
3 cups sifted
    CREAM OF THE WEST Flour
1 teaspoon baking powder
½ teaspoon salt
2 teaspoons vanilla

Cream butter and sugar. Add well beaten eggs. Blend in the crushed and drained peaches, raisins, cut up cherries and cocoanut. Stir in sifted dry ingredients; add vanilla. (A little peach juice may be added if the batter seems dry.)

Pour into a large round or square pan which has been lined (at least 9 inches in diameter and 3 inches deep). Bake at 275° F. for about 3 hours.

MOLASSES FRUIT CAKE

1 cup butter
1 cup granulated sugar
2 cups molasses
4 eggs
4 cups sifted
    CREAM OF THE WEST Flour
2 teaspoons baking powder
2 teaspoons baking soda
1 teaspoon salt
4 teaspoons mixed spices
2 cups currants or chopped raisins
1 cup dates, finely chopped
1 cup nuts, finely chopped
1 cup mixed peel

Cream butter, sugar and molasses together. Then add eggs and beat well for about 10 minutes.

Sift together the flour, baking powder, baking soda, salt and spices.

Put fruit in a separate bowl and use ½ cup of the flour mixture to dredge it.

Add remaining sifted dry ingredients to the egg mixture. Then add the fruit. Combine well.

Pour into a large round baking pan which has been lined (about 9 or 10 inches in diameter and 3 inches deep).

Bake at 300° F. for 3 hours.

EGGLESS FRUIT CAKE

1 cup margarine
2 cups granulated sugar
4¼ cups sifted
    CREAM OF THE WEST Flour
1½ cups raisins
1½ cups currants
¾ cup mixed peel
1 teaspoon salt
1½ teaspoons each of cinnamon, ginger, nutmeg and cloves
2 teaspoons baking soda
2 cups milk

Cream margarine and sugar well. Dust fruit with ¼ cup of flour. Sift together remaining flour, salt, spices and soda. Add dry ingredients to creamed mixture, alternately with the milk. Stir in floured fruit.

Use a lined bake pan which is 9 or 10 inches in diameter and at least 3-inches deep. Bake at 325° F. for 2½ hours.

YOU ARE A CHRISTMAS CAKE

1 cup of butter of faith—to make life run smoothly.
1 cup of sugar—life needs its sweetness.
5 eggs to make it light—this is prayer, which uplifts.

½ pound of nuts—humour. Nuts to crack like good humour—be sure they are clean!

¼ pound of cherries—colour the cake like music on a dull morning.

1 pound of raisins are old friends, always a delight.

1 pound of currants are new friends, always interesting.

¼ teaspoon of allspice puts tang in it like initiative.

¼ teaspoon of cinnamon is ambition.

2 teaspoons of baking powder to make it rise. This is the Holy Spirit.

½ cup of pure fresh whole milk—the perfect food which is the Word of God.

½ teaspoon of salt called Wisdom.

3 cups of CREAM OF THE WEST Flour sifted finely to fold the whole cake together—Love blends all life into one.

Method:—Mix all well together and bake in the slow oven of experience. When well done, allow to cool. Add frosting to surround it with beauty. Add red candles to light for all to see; then slice the cake and share it with others.

"We thought the recipe itself was quite delightfully phrased, and it produces a very nice cake indeed." SALLY WEST.

OLD TIME PORK CAKE FOR CHRISTMAS

1 cup finely ground salt pork
1 cup hot strong coffee
1 cup granulated sugar
1 teaspoon each of allspice, nutmeg and cinnamon
1 teaspoon baking soda
2 eggs, well beaten
⅔ cup molasses
3 cups sifted CREAM OF THE WEST Flour
2 cups raisins
1 cup currants
2 cups mixed peel

Place pork in a bowl and pour hot coffee over it. Let stand until cold.

Combine sugar, spices and soda; stir into pork mixture and then add well beaten eggs and molasses.

Sprinkle 2 tablespoons flour over the fruit. Add remaining flour to the pork mixture, stirring until well blended. Add the floured fruit.

Use a large 9-inch or 10-inch baking pan and line it with three layers of brown paper. Bake at 275° F. for about 3 hours.

A busy housewife after a hard day on her feet might be heard to say—
"My heel is galled and I have a sparble in my shoe."
—Sparble—from the old English shoemaker's name for tack or 'sparrow bill'.

ECONOMY CHRISTMAS CAKE

1 cup butter
2 cups brown sugar
4 eggs
½ cup molasses
3 tablespoons raspberry jam
1 apple (grated)
1¼ cups cooked dates
1 cup mixed peel
3 cups seedless raisins
3 cups currants
5 cups sifted CREAM OF THE WEST Flour
1 teaspoon salt
1 teaspoon each of nutmeg, cinnamon, cloves and ginger
1½ teaspoons baking soda
1 cup hot coffee

Cream butter, add the sugar and eggs; beat well. Add the molasses, jam and fruit; mix well. Sift the flour, salt and spices together; add them to the fruit mixture and blend thoroughly. Dissolve the soda in the hot coffee and add to the batter; mix well. Line a large 10-inch bake pan with several layers of brown paper. Bake at 300° F. for about 3 hours. (The cake may be covered in the oven. If you do so, remove the cover to brown the top.)

CHERRY CAKE

1 cup butter
1 cup granulated sugar
3 eggs
½ teaspoon lemon flavouring
3 cups sifted CREAM OF THE WEST Flour

2 teaspoons baking powder
½ teaspoon salt
½ cup milk
¾ cup red cherries
¾ cup green cherries

Cream butter and sugar. Add unbeaten eggs one at a time, beating well after each addition. Add flavouring. Sift flour, baking powder and salt together three times and add them to the creamed mixture alternately with the milk; combine thoroughly. Add cherries.

Bake in a greased and lined 10-inch pan (which is 3 inches deep). Have oven at 300° F. and bake for 2 hours.

BAKED POT CAKE

1½ cups butter
1½ cups granulated sugar
3 eggs
2 teaspoons vanilla or almond extract
3½ cups sifted CREAM OF THE WEST Flour
3 teaspoons baking powder
1 teaspoon salt
1 can evaporated milk (15 oz.)
1½ cups cocoanut
3 cups raisins
1½ cups candied cherries

Cream butter and sugar; add eggs and flavouring extract; beat well. Sift dry ingredients and add to creamed mixture, alternately with milk. Add cocoanut, floured raisins and cherries.

Pour into a well lined pan (9 inches in diameter and 3 inches deep). Bake at 300° F. for 2½ hours. Allow to cool for 30 minutes before removing from the pan.

In many Newfoundland homes to-day a cast iron bake-pot is still a favorite cooking utensil and is used for baking cakes, stews and bread.

HOT MILK POUND CAKE

1½ cups butter or shortening
2 cups granulated sugar
3 eggs
3½ cups sifted CREAM OF THE WEST Flour
1½ teaspoons baking powder
½ teaspoon salt
1 cup hot milk

1 teaspoon lemon flavouring
3 cups raisins
2½ cups cherries

Cream butter; add the sugar and blend well. Beat in the eggs one at a time.

Gradually mix in the sifted dry ingredients. Add the hot milk (not boiling).

Fold in the floured fruit.

Grease a 9-inch or 10-inch cake pan; line it with heavy paper. Pour batter into this. Bake in a 325° F. oven for 2 to 2½ hours.

JAM CAKE

½ cup shortening
1 cup granulated sugar
2 eggs
1 cup jam (blackberry, raspberry or strawberry)
3 cups sifted CREAM OF THE WEST Flour
½ teaspoon salt
1 teaspoon cinnamon
1 teaspoon nutmeg
1 teaspoon baking soda
1 cup buttermilk
1 cup raisins, floured

Cream shortening; slowly beat in the sugar. Add unbeaten eggs one at a time and beat after each addition. Add jam and mix well. Sift together the flour, salt and spices. Stir soda into the buttermilk. Then add the dry ingredients to the creamed mixture, alternately with the buttermilk. Stir well. Fold in the raisins. Bake in a greased 9-inch square pan at 350° F. for 40 minutes. Then lower the temperature to 300° F. and bake for one hour.

BLUEBERRY CAKE

½ cup margarine
1 cup granulated sugar
1 egg, separated
2 cups sifted CREAM OF THE WEST Flour
3 teaspoons baking powder
½ teaspoon salt
¾ cup milk
1 teaspoon vanilla
1½ cups fresh blueberries

Cream together the margarine and sugar; add the egg yolk and beat well. Sift flour, baking powder and salt. Add alternately with milk to the creamed mixture. Beat egg white until stiff; fold into the cake batter with the vanilla. Add fresh blueberries and combine gently.

Pour into a greased 8-inch cake pan and bake at 375° F. for 45 to 50 minutes.

BLUEBERRY SPICE CAKE

- 1/2 cup butter
- 1 1/4 cups brown sugar
- 2 eggs, beaten
- 2 1/2 cups sifted CREAM OF THE WEST Flour
- 1 teaspoon baking powder
- 1 teaspoon salt
- 1 teaspoon ground cinnamon
- 1 teaspoon grated nutmeg
- 2/3 cup milk
- 3/4 cup fresh blueberries
- 1/2 cup raisins

Cream butter and blend in sugar gradually. Add beaten eggs a little at a time and beat after each addition. Add sifted dry ingredients to butter mixture alternately with the milk. Fold in floured blueberries and raisins.

Turn into a buttered and flour coated 9-inch square pan. Bake for 50 minutes at 350° F.

EGGLESS, MILKLESS, BUTTERLESS CAKE

- 1 cup brown sugar
- 1 cup water
- 1 cup raisins
- 3 tablespoons of drippings
- 1/2 teaspoon salt
- 1 1/2 cups sifted CREAM OF THE WEST Flour
- 3/4 teaspoons baking soda
- 1 teaspoon cinnamon
- 1/2 teaspoon ginger

Combine the sugar, water, raisins, drippings and salt. Cook together until the mixture thickens slightly; stirring constantly. Let cool.

Sift the flour, soda, cinnamon and ginger into the cooled mixture; combine well.

Pour into a greased 8-inch or 9-inch square pan. Bake at 350° F. for 1 hour.

Note: Add 1 cup of chopped dates, 1 cup of mixed peel and 1/2 cup of chopped nuts to make a delicious fruit cake with wonderful keeping qualities.

Drop the batter onto greased cookie sheets and bake for 15 minutes at 350° F. and you have soft delicious Hermits.

Double the recipe and you have something worthwhile.

MOM'S DANDY CAKE

- 1 1/2 cups margarine
- 1 1/2 cups granulated sugar
- 3 eggs
- 1 teaspoon vanilla
- 1 teaspoon lemon extract
- 1 teaspoon almond extract
- 3 cups sifted CREAM OF THE WEST Flour
- 2 teaspoons baking powder
- 1 teaspoon salt
- 1 cup hot milk
- 1 cup cherries, raisins or mixed fruit

Cream margarine and sugar until light and fluffy; add eggs one at a time and beat well after each. Add flavourings. Sift flour, baking powder and salt three times. Dredge the fruit. Add the sifted dry ingredients to the creamed mixture alternately with the hot milk. Then fold in floured fruit.

Bake in ring pan for one hour at 350° F. If a loaf pan is used, bake for 1 1/2 hours. Ice with cherry almond or butter icing.

TOMATO SOUP CAKE

- 3/4 cup butter
- 1 1/2 cups granulated sugar
- 1 can tomato soup (10 ounce)
- 1 can water (10 ounce)
- 3 cups sifted CREAM OF THE WEST Flour
- 1 teaspoon baking soda
- 3 teaspoons baking powder
- 1/2 cup cherries
- 3 cups currants or raisins

Cream butter and sugar together. In separate bowl dilute soup with water; mix well. Sift dry ingredients together and add them to the creamed mixture alternately with the liquid. Stir in cherries and currants or raisins. Bake in a greased 13-inch x 9-inch x 2-inch pan at 350° F. for 1 hour and 20 minutes.

NOTES:

_____

_____

_____

COOKIES, SQUARES AND SMALL CAKES

For youngsters (of all ages) home isn't quite complete without a bulging cookie jar in the kitchen. Here is a wide selection of "goodies" for you to try.

COOKIES:

BROWN SUGAR COOKIES
GRANDMOTHER'S GINGER CAKES
MOLASSES DROP COOKIES
MOLASSES OATMEAL COOKIES
DATE OATMEAL COOKIES
JUMBO RAISIN COOKIES
OAT AND RAISIN COOKIES
RAISIN AND NUT DROP COOKIES
PINEAPPLE RAISIN COOKIES
MINCE MEAT DROP COOKIES
JAM DROPS
POTATO COOKIES
CARROT COOKIES

DATE FILLED COOKIES
DATE ROLLS
THREE FRUIT ROLLED OAT COOKIES
GINGERSNAPS
ICE BOX COOKIES
SHORT BREAD
OLD FASHIONED SCOTCH CAKES
CHEESE PASTRIES
GINGER SCHROLLS
BRICKS WITHOUT STRAW
COTTON TOPS
CHOCOLATE SNOW BALLS

SQUARES:

RAISIN BARS
RAISIN SQUARES
DATE SQUARES
FRUIT SQUARES
ORANGE SQUARES

BLUEBERRY SQUARES
MINCEMEAT SQUARES
CRANBERRY SQUARES
PEANUT BUTTER CHOCOLATE SQUARES

SMALL CAKES:

BROWNIES
TEA CAKES

CREAM PUFFS

BROWN SUGAR COOKIES

3/4 cup butter
1 cup brown sugar (tightly packed)
2 eggs
2 teaspoons vanilla
1/2 teaspoon baking soda, dissolved
     in 1 teaspoon boiling water
2 cups sifted
     CREAM OF THE WEST Flour
1/2 teaspoon baking powder
     Few grains salt
     Few chopped nuts

Cream butter and sugar; add eggs and beat well. Blend in vanilla and the soda dissolved in boiling water. Add sifted dry ingredients and chopped nuts.

Drop on greased cookie sheets. Bake at 350° F. for 15 minutes or until golden brown.

GRANDMOTHER'S GINGER CAKES

1 cup brown sugar
1 teaspoon ginger
2 teaspoons baking soda
2 teaspoons cream of tartar
1/2 teaspoon salt
2 eggs, well beaten
1 cup molasses
1/2 teaspoon lemon extract
4 cups sifted CREAM OF THE
     WEST Flour (approximately)

Combine brown sugar, ginger, soda, cream of tartar and salt. Add well beaten eggs, molasses and lemon extract; beat until smooth. Cover and let rise for 2 hours. Then add enough sifted flour to form a soft dough (about 4 cups). Roll out on a floured board; cut into large thick cookies. Place on a greased cookie sheet and bake at 350° F. for 10 to 12 minutes.

Note: Flavour and texture will improve if cookies are kept in a covered cake tin for two days before serving.

"The sender of this recipe points out it is very old. Also that it is very good and improves with a little aging." SALLY WEST.

MOLASSES DROP COOKIES

3/4 cup butter or lard
3/4 cup brown sugar
1 egg
3/4 cup molasses
3/4 cup sour cream or sour milk
3 1/2 cups sifted
     CREAM OF THE WEST Flour
1 teaspoon baking powder
1 teaspoon baking soda
1 teaspoon salt
2 teaspoons cinnamon
2 teaspoons ginger
1/2 teaspoon ground cloves

Cream the fat, add the brown sugar and egg, beat for 2 minutes. Add molasses and sour milk. Sift dry ingredients and add to the creamed mixture; combine well.

Drop by spoonfuls onto a greased baking sheet. Space 2 inches apart.

Bake at 350° F. for 15 minutes.

MOLASSES OATMEAL COOKIES

2 1/2 cups rolled oats
1 cup sifted
     CREAM OF THE WEST Flour
1/2 cup sugar
2 teaspoons baking powder
1/2 teaspoon baking soda
1/2 teaspoon salt
1/2 teaspoon each of nutmeg, cloves
     and cinnamon
1/3 cup raisins
2/3 cup melted fat
3/4 cup molasses
1 tablespoon milk
1 egg, beaten

Measure rolled oats into a bowl. Sift dry ingredients over them; add the raisins and combine well.

Melt the fat, and then add the molasses, milk and beaten egg.

Pour the liquid ingredients over the dry mixture and blend well.

Drop on greased pans. Bake for 15 minutes at 350° F.

DATE OATMEAL COOKIES

1 1/4 cups dates
1/2 cup granulated sugar
1/2 cup water
1/2 cup shortening
1/2 cup brown sugar
1/2 teaspoon baking soda
1/4 cup boiling water
1/2 teaspoon salt
1 1/4 cups sifted
     CREAM OF THE WEST Flour
1/2 cup oatmeal

Cook dates gently with granulated sugar and water until thick and smooth.

Cream shortening and gradually work in brown sugar. Combine soda, boiling water and salt. Add to creamed mixture. Stir in flour and oatmeal; mix well to form a soft dough.

Roll to ⅛ inch thickness (adding more water if dough does not roll easily). Cut into 2 inch rounds. Spread one round with date mixture to within ¼ inch of edge. Place another round on top and press edges firmly together.

Bake in a 350° F. oven for about 15 minutes or until nicely browned.

JUMBO RAISIN COOKIES

1   **cup boiling water**
2   **cups raisins**
1   **cup shortening**
2   **cups granulated sugar**
3   **eggs**
1   **teaspoon vanilla**
4   **cups sifted**
    CREAM OF THE WEST Flour
1   **teaspoon baking powder**
1   **teaspoon baking soda**
2   **teaspoons salt**
1½ **tesapoons cinnamon**
½ **teaspoon nutmeg**
¼ **teaspoon allspice**
1   **cup chopped nuts**

Boil water and raisins together for 5 minutes. Cool. Cream shortening and sugar; add eggs and beat well. Blend in cooled raisin mixture and vanilla. Sift dry ingredients and add to the creamed mixture; blend well. Chill.

Drop from a teaspoon onto greased and floured baking sheets. Bake at 400° F. for 12 to 15 minutes.

Note: This recipe makes from 6 to 7 dozen cookies.

OAT AND RAISIN COOKIES

¾ **cup shortening**
1¼ **cups lightly packed brown sugar**
1¾ **cups sifted**
    CREAM OF THE WEST Flour
½ **teaspoon salt**
1¼ **cups rolled oats**
1   **teaspoon baking soda**
¼ **cup boiling water**
1   **teaspoon vanilla**
¾ **cup finely chopped raisins**

Cream shortening and sugar well. Blend in sifted flour, salt and rolled oats. Add soda dissolved in boiling water; blend well. Add vanilla and chopped raisins.

Drop dough onto ungreased cookie sheets and flatten with tines of a wet fork.

Bake at 375° F. for 12 minutes.

RAISIN AND NUT DROP COOKIES

1   **cup butter or shortening**
2   **cups brown sugar**
2   **eggs, beaten**
3   **cups sifted**
    CREAM OF THE WEST Flour
2   **teaspoons baking soda**
½ **teaspoon salt**
½ **teaspoon cinnamon**
½ **teaspoon cloves**
1   **cup sour milk**
1   **cup chopped raisins**
1   **cup chopped nuts**

Cream butter and brown sugar until light; add beaten eggs and combine well. Add the sifted dry ingredients alternately with the milk. Blend in floured raisins and nuts. Drop batter from a teaspoon onto lightly greased cookie sheets, leaving about 2 inches between cookies. Bake at 350° F. for 10 to 12 minutes.

This makes about 5 dozen cookies and they keep very well in a closed can.

PINEAPPLE RAISIN COOKIES

½ **cup shortening**
1   **cup brown sugar**
1   **egg, beaten**
1   **teaspoon vanilla**
¾ **cup crushed pineapple (not drained)**
2   **cups sifted**
    CREAM OF THE WEST Flour
½ **teaspoon baking powder**
½ **teaspoon baking soda**
½ **teaspoon salt**
½ **cup raisins, floured**

Blend shortening and sugar well. Add egg, vanilla and pineapple. Sift in the dry ingredients and add floured raisins. Drop on greased baking sheets. Bake at 375° F. for 12 to 15 minutes.

MINCE MEAT DROP COOKIES

1¼ **cups sifted**
    CREAM OF THE WEST Flour

2½ teaspoons baking powder
¼ teaspoon salt
¼ cup shortening or butter
½ cup granulated sugar
1 egg, beaten
1 cup mince meat

Sift flour, baking powder and salt together. Cream butter, add sugar; cream until light and fluffy. Add beaten egg and mince meat. Blend in sifted dry ingredients. Drop by spoonfuls onto greased pan. Bake at 375° F. for 10 to 15 minutes.

JAM DROPS

⅔ cup butter
½ cup sugar
1 egg
½ cup thick jam
1 teaspoon vanilla
½ cup cocoanut
½ cup nutmeats
1¾ cups sifted
        CREAM OF THE WEST Flour
2 teaspoons baking powder
½ teaspoon salt

Cream butter and sugar well; add egg and beat. Blend in the jam, vanilla, nuts and cocoanut. Add sifted dry ingredients. Drop by spoonfuls onto a greased cookie sheet. Bake at 375° F. for 10 to 15 minutes.

POTATO COOKIES

⅔ cup shortening
1 cup sugar
1½ cups hot mashed potatoes
2 cups sifted
        CREAM OF THE WEST Flour
2 teaspoons baking powder
1 teaspoon salt
1 teaspoon cinnamon
½ teaspoon cloves
½ teaspoon nutmeg
½ cup raisins
¼ cup broken nutmeats

Combine shortening and sugar thoroughly; blend in the mashed potatoes. Add the sifted dry ingredients and then the raisins and nutmeats. Drop by teaspoons onto greased cookie sheets. Bake at 350° F. for 12 to 15 minutes.

CARROT COOKIES

1 cup shortening
¾ cup sugar
1 egg, beaten
1 cup cooked mashed carrots
2 cups sifted
        CREAM OF THE WEST Flour
2 teaspoons baking powder
½ teaspoon salt
½ teaspoon vanilla
        Few drops almond extract

Cream shortening and sugar; add beaten egg. Add mashed carrots alternately with the sifted dry ingredients. Blend in flavouring extracts.

Drop from a teaspoon onto greased baking sheets. Bake at 375° F. for 10 to 12 minutes. Ice with orange icing, if desired.

DATE FILLED COOKIES

Date Filling:
2 cups finely chopped dates
¾ cup sugar
¾ cup water
½ cup chopped nuts, if desired

Cook dates, sugar and water until the mixture thickens, stirring constantly. Add nuts, if used, and cool.

1 cup shortening
2 cups brown sugar
3 eggs
½ cup water
1 teaspoon vanilla
3½ cups sifted
        CREAM OF THE WEST Flour
1 teaspoon baking soda
½ teaspoon salt
⅛ teaspoon cinnamon

Cream shortening and sugar; add eggs and beat well. Stir in the water and vanilla. Add the sifted dry ingredients and blend well. Drop batter from a teaspoon onto greased bakery sheets. Place about ½ teaspoon of filling in the centre of each cookie and cover with another teaspoon of batter.

Bake at 350° F. until nicely browned (10 to 12 minutes).

This recipe makes about 5 or 6 dozen cookies.

The shortest conversation held by two fishermen—
    "Ar'n?"
    "Nar'n."
    (Meaning "Did you get any fish?"
        "No—none.")

DATE ROLLS

1   cup butter
1   cup brown sugar
2   eggs, well beaten
1   cup cocoanut
½   cup chopped nuts
2   cups sifted
       CREAM OF THE WEST Flour
2   teaspoons baking powder
       Few grains of salt
1   teaspoon vanilla
       Pitted dates

Cream butter and sugar; then add beaten eggs and combine well. Blend in remaining ingredients in order given. Roll mixture around pitted dates. Bake in a 375° F. oven until brown (about 10 to 12 minutes).

THREE FRUIT ROLLED OAT COOKIES

½   cup brown sugar
½   cup granulated sugar
½   cup melted shortening
1   egg, beaten
½   teaspoon salt
½   cup cocoanut
½   cup chopped walnuts
½   cup chopped raisins
1   teaspoon vanilla
1   banana, mashed
1   cup sifted
       CREAM OF THE WEST Flour
½   teaspoon baking soda
2   cups rolled oats

Combine ingredients in the order given, blending after each addition. Drop from a teaspoon onto greased baking sheets. Press down with floured fork or spoon. Bake in a 350° F. oven for 12 to 15 minutes.

GINGERSNAPS

4   cups sifted
       CREAM OF THE WEST Flour
2   teaspoons baking powder
1   teaspoon baking soda
1   teaspoon salt
2   teaspoons ginger
1   teaspoon cinnamon
1   cup shortening
1   cup sugar
1   cup molasses
¼   cup cold tea (medium strength)

Sift flour, baking powder, baking soda, salt and spices together three times.

Cream shortening; add sugar and molasses. Beat until light and fluffy.
Add sifted dry ingredients and cold tea alternately to the creamed mixture. Blend well.
Turn dough onto a lightly floured board and roll to ⅛-inch thickness. Cut with a lightly floured cookie cutter.
Bake at 375° F. for 10 to 12 minutes.
Makes about 8 dozen cookies.
Note: Dough may be covered and chilled before rolling, if you wish.

Another fishermen's conversation.
"How's the fishery this year?"
"Not so good. Them that got ar'n,
ain't no better than them that got
nar'n. Cause them that got ar'n,
ain't no bit of size!"

ICE BOX COOKIES

1   cup butter or shortening
1   cup granulated sugar
1   cup brown sugar
2   eggs, beaten
1   teaspoon vanilla
3½   cups sifted
         CREAM OF THE WEST Flour
1   teaspoon baking soda
⅛   teaspoon salt
1   cup chopped nuts
1   tablespoon caraway seeds

Cream butter and sugar until light and fluffy. Add beaten eggs and vanilla and beat well. Sift dry ingredients together and add them to the creamed mixture; blend well. Add nuts and caraway seeds. Form into two long rolls which are about 2 inches in diameter; cover with waxed paper. Leave in the ice box or other cool place overnight. Slice very thin and bake at 375° F. for 10 minutes or until lightly browned.

SHORT BREAD

¼   cup granulated sugar
½   cup butter
1   cup sifted
       CREAM OF THE WEST Flour

Cream butter and sugar well. Sift flour three times.
Add to the creamed mixture and combine. Roll out on a lightly floured board, cut in desired shapes. Bake at 350° F. for 20 minutes.

OLD FASHIONED SCOTCH CAKES

1 cup butter
½ cup granulated sugar
2 cups CREAM OF THE WEST Flour
½ cup potato flour
½ teaspoon salt

Cream butter and sugar. Add sifted dry ingredients and blend well. Grease a baking sheet or two 8-inch square pans. Put mixture in pan and press evenly with a fork and cut into squares before placing in oven.

Bake at 325° F. for 20 to 25 minutes. Cut again after they are baked.

CHEESE PASTRIES

1 cup sifted
   CREAM OF THE WEST Flour
¼ teaspoon salt
½ cup grated cheese
½ cup butter
3 tablespoons milk

Sift flour and salt; add cheese. Rub in the butter. Add milk and stir lightly to make a stiff dough.

Roll to ⅛-inch thickness; cut into 2-inch rounds. Place spoonfuls of marmalade on half of the rounds; top each with a second round of pastry. Press the edges together with a fork.

Bake at 425° F. for 10 minutes.

GINGER SCHROLLS

¼ cup margarine
6 tablespoons brown sugar
¼ cup molasses
½ cup sifted
   CREAM OF THE WEST Flour
1 teaspoon ginger
1 teaspoon lemon juice
1 teaspoon vanilla

Mix all ingredients together in order listed. Grease cookie sheets and drop batter on them by small spoonfuls, leaving space to allow for spreading. Bake at 375° F. for 5 minutes.

Cool slightly and then shape by rolling each around the handle of a wooden spoon. Cool thoroughly. Fill schrolls with whipped cream a few minutes before serving.

BRICKS WITHOUT STRAW

(Cookies)

1 cup dry bread crumbs (finely rolled)
½ cup cocoanut
   Few grains salt
½ cup sugar
2 egg whites, beaten
1 teaspoon almond flavouring

Combine bread crumbs, cocoanut, salt and sugar. Fold into beaten egg whites and add flavouring.

Shape into balls and bake in a 350° F. oven until nicely browned (about 15 minutes).

"Our contributor tells us how she came to invent this recipe: 'You known how there are always crumbs on the board when you cut bread. Many throw them out but I began saving them for the birds and it's quite amazing how they mount up. Then one day I was stumped for small cakes and I made up this recipe'." SALLY WEST.

COTTON TOPS

5 tablespoons shortening
1 cup sugar
6 tablespoons cocoa
1 egg
1½ cups sifted
   CREAM OF THE WEST Flour
1½ teaspoons baking powder
½ teaspoon cinnamon
⅓ cup milk
½ teaspoon vanilla
   Marshmallows

Cream shortening; blend in sugar and cocoa. Add egg and beat well. Add sifted dry ingredients alternately with the milk. Add vanilla. Drop on cookie pans, bake at 375° F. for 15 minutes. Place ½ marshmallow on top of each cookie and bake an additional 5 minutes.

CHOCOLATE SNOW BALLS

Boil for 3 to 4 minutes:
¼ cup butter
½ cup evaporated milk
2 cups granulated sugar
Add
2 tablespoons cocoa
Let cool a little, then add:
2 cups cocoanut
2 cups rolled oats
1 teaspoon vanilla

Roll in balls and then in more cocoanut.
NO COOKING NEEDED.

RAISIN BARS

½ cup butter
½ cup granulated sugar
1 egg, beaten
2 cups sifted
   CREAM OF THE WEST Flour
2 teaspoons baking powder
¼ cup milk

Cream butter and sugar; add beaten egg. Then blend in sifted dry ingredients alternately with the milk. Spread half of this mixture in a greased 8 or 9 inch square pan. Add raisin filling, then top with second half of the batter. Bake at 350° F. until golden brown (about 40 minutes).

RAISIN FILLING

2½ cups raisins
¾ cup brown sugar
2 tablespoons
   CREAM OF THE WEST Flour
½ cup water
¼ teaspoon lemon extract

Place raisins in a saucepan; add sugar and flour. Then add water and boil together until thick. Stir in flavouring. Cool slightly and then use as directed above.

RAISIN SQUARES

⅓ cup shortening
⅔ cup brown sugar
2 tablespoons molasses
1 egg
½ cup sifted
   CREAM OF THE WEST Flour
¼ teaspoon baking soda
¼ teaspoon salt
¾ cup quick cooking rolled oats
1 cup seedless raisins

Melt shortening; pour into a bowl. Stir in sugar and molasses. Add egg and beat well. Sift flour, soda and salt into the shortening mixture. Then blend in rolled oats and raisins which have been rinsed and drained.

Turn into a greased 8-inch square pan. Bake at 350° F. for 25 to 30 minutes. Cool and cut into squares.

DATE SQUARES

Filling:
2 cups dates
1 cup brown sugar
1 cup hot water

Combine and cook until dates are very soft. Set aside to cool.

Crumb:
1½ cups sifted
   CREAM OF THE WEST Flour
1½ teaspoons baking soda
½ teaspoon salt
1½ cups rolled oats
1 cup brown sugar
¾ cup butter

Sift flour, soda and salt into a large bowl. Stir in rolled oats and sugar. Rub in the butter until a coarse crumb is formed.

Press half of this mixture into a greased 8-inch x 12-inch pan. Cover with date filling, then add remaining crumb mixture. Bake at 375° F. for 25 minutes. Cut into squares while hot.

FRUIT SQUARES

2½ cups sifted
   CREAM OF THE WEST Flour
½ teaspoon baking powder
¼ teaspoon salt
½ cup lard
½ cup butter
¼ cup ice water (about)

Sift dry ingredients; cut in lard and butter; add enough ice water to make a stiff dough. Form into a ball and chill.

Filling:
4 apples, finely chopped
3 cups currants
1 cup granulated sugar
½ teaspoon salt
1 teaspoon cinnamon
2 tablespoons
   CREAM OF THE WEST Flour
1 tablespoon butter
½ cup water
1 teaspoon almond extract

Combine all ingredients except the almond extract. Simmer until the apples are tender and the mixture is thickened. Cool and then add the almond extract.

Roll out half of the dough and line a large pan (about 15 x 11 inches). Bring dough up on the sides. Spread filling over this. Cover with remaining rolled out dough, pinching moistened edges together. Prick with a fork at 1-inch intervals.

Bake at 500° F. for 10 minutes, then reduce heat to 350° F. and continue baking for 25 minutes.

Sprinkle with ¼ cup powdered sugar and cut in 2-inch squares.

ORANGE SQUARES

2 cups sifted
CREAM OF THE WEST Flour
¾ cup granulated sugar
1 teaspoon baking powder
½ teaspoon salt
2 cups cocoanut
1 cup butter

Sift dry ingredients together. Add cocoanut. Rub in butter until mixture is crumbly. Press half of this mixture over bottom of a greased pan (about 9-inches square)

For the filling:

Combine:
1 cup granulated sugar
2 teaspoons custard powder
1 orange (juice, pulp and grated rind)
1 cup hot water

Boil filling until it thickens. Then add 1 tablespoon butter and spread over layer of crumb in the pan.

Top with remaining half of the crumb.

Bake at 350° F. for 25 to 30 minutes. Cut in squares when cool.

BLUEBERRY SQUARES

3 tablespoons butter
⅓ cup sugar
2 egg yolks
⅔ cup sifted
CREAM OF THE WEST Flour
1 teaspoon baking powder
¼ teaspoon salt
¼ cup milk
¼ teaspoon vanilla

Cream butter and sugar; beat in the egg yolks. Add sifted dry ingredients alternately with the milk and vanilla.

Pour into a greased 8-inch square pan. Bake at 350° F. for 18 to 20 minutes.

Topping:
2 egg whites
6 tablespoons sugar
¼ teaspoon salt
1 cup fresh blueberries

Beat eggs until peaked; beat in sugar and salt. Fold blueberries into the meringue and spread over the baked cake portion.

Return to a 300° F. oven and bake until topping has browned slightly (12 to 15 minutes).

MINCEMEAT SQUARES

1½ cups sifted
CREAM OF THE WEST Flour
1 teaspoon baking soda
½ teaspoon salt
1½ cups rolled oats
1 cup brown sugar
½ cup butter
2 cups mincemeat

Sift flour, soda and salt together; add the rolled oats and brown sugar and mix well. Cut butter into the dry mixture until it is in fine crumbs. Press three-quarters of this mixture into a greased 9-inch square pan and spread the mincemeat evenly.

Sprinkle the remaining crumb mixture over the mincemeat.

Bake at 350° F. for 30 minutes. Cool and cut into squares.

CRANBERRY SQUARES

2 cups rolled oats
1 cup brown sugar
1 cup sifted
CREAM OF THE WEST Flour
1 teaspoon baking powder
¾ cup melted butter
2½ cups cranberry jam or freshly cooked and sweetened cranberries

Combine rolled oats, sugar, flour and baking powder. Add melted butter and mix well. Press half of this mixture over bottom of greased baking pan (about 8 x 12 inches). Spread with cranberry jam or freshly cooked and sweetened cranberries. Add remaining rolled oat mixture.

Bake at 350° F. for 30 minutes. Remove from oven and cut into squares.

PEANUT BUTTER CHOCOLATE SQUARES

Cut crusts from 16 slices of white bread. Spread 8 of these slices with a thin layer of peanut butter and press a plain slice on top of each. Cut into 1-inch squares.

Now, boil together for 2 or 3 minutes.

2 cups granulated sugar
4 tablespoons cocoa
8 tablespoons water

Dip squares into the syrup and then roll in cocoanut. Place on waxed paper to cool.

BROWNIES

¼ cup butter
¾ cup granulated sugar
2 squares melted unsweetened
   chocolate
2 eggs, slightly beaten
½ cup sifted
   CREAM OF THE WEST Flour
1 cup chopped nuts
1 teaspoon vanilla

Cream butter and sugar; add melted chocolate and mix well. Add slightly beaten eggs. Stir in flour, chopped nuts and vanilla. Bake in a greased 8-inch square pan at 350° F. for 25 to 30 minutes.

TEA CAKES

⅓ cup shortening
1 cup granulated sugar
2 eggs, well beaten
1⅔ cups sifted
   CREAM OF THE WEST Flour
1½ teaspoons baking powder
¼ teaspoon salt
⅔ cup milk
1 teaspoon vanilla

Cream shortening with sugar until fluffy; add well beaten eggs. Sift dry ingredients and add them alternately with the milk in small amounts. Stir in the vanilla.

Fill greased muffin pans ⅔ full. Bake at 375° F. for 15 to 18 minutes.

CREAM PUFFS

½ cup boiling water
¼ cup butter
¼ teaspoon salt
½ cup sifted
   CREAM OF THE WEST Flour
2 eggs

Add butter and salt to boiling water in a saucepan and bring to a boil. Add flour all at once and stir vigorously until mixture forms a stiff ball. Remove from heat.

Add eggs, one at a time, and beat each time until mixture is smooth.

Shape puffs on a greased cookie sheet.

Bake at 425° F. for 15 minutes and then at 350° F. for 25 minutes.

Cool, cut slit in side of each puff and fill. Use whipped cream, ice cream or your favourite filling.

NOTES:

DESSERTS

Puddings make a hearty ending to an enjoyable meal, and they've long been a favourite dessert in Newfoundland. Here are some old favourites with some new twists, too.

SIMPLE PUDDINGS:

BAKED CUSTARD

RAISIN BREAD PUDDING

ORANGE PUFF CUSTARD

HOMEMADE VANILLA ICE CREAM

CHOCOLATE PUDDING

CHOCOLATE DUMPLINGS

HONEYCOMB PUDDING

ONE BOWL PLAIN PUDDING

EGG PATTIES

STEAMED PUDDINGS:

SEVEN CUP PUDDING

OLD FASHIONED FIGGED DUFF

OLD FASHIONED MOLASSES PUDDING

PLUM PUDDING

CHRISTMAS PUDDING

CRANBERRY PUDDING

STEAMED PARTRIDGEBERRY PUDDING

STEAMED FIG PUDDING

STEAMED APPLE PUDDING

BLACKBERRY PUDDING

STEAMED PEACH PUDDING

UPSIDE DOWN PUDDINGS:

PINEAPPLE GINGERBREAD
   UPSIDE-DOWN CAKE

BLUEBERRY UPSIDE DOWN CAKE

ORANGE UPSIDE DOWN PUDDING

FRUIT PUDDINGS:

APPLE COBBLER

APPLE DELIGHT

QUICK APPLE PUDDING

APPLE DUMPLINGS

GRANDMOTHER'S APPLE CROW'S NEST

DANISH APPLE PUDDING

RASPBERRY DOUBLE BOILER PUDDING

RHUBARB CAKE

ROYAL RHUBARB CAKE

BLUEBERRY COBBLER

BLUEBERRIES WITH DOUGHBOYS

BLUEBERRY ROLY-POLY

BLUEBERRY BUCKLE

OLD FASHIONED BLUEBERRY PUDDING

BLUEBERRY CRUNCH

BAKED PARTRIDGEBERRY PUDDING

BAKEAPPLE DESSERT

NEWFOUNDLAND MARSH-BERRY CAKE

PARTRIDGEBERRY PUDDING

BAKED CUSTARD

4 eggs
1/4 cup granulated sugar
1/2 teaspoon salt
1 15 oz. can evaporated milk
1 cup water
1 teaspoon vanilla
1/4 cup sifted brown sugar

Beat eggs, granulated sugar, salt, evaporated milk, water and vanilla together in a bowl.

Spread sifted brown sugar over the bottom of a 1 1/2-quart casserole. Pour custard over brown sugar.

Place casserole in a pan of hot water and bake in a 350° F. oven for 50 to 60 minutes, or until knife inserted in the centre comes out clean.

Cool for one hour; then invert custard over a plate. Brown sugar will form a sauce.

This makes 6 servings.

> *Hauler's Bread. It was the custom for the men of one church to get together in the fall and cut and haul wood for the church and parsonage. In return the minister's wife would serve an especially rich raisin bread, called hauler's bread or Methodist bread.*

RAISIN BREAD PUDDING

2 cups milk
5 slices raisin bread
  Butter
2 eggs
1/2 cup granulated sugar
1/4 teaspoon salt
1/4 cup powdered food beverage (Ovaltine or Instant Coffee)

Scald milk. Remove crusts from bread, lightly butter and cut bread into cubes. Put into a one-quart baking dish.

Beat eggs slightly; stir in sugar, salt and powdered food beverage. Add scalded milk and blend until mixture is smooth. Strain over raisin bread.

Oven poach in a 350° F. oven for one hour or until custard is set.

Serve warm with pouring cream.

ORANGE PUFF CUSTARD

2 tablespoons butter
1/4 cup granulated sugar
2 tablespoons
  CREAM OF THE WEST Flour
2 eggs, separated
1/4 teaspoon salt
1/4 cup orange juice
1 teaspoon lemon juice
1 1/2 teaspoons grated lemon rind
1/2 cup milk
1/2 cup boiling water.

Cream butter. Mix well with sugar and flour. Add egg yolks and salt; beat well. Add juice and rind, stir until smooth. Blend in milk and water. Fold in beaten egg whites. Put in a 1 1/2-quart pyrex bowl; set in a shallow pan of hot water and bake at 300° F. for 45 minutes.

HOMEMADE VANILLA ICE CREAM

1 1/2 teaspoons cornstarch
3 cups milk
3/4 cup granulated sugar
1/4 teaspoon salt
2 eggs, beaten
2 cups whipping cream
1 1/2 teaspoons vanilla

Mix cornstarch to a thin, smooth paste by combining it with about one tablespoon of the milk. Add 2 cups of the milk, sugar and salt. Cook over boiling water for 20 minutes, stirring occasionally. Beat eggs until light; add hot milk mixture to them. Return to double boiler and cook for 2 minutes, stirring constantly. Cool and put through a sieve. Add remaining milk, cream and vanilla.

Pour mixture into freezer can. Freeze until very firm. Use 8 parts cracked ice to one part salt.

When sufficiently frozen, remove the dasher; cover and seal well. Pour brine from the freezer; repack the ice cream container in cracked ice, covering the top. Wrap in newspapers or sacking until ready to use.

> *Nish—delicate, tender*
> *—applied to ice or even to pastry.*

CHOCOLATE PUDDING

1 cup sifted
  CREAM OF THE WEST Flour
2 teaspoons baking powder
1/2 teaspoon salt

3/4 cup granulated sugar
2 tablespoons cocoa
2 tablespoons shortening
1/2 cup milk
1 teaspoon vanilla
1/4 cup cocoa
3/4 cup brown sugar
1 3/4 cups hot water

Sift flour, baking powder, salt, sugar and 2 tablespoons cocoa into a bowl. Blend in the shortening, then add the milk and vanilla and mix until well blended. Spread batter in a greased 8-inch square pan. Combine 1/4 cup cocoa and brown sugar; add hot water and stir until cocoa dissolves.

Pour sauce over the batter. Do not stir. Bake at 350° F. for 45 minutes.

CHOCOLATE DUMPLINGS

Dumplings:

3 tablespoons shortening
1/2 cup granulated sugar
2 tablespoons cocoa
1 egg, beaten
1 cup sifted
    CREAM OF THE WEST Flour
2 teaspoons baking powder
1/2 teaspoon salt
1/3 cup milk
1 teaspoon vanilla

Cream shortening, sugar and cocoa; add beaten egg. Add sifted dry ingredients and milk alternately to the creamed mixture. Add vanilla.

Sauce:

Combine:

3/4 cup brown sugar
1/2 cup cocoa
2 tablespoons
    CREAM OF THE WEST Flour
    Few grains salt

Add 2 cups boiling water and cook until thick. Remove from heat and stir in 2 tablespoons butter.

Drop dumpling mixture by spoonfuls on top of the sauce. Cover and cook for 20 minutes.

Note: If you prefer, the dumplings may be baked in a covered casserole at 425° F.

HONEYCOMB PUDDING

1 cup sifted
    CREAM OF THE WEST Flour
1/2 cup granulated sugar
1/2 cup milk
1/2 cup butter
1 cup molasses
1 teaspoon baking soda
4 eggs

Sift flour and sugar together. Scald the milk and melt the butter in it. Pour this over the sifted flour and sugar. Heat the molasses and stir in the soda until it foams. Beat the eggs until thick. Add the foaming molasses and beaten eggs to the hot milk mixture; stir all together. Bake in a 1 1/2 or 2-quart pudding dish for 30 to 40 minutes at 375° F. Serve hot with Creamy Sauce.

CREAMY SAUCE

1/2 cup butter
1 cup powdered sugar
1/4 cup cream
1 teaspoon vanilla

Beat butter to a cream. Add sugar gradually and beat until very light and smooth. Blend in the cream and vanilla.

If the sauce becomes too thick, place bowl in hot water and stir until smooth.

ONE BOWL PLAIN PUDDING

1 cup sifted
    CREAM OF THE WEST Flour
2 teaspoons baking powder
1/4 teaspoons salt
2 tablespoons butter or margarine
1/3 cup milk

Sift dry ingredients into bowl in which pudding is to be steamed. Rub in butter or margarine; add milk to make a soft dough. Spread over bottom of the bowl and place in a steamer for 25 minutes; keep water boiling rapidly.

Serve hot with Molasses Sauce or Partridgeberry Sauce.

MOLASSES SAUCE

1 cup molasses
1 tablespoon butter
    Pinch of nutmeg

Boil together for 3 minutes.

PARTRIDGEBERRY SAUCE

1 cup partridgeberries
3/4 cup granulated sugar
3/4 cup water

Boil together until the berries are soft and the sauce has thickened (about 20 minutes).

EGG PATTIES

4 eggs
1/2 cup granulated sugar
2 cups sifted
CREAM OF THE WEST Flour
2 teaspoons baking powder
1/2 teaspoon salt

Beat eggs; add sugar and continue beating until thick. Add twice-sifted dry ingredients to the egg mixture and mix to a smooth paste. Drop by spoonfuls into hot deep fat and fry until golden brown.

SAUCE FOR PATTIES

1/2 cup granulated sugar
1 tablespoon butter
1 cup boiling water
2 teaspoons custard powder or cornstarch
2 tablespoons cold water

Combine sugar, butter and boiling water in top part of double boiler. Blend until butter melts and sugar is dissolved. Dissolve custard powder or cornstarch in cold water; add some of the hot mixture to this. Then add this mixture to the sauce and cook over hot water until thickened.

Cool and serve over the patties.

SEVEN CUP PUDDING

1 cup butter
1 cup granulated sugar
1 cup sifted
CREAM OF THE WEST Flour
1 cup raw chopped apples
1 cup stale bread crumbs
1 cup currants
1 cup milk
1/2 teaspoon baking soda

Mix all ingredients together in a large bowl until well combined. Put in a pudding cloth and boil for 1 1/2 hours.

Serve hot with sauce.

OLD FASHIONED FIGGED DUFF

3 cups bread crumbs
1 cup raisins
1/2 cup brown sugar
Few grains salt
1 teaspoon each of ginger, allspice and cinnamon

1/4 cup melted butter
3 tablespoons molasses
1 teaspoon baking soda
1 tablespoon hot water
1/2 cup sifted
CREAM OF THE WEST Flour

Soak stale bread and crusts in water for a few minutes. Squeeze out the water and rub between the hands to make crumbs. Measure without pressing down in the cup. Combine the bread crumbs, raisins, sugar, salt and spices and mix with a fork. Add melted butter, molasses, and soda which has been dissolved in the hot water. Now add the flour and combine well.

Pour mixture into a dampened pudding bag; tie tightly leaving a little slackness to allow the pudding to expand.

Boil for 1 1/2 hours. (May be done with corned beef or pork.)

Serve with heated molasses.

Note: Serve with Corned Beef and Cabbage Dinner.

OLD FASHIONED MOLASSES PUDDING

1 cup molasses
1/2 cup granulated sugar
1 teaspoon cinnamon
1 teaspoon cloves
1 teaspoon allspice
1/2 cup hot water
1 teaspoon baking soda
1/2 cup butter, melted
1/2 pound raisins
3 cups sifted
CREAM OF THE WEST Flour
1/2 teaspoon salt

Mix together molasses, sugar and spices in a bowl. Dissolve baking soda in hot water and add to first mixture. Then add melted butter and raisins; mix well. Add sifted flour and salt a little at a time. Pour into a pudding bag or greased mould and steam for 2 to 2 1/2 hours. (If a mould is used, cover tightly with a cloth.)

PLUM PUDDING

2/3 cup margarine
3/4 cup brown sugar
2 eggs, beaten
3/4 teaspoon baking soda
1 cup grated raw apple
3/4 cup grated raw carrots
1 cup grated raw potato

1½ cups 3-day old bread, crumbled
1⅜ cups sifted
    CREAM OF THE WEST Flour
1 teaspoon baking powder
1½ teaspoon salt
1½ teaspoon cinnamon
½ teaspoon each of ground cloves,
    ground ginger, allspice and
    grated nutmeg
¼ cup orange or other fruit juice or
    syrup from canned fruit
1½ cups seedless raisins (floured)
1½ cups currants (floured)
⅓ cup chopped candied peel
¼ cup chopped nuts (if desired)

Cream margarine and blend in sugar gradually.

Dissolve soda in well beaten eggs and add to the creamed mixture, a little at a time; beat well after each addition. Stir in grated apples, carrots and potatoes, and the bread crumbs.

Sift dry ingredients and add to the above mixture, alternately with the fruit juice. Combine well.

Wash and dry the raisins and currants; lightly flour. Add the floured fruit, peel and nuts to the plum pudding and combine well. Turn into well greased 10-inch pudding mould and tie on cover of water proof paper. Steam for 3½ hours. (The pudding may be tied in a pudding bag and boiled for 3½ hours, if preferred.)

Store in a cool place. For serving, reheat by steaming one hour.

Figged—duff or figgity-pudding, raisin or plum pudding.

CHRISTMAS PUDDING

2¼ cups sifted
    CREAM OF THE WEST Flour
2 teaspoons baking soda
2 cups raisins
3 cups whole candied cherries
4 cups cut mixed peel
1½ cups currants
2 eggs, well beaten
2 cups ground suet
1⅓ cups brown sugar
2 tablespoons molasses
2 cups fine dry bread crumbs
2 cups buttermilk
1½ cups almonds

Sift flour and soda together. Mix raisins, cherries, mixed peel and currants; sprinkle fruit with ½ cup of the flour mixture.

Beat eggs well; add ground suet, brown sugar and molasses. Blend in remaining flour mixture and the bread crumbs, alternately with the buttermilk. Stir in floured fruit and the almonds.

Pour into a two-quart mould that has been well greased. Cover with waxed paper and a cloth; tie securely.

Steam for 3 hours.

Serve piping hot.

CRANBERRY PUDDING

1 cup chopped cranberries (fresh)
2 tablespoons butter
1 cup boiling water
½ cup granulated sugar
½ cup light molasses
1 egg, well beaten
1½ cups sifted
    CREAM OF THE WEST Flour
1 teaspoon baking soda
1 teaspoon salt

Put cranberries and butter in a mixing bowl; add boiling water. Then add the sugar, molasses and beaten egg. Stir until well mixed. Add the sifted dry ingredients.

Pour into a well greased one-quart pudding bowl; cover tightly. Steam for 2 hours.

Serve with a foamy sauce.

STEAMED
PARTRIDGEBERRY PUDDING

1½ cups sifted
    CREAM OF THE WEST Flour
3 teaspoons baking powder
¼ teaspoon salt
¼ cup margarine
1¼ cups fresh partridgeberries
¾ cup milk (made up from dried milk
    powder)

Sift dry ingredients into a bowl; rub in the margarine. Add the berries and then the milk, stirring lightly to make a batter.

Pour into a greased one-quart mould. Place over boiling water and steam for 1 hour.

Serve with a sauce made as follows:

1 cup brown sugar
1 tablespoon
    CREAM OF THE WEST Flour

½ cup water
1 tablespoon butter

Combine sugar and flour; add water and boil until thickened. Remove from heat and add the butter.

Note: For a richer batter, add ¼ cup granulated sugar to the dry ingredients; reduce milk to ½ cup and add 1 beaten egg.
Blueberries may be used in place of partridgeberries.

STEAMED FIG PUDDING

¼ cup shortening
1 cup granulated sugar
1 egg
2 cups sifted
   CREAM OF THE WEST Flour
4 teaspoons baking powder
⅓ teaspoon salt
1 cup milk
½ teaspoon vanilla or lemon extract
1½ cups chopped figs

Cream shortening; add sugar and beaten egg. Then add sifted flour, baking powder and salt. Stir in the milk, flavouring extract and figs.

Pour into a large 9-inch or 10-inch pudding mould and steam for 2 to 2½ hours.

STEAMED APPLE PUDDING

1½ cups sifted
   CREAM OF THE WEST Flour
1½ teaspoons baking powder
½ teaspoon salt
1½ teaspoons granulated sugar
4 tablespoons margarine
½ cup cold water

Sift dry ingredients together three times. Cut in margarine. Add water to make a dough for rolling.

Using a lightly floured board or pastry cloth, roll ⅓ of the pastry into a 6-inch circle. Roll remaining pastry into an 11-inch circle and fit it into a greased 6-inch pudding bowl, flattening the folds against the sides.

FILLING

2½ cups chopped apples (peeled and cored)
¾ cup granulated sugar
1 teaspoon lemon juice or ½ teaspoon lemon extract

Mix together and put in pastry lined bowl. Moisten edge with cold water and place small circle of pastry on top; seal carefully. Place in a kettle with boiling water half way up side of the bowl. Turn a 7-inch plate over the top to keep out the moisture. Cover kettle and steam for 2 hours. Turn out on a platter and serve hot. No sauce required but it is delicious with cream when available.

N.B. Filling may be varied by using half apples and half partridgeberries or other fresh fruit in season.

BLACKBERRY PUDDING

1 egg
⅔ cup molasses
3 tablespoons melted shortening
1 teaspoon vanilla
1¾ cups sifted
   CREAM OF THE WEST Flour
1 teaspoon baking powder
½ teaspoon baking soda
½ teaspoon salt
1 teaspoon cinnamon
½ teaspoon mace
¼ teaspoon ginger
½ cup cold water
1 cup blackberries

Beat egg and then stir in the molasses, melted shortening and vanilla. Sift the dry ingredients and add them alternately with the water. Fold in the blackberries.

Put in a pudding bag and boil for 3 hours or pour into an 8-inch mould and steam for 3 hours.

STEAMED PEACH PUDDING

2 cups sifted
   CREAM OF THE WEST Flour
3 teaspoons baking powder
½ teaspoon salt
2 tablespoons butter
1 cup milk
3 cups sliced peaches and juice

Sift dry ingredients; rub in butter. Add milk to form a very soft dough. Place peaches and juice in the bottom of a two-quart baking dish which has been greased. Spread dough over the fruit; cover with a plate. Steam pudding over rapidly boiling water for 1½ hours. Serve with hard sauce or whipped cream.

PINEAPPLE GINGERBREAD UPSIDE-DOWN CAKE

½ cup molasses
¼ cup butter or margarine
1 can sliced pineapple
Few raisins and nuts

Pour molasses over bottom of a deep 9-inch baking pan; dot with butter. Arrange pineapple slices over this and fill centres with nuts and raisins. Heat this on top of stove until butter melts.

3 tablespoons butter or margarine
½ cup brown sugar
1 egg
1½ cups sifted
CREAM OF THE WEST Flour
1 teaspoon baking soda
¼ teaspoon salt
1 teaspoon ginger
1 teaspoon cinnamon
½ cup molasses
½ cup milk

Cream butter and sugar; add egg and beat well. Add sifted flour, soda, salt and spices alternately with the molasses and milk.

Pour batter over the mixture in the baking pan. Bake in a 350° F. oven for 45 minutes.

BLUEBERRY UPSIDE DOWN CAKE

3 tablespoon butter
⅓ cup firmly packed bro wn sugar
1¾ cups fresh blueberries
½ teaspoon grated lemon rind
2 teaspoons lemon juice
1⅓ cups sifted
CREAM OF THE WEST Flour
2 teaspoons baking powder
¼ teaspoon salt
¾ cup granulated sugar
1 teaspoon cinnamon
½ teaspoon nutmeg
⅛ teaspoon cloves
¼ cup margarine
1 egg
½ cup milk
1 teaspoon vanilla

Melt butter in an 8-inch square pan. Remove from heat and add brown sugar; blend well. Spread blueberries over the brown sugar mixture and sprinkle with lemon rind and juice.

Combine sifted flour, baking powder, salt, granulated sugar and spices. Cream margarine. Add sifted flour mixture, unbeaten egg, milk and vanilla. Stir until flour is dampened, then beat vigorously for 1 minute. Spoon batter over blueberries.
Bake at 350° F. for 50 to 60 minutes.

Cook cake in pan for 5 minutes and then invert on a large, flat dessert platter. Serve warm with whipped cream or ice cream.

ORANGE UPSIDE DOWN PUDDING

1 tablespoon butter
½ cup granulated sugar
⅔ cup boiling water
2 teaspoons grated orange rind
½ cup orange juice
2 tablespoons butter
⅔ cup granulated sugar
1 egg
1½ cups sifted
CREAM OF THE WEST Flour
1½ teaspoons baking powder
½ teaspoon salt
⅔ cup milk

Blend together first five ingredients and pour into a greased 9-inch square baking dish.

Cream 2 tablespoons butter and ⅔ cup granulated sugar; add unbeaten egg and beat well. Mix and sift dry ingredients twice and add to creamed mixture, alternately with the milk. Drop by spoonfuls over orange mixture.

Bake in a 400° F. oven for 5 minutes, then reduce heat to 350° F. and bake for 35 minutes.

APPLE COBBLER

6 apples, peeled and sliced
¾ cup brown sugar
1 tablespoon butter
1½ cups sifted
CREAM OF THE WEST Flour
2 teaspoons baking powder
¼ teaspoon salt
2 tablespoons shortening
1 egg, well beaten
6 tablespoons milk
¼ cup granulated sugar
2 tablespoons boiling water
½ teaspoon vanilla

Arrange apples in a greased baking dish (2-quart size). Sprinkle with brown sugar and dot with butter.

Sift flour, baking powder and salt together; cut in the shortening. Combine well beaten egg and the milk; add to the flour mixture and mix lightly to a soft dough.

Arrange dough over the apples and pat down gently to completely cover the apples. Bake at 425° F. for 15 minutes.

Remove from oven and lower temperature to 350° F. Pour the sugar, boiling water and vanilla mixture over the top. Return to the 350° F. oven and bake for another 20 minutes.

Serve plain or with cream.

APPLE DELIGHT

¼ cup butter
¼ cup granulated sugar
1   egg
2   cups sifted
     CREAM OF THE WEST Flour
3½ teaspoons baking powder
½ teaspoon salt
⅔ cup milk
4 to 6 apples
½ cup brown sugar
1   teaspoon cinnamon

Cream butter and granulated sugar well; add egg and beat until light. Add sifted flour, baking powder and salt alternately with the milk. Spread batter over bottom of a greased 8-inch or 9-inch square pan.

Peel and core apples, cut in thin wedges. Press sharp edges of apple pieces into the dough. Mix the brown sugar and cinnamon; sprinkle over the apples.

Bake at 375° F. for 35 to 40 minutes.

Serve warm with foamy lemon sauce.

QUICK APPLE PUDDING

2   tablespoons butter
¼ cup granulated sugar
1 cup sifted
     CREAM OF THE WEST Flour
1   teaspoon baking powder
⅓ teaspoon salt
1   cup chopped apples
6   tablespoons milk

Cream butter and sugar. Sift dry ingredisent and stir in the chopped apples. Add this to the creamed mixture alternately with the milk. Pour into a 1½ or 2 quart casserole.

SAUCE

1   cup brown sugar
1   tablespoon butter
     Few grains salt
1½ cups boiling water
1   teaspoon vanilla

Combine sugar, butter and salt; add boiling water and stir until sugar dissolves and the butter is melted. Add the vanilla.

Pour sauce over the batter. Bake at 400° F. for 30 to 35 minutes.

APPLE DUMPLINGS

2   cups sifted
     CREAM OF THE WEST Flour
4   teaspoons baking powder
½ teaspoon salt
3   tablespoons shortening
¾ cup milk

Sift dry ingredients into a bowl. Cut in shortening and add milk to make a soft dough. Roll out to ¼ inch thickness, cut in six squares.

6 apples, pared and cored
Jam
Sugar
Cinnamon
Butter

Place an apple in centre of each square of pastry. Fill apple centres with jam, add a little sugar and cinnamon; top with a dot of butter.

Fold opposite corners of pastry to the centre; dampen edges and seal. Prick each with a fork.

Place one inch apart in a greased baking dish. Bake at 350° F. for 30 minutes. Serve warm with cream.

GRANDMOTHER'S APPLE CROW'S NEST

4   medium sized tart apples
1   tablespoon butter
½ cup granulated sugar
1   teaspoon cinnamon

Slice apples into a greased 9-inch or 10-inch pie plate; dot with butter. Combine sugar and cinnamon; sprinkle 2 tablespoons of this over the apples and set aside the rest.

1   cup sifted
     CREAM OF THE WEST Flour
2   teaspoons baking powder

¼ teaspoon salt
¼ cup granulated sugar
3 tablespoons shortening
¼ cup milk

Sift together flour, baking powder, salt and sugar. Cut in shortening. Add enough milk to make a soft dough. Pat out to desired size and cover apple mixture with the dough.

Bake at 400° F. for 25 to 30 minutes or until apples are tender.

When baked, turn out upside down on a plate and work remaining sugar and cinnamon mixture into the apples with a fork.

Serve hot with whipped cream, topped with a little cinnamon and a few finely chopped nuts.

DANISH APPLE PUDDING

6 medium sized apples
4 tablespoons butter
3 eggs
3 tablespoons
  CREAM OF THE WEST Flour
  Grated rind of 1 lemon
  Pinch of salt
2 cups milk
¼ cup icing or fruit sugar

Peel apples and cut in splices. Melt butter, add apples and cook over medium heat for 10 minutes, stirring occasionally. Beat whole eggs, add flour, lemon rind, salt and milk; mix well. Pour apples into buttered 1½-quart baking dish and pour egg mixture over them.

Place in a pan of hot water and bake at 350° F. for 45 minutes. When ready, sprinkle with the icing sugar and put back in the oven until brown.

RASPBERRY
DOUBLE BOILER PUDDING

1¼ cups canned or stewed
  raspberries, with syrup
¼ cup granulated sugar
1½ tablespoons
  CREAM OF THE WEST Flour

Put raspberries and syrup in top part of a double boiler. Combine sugar and cornstarch; add to the raspberries and mix well. Set aside.

3 tablespoons shortening
⅓ cup granulated sugar

1 egg
1⅛ cups sifted
  CREAM OF THE WEST Flour
1½ teaspoons baking powder
¼ teaspoon salt
½ cup milk
¼ teaspoon vanilla
½ teaspoon grated lemon rind

Cream shortening and sugar; add egg and beat well. Add sifted dry ingredients alternately with the milk. Stir in vanilla and grated lemon rind.

Turn batter over raspberries in top part of double boiler. Cover closely. Cook over rapidly boiling water for 1¼ hours or until batter is done.

Serve with custard sauce or thin cream.

RHUBARB CAKE

1½ cups finely chopped fresh rhubarb
  Boiling water
¼ cup shortening
¾ cup granulated sugar
1 egg
1½ cups sifted
  CREAM OF THE WEST Flour
¾ teaspoon baking powder
¼ teaspoon baking soda
¼ teaspoon salt
¼ cup chopped nuts
½ cup milk

Cover rhubarb with boiling water; let stand 5 minutes; drain.

Cream shortening and sugar; add egg and beat well. Sift dry ingredients, and add them to the creamed mixture alternately with the milk. Fold in drained rhubarb and chopped nuts.

Pour batter into a greased 8-inch square pan.

Bake for 40 minutes at 350° F.

Serve warm with rhubarb sauce.

RHUBARB SAUCE

Cover 1½ cups chopped rhubarb with cold water. Bring to a boil. Drain. Blend ½ cup granulated sugar and 1 tablespoon CREAM OF THE WEST Flour into the rhubarb. Cook until thickened; stirring constantly. Remove from the heat; stir in 1 tablespoon butter and serve hot over Rhubarb Cake.

ROYAL RHUBARB CAKE

Arrange in a greased 9-inch square pan:

2 cups rhubarb, diced in 1/2-inch pieces

Sprinkle with a mixture of:

2/3 cup granulated sugar
1 tablespoon CREAM OF THE WEST Flour
1 teaspoon grated orange rind
1 teaspoon cinnamon

Sift together into a bowl:

1 cup sifted CREAM OF THE WEST Flour
2 teaspoons baking powder
2 tablespoons granulated sugar
1/2 teaspoon salt

Cut in 1/4 cup shortening until mixture looks like meal.

Combine:

1 egg, well beaten
3 tablespoons milk

Add egg mixture to dry ingredients to make a dough. Drop by spoonfuls over rhubarb mixture and spread.

Bake at 350° F. for 25 minutes.

Combine:

2 tablespoons orange juice
1 tablespoon granulated sugar

At end of 25 minutes baking period, remove cake from the oven and pour this mixture over it. Return to oven and bake an additional 15 minutes at 350° F.

Serve warm with cream or hard sauce.

Note: This is equally good with apples or blueberries instead of rhubarb.

BLUEBERRY COBBLER

Combine:

3 cups fresh blueberries
1/3 to 1/2 cup granulated sugar
1 tablespoon lemon juice
1/4 teaspoon salt
2 tablespoon melted butter

Spread this mixture over bottom of an 8-inch square pan. Sprinkle with 1/2 teaspoon cinnamon.

Make a biscuit dough as follows:

1 1/2 cups sifted CREAM OF THE WEST Flour
3 teaspoons baking powder
3/4 teaspoon salt
3 tablespoons skim milk powder
6 tablespoons shortening
3/4 cup water

Sift dry ingredients together; cut in shortening. Add water to form a soft dough. Drop by spoonfuls onto blueberry mixture. Bake at 400° F. for 35 minutes or until berries are tender.

Serve with milk or cream.

BLUEBERRIES WITH DOUGHBOYS

1 cup granulated sugar
1/2 cup water
1 quart blueberries

Make a syrup of the sugar and water by boiling for 5 minutes. Then add blueberries and boil until tender.

Add doughboys when blueberries are cooked.

DOUGHBOYS

2 cups sifted CREAM OF THE WEST Flour
3 teaspoons baking powder
1/2 teaspoon salt
1 tablespoon granulated sugar
1 tablespoon butter
2/3 cup milk (about)

Sift dry ingredients together and then cut in the butter. Add enough milk to make into doughboys. Drop from a tablespoon into boiling blueberry mixture. Cover and cook rapidly for 15 minutes (no peeking).

Serve hot with whipped cream.

BLUEBERRY ROLY-POLY

2 cups sifted CREAM OF THE WEST Flour
3 teaspoons baking powder
1/2 teaspoon salt
1 tablespoon granulated sugar
4 tablespoons butter or margarine
3/4 cup milk (about)

Sift dry ingredients together; cut in the butter or margarine; add enough milk to make a soft dough. Turn out on a lightly floured board, knead lightly for a few seconds and roll to a rectangle measuring about 9 inches by 12 inches.

Spread with this mixture:

2 cups fresh blueberries
3/4 cup granulated sugar
1 tablespoon lemon juice

Roll up like a jelly roll; sealing ends and edges well. Bake in a greased loaf pan (about 9 x 5 inches) at 425° F. for 25 to 30 minutes.

Serve hot with cream.

BLUEBERRY BUCKLE

- ¼ cup shortening
- ½ cup granulated sugar
- 1 egg
- 1 cup sifted CREAM OF THE WEST Flour
- 1½ teaspoons baking powder Few grains salt
- ⅓ cup milk
- 2 cups blueberries

Cream shortening; add sugar and cream thoroughly. Add egg and mix well. Sift the flour, baking powder and salt. Add them alternately with the milk to the first mixture.

Pour into a greased 8-inch or 9-inch square pan. Spread blueberries over the cake batter.

TOPPING

- ½ cup granulated sugar
- ⅓ cup sifted CREAM OF THE WEST Flour
- ½ teaspoon cinnamon
- ¼ cup butter

Rub butter into the dry ingredients. Sprinkle mixture over the blueberries. Bake at 350° F. for 45 to 50 minutes.

OLD FASHIONED BLUEBERRY PUDDING

- 3 cups fresh blueberries
- ⅓ cup cold water
- 1 teaspoon gelatin
- ¼ cup boiling water
- ½ cup granulated sugar
- 1 teaspoon lemon juice
- 7 thin slices bread
- ½ cup melted butter

Place fresh blueberries in a saucepan with cold water and cook for 5 minutes or until berries are tender. Remove from the fire. Soften gelatin in ¼ cup of juice from the cooked blueberries; let stand for 5 minutes. Add boiling water to dissolve the gelatin. Combine blueberries and juice, dissolved gelatin, sugar and lemon juice.

Remove crusts from bread. Brush both sides of each slice generously with melted butter.

Cover bottom and sides of a one-quart dish with buttered bread, cutting slices to make a neat effect. Cut remaining bread into small squares. Pour ⅓ of the blueberry mixture into the bread lined dish; top with squares of bread. Add two more layers each of blueberries and bread.

Cool all day and serve with whipped or sour cream.

> *Blueberry pudding was usually referred to as 'John Casey', especially if it was served with molasses 'coady' or sauce.*

BLUEBERRY CRUNCH

- 2 cups blueberries
- ¼ cup granulated sugar
- 1 cup sifted CREAM OF THE WEST Flour
- 1 cup brown sugar
- ¼ teaspoon salt
- ½ teaspoon cinnamon
- ½ cup margarine

Put blueberries in an 8-inch baking dish; sprinkle with granulated sugar. Mix together the flour, brown sugar, salt and cinnamon. Rub margarine into the flour mixture until crumbly. Sprinkle this mixture over the berries and bake in a 350° F. oven for 30 minutes.

Note: Apples or rhubarb may be used instead of blueberries.

BAKED PARTRIDGEBERRY PUDDING

- 2 cups sifted CREAM OF THE WEST Flour
- 1 cup granulated sugar
- 2½ teaspoons baking powder
- ½ teaspoon salt
- 3 tablespoons melted shortening
- ⅔ cup milk
- 1 teaspoon vanilla
- 1 egg
- 2 cups partridgeberries

Sift dry ingredients into a mixing bowl, add shortening, milk, vanilla and egg. Beat 2 minutes. Stir in partridgeberries.

Bake in a greased 9-inch square pan at 350° F. for 40 minutes.

Serve with sauce.

BAKEAPPLE DESSERT

½ cup margarine
1 cup brown sugar
1 cup sifted
  CREAM OF THE WEST Flour
2 cups rolled oats
1 teaspoon baking soda
1½ cups fresh bakeapples
  (sweetened)
      or
1½ cups bakeapple jam

Place margarine, sugar, flour, rolled oats and baking soda in bowl. Rub with finger tips until fine and crumbly. Spread half of mixture into pie dish. Spread with bakeapples or bakeapple jam. Cover with remaining crumb mixture and gently press down with hands until even. Bake in moderate 350° F. oven until golden brown. Serve hot.

NEWFOUNDLAND MARSH-BERRY CAKE

½ cup shortening
1 cup granulated sugar
1 egg
2 cups sifted
  CREAM OF THE WEST Flour
2 teaspoons baking powder
½ teaspoon salt
½ teaspoon vanila
¾ cup milk
1 cup marsh-berries

Cream shortening and sugar until light and fluffy. Add the egg, beating until thoroughly blended. Sift together the flour, baking powder, and salt. Stir the vanilla into the milk. Add the dry ingredients alternately with the liquid to the creamed mixture, mixing well after each addition. Fold in the marsh-berries. Pour the batter into a greased 9-inch square pan.

Sprinkle with 2 tablespoons sugar. Bake for 50 to 55 minutes at 350° F.

For dessert serve the cake warm or cold with a hot Lemon Sauce:

LEMON SAUCE

1 cup granulated sugar
3 tablespoons
  CREAM OF THE WEST Flour
  Dash of salt
2 cups boiling water
  Grated rind and juice of 1 lemon
2 tablespoons butter

Mix the sugar, flour and salt. Add the boiling water gradually, stirring constantly to keep the mixture smooth. Boil 5 minutes, then remove from the heat. Add the grated lemon rind and juice and the butter. Serve hot.

PARTRIDGEBERRY PUDDING

1 cup partridgeberries
1 cup granulated sugar
¾ cup butter
½ cup brown sugar
1 egg
1½ cups sifted
  CREAM OF THE WEST Flour
1 teaspoon baking powder
¼ teaspoon salt
1 teaspoon vanilla

Combine partridgeberries and sugar; cook together until berries are tender. Put in a 1½-quart casserole.

Cream butter and brown sugar; add egg and beat until light. Add sifted dry ingredients and vanilla.

Spread batter over the fruit mixture.

Bake at 375° F. for 25 to 30 minutes. Serve with whipped cream.

NOTES:

_____
_____
_____
_____
_____
_____
_____
_____
_____
_____

PASTRY AND PIES

It takes a knowing touch to make good pastry—but it's well worth the effort when your pies come from the oven—golden-brown, flaky and tender.

PASTRY:

PASTRY
PASTRY
PASTRY
HOT WATER PASTRY

NEVER FAIL PASTRY
SWEET PASTRY FOR TARTS
PUFF PASTRY

PIES:

CRANBERRY PIE
RAISIN PIE
FRESH BLUEBERRY PIE
RHUBARB PIE
LEMON MERINGUE PIE
LEMON CAKE PIE

RHUBARB CREAM PIE
BANANA CREAM PIE
RAISIN BUTTERMILK PIE
PUMPKIN PIE
SPICE CRUMB APPLE PIE

TARTS, Etc.:

LASSY TART
BUTTER TARTS

EGG TARTS
CRUNCHY PARTRIDGEBERRY APPLE TARTS

PASTRY

1   cup butter
1/3 cup granulated sugar
1   egg, beaten
3   cups sifted
    CREAM OF THE WEST Flour
1/2 teaspoon baking powder

Cream butter and sugar until well blended. Add the beaten egg and combine well. Sift the flour and baking powder together. Add the dry ingredients to the creamed mixture, cutting in with a pastry blender or two knives until mixture resembles fine cornmeal. Form into three balls of dough; wrap in waxed paper and chill.

Roll out to 1/8 inch thickness. Makes one 2-crust pie and one pie shell.

Bake shells at 450° F. for 8 to 10 minutes; bake 2-crust pies at this temperature for 10 minutes and then lower temperature to 350° F. and continue baking until done.

Scrumptious—wonderful, fine, imposing.

PASTRY

5   cups sifted
    CREAM OF THE WEST Flour
2   tablespoons brown sugar
1½ teaspoons salt
1   pound lard
1   egg
2   tablespoons vinegar
    Cold water

Sift flour, sugar and salt; rub in the lard. Beat egg in a measuring cup; add vinegar and then add enough cold water to make 3/4 cup. Add it to the flour mixture and stir lightly to a soft dough.

Wrap in waxed paper and then in a tea towel. Store in a cold place until needed.

PASTRY

3   cups sifted
    CREAM OF THE WEST Flour
1/4 teaspoon salt
1   cup butter
6 to 8 tablespoons cold water

Sift flour and salt; cut in butter. Sprinkle with cold water and mix lightly to a soft dough. Chill before using.

Sufficient for one 2-crust pie and one pie shell.

HOT WATER PASTRY

2   cups shortening
1   cup boiling water
6   cups sifted
    CREAM OF THE WEST Flour
2   teaspoons baking powder
2   teaspoons salt

Pour boiling water over the shortening; beat until creamy. Cool. Add sifted dry ingredients all at once; cut in with two knives or a pastry blender. Chill thoroughly before rolling.

Sufficient for 3 two-crust pies.

Liveyers—those who belong or "live here."

NEVER FAIL PASTRY

6   cups sifted
    CREAM OF THE WEST Flour
2   teaspoons salt
1   teaspoon baking powder
1   pound shortening
2   teaspoons vinegar
1   egg, beaten
    Cold water

Sift dry ingredients into a bowl; cut in the shortening. Combine vinegar and beaten egg in an 8-ounce measuring cup; fill the cup with cold water. Add to the flour mixture and stir lightly to form a soft dough.

This pastry may be kept in the ice box or used at once.

Sufficient for 3 double crust pies or 6 pie shells.

SWEET PASTRY FOR TARTS

1/2 cup butter
3/4 cup brown sugar
2   egg yolks
1½ cups sifted
    CREAM OF THE WEST Flour
1   teaspoon baking powder
    Pinch salt

Cream butter, sugar and egg yolks until smooth. Add sifted dry ingredients and stir until well blended.

Pat mixture into cup cake pans; reserving some to use as a topping, if desired. Fill two-thirds full with raisin filling, mincemeat or other filling. For top, roll reserved dough to 1/8-inch thickness and cut to cover each tart. Press edges together and prick top to allow steam to escape.

Bake at 400° F. for 15 to 18 minutes.

PUFF PASTRY

½ **pound butter**
2 **cups sifted**
   CREAM OF THE WEST Flour
   Ice-cold water
   Jam or jelly

Divide the butter into 3 equal portions. Dredge each with sufficient flour to roll into a thin sheet.

Add enough cold water to the 2 cups of sifted flour to make a soft but not sticky dough. Roll out until quite thin.

Place one sheet of butter on the dough; fold edges of pastry over the butter on every side. Roll out with short, light strokes until pastry is its original size. (Do not go quite to the edge when rolling so that the air will not be forced out.) Chill 10 minutes.

Repeat with the second sheet of butter and third sheet of butter; chilling for 10 minutes after each rolling.

Roll out until quite thin; cut in squares. Put a teaspoon of jam or jelly on each square; dampen the edges; fold corner-wise to make triangles; seal.

Bake at 500° F. for 10 minutes; reduce temperature to 350° F. and bake for another 15 to 20 minutes.

"The secret is to keep the materials cool throughout. Handle as little as possible, using tips of fingers. The triangles should be very flaky and rise an inch or more, be golden-brown in colour." SALLY WEST.

CRANBERRY PIE

1½ **cups cranberries**
1 **cup granulated sugar**
2 **tablespoons**
   CREAM OF THE WEST Flour
1 **cup cold water**
1 **teaspoon vanilla**
½ **teaspoon almond extract**

Cut cranberries in half. Combine sugar and flour; add to cranberries, in a saucepan. Add cold water and bring mixture to a boil; simmer until it thickens slightly. Remove from heat and add flavourings.

Pour into unbaked 8½-inch pie shell; cover with top crust. Bake at 425° F. for 10

minutes; reduce heat to 350° F. and complete baking.

RAISIN PIE

1 **cup brown sugar**
2 **tablespoons**
   CREAM OF THE WEST Flour
   Few grains salt
1 **cup water**
   Grated rind of one lemon
   Juice of one lemon
2 **cups raisins, chopped or ground**
   Pastry

Combine sugar, flour and salt in top part of a double boiler. Add the water, lemon rind and juice, and the raisins. Cook over hot water for 15 minutes, stirring occasionally. Cool.

Meantime, line a 9-inch pie plate with pastry and prepare pastry strips for top of the pie.

Add cooled filling and top with pastry strips in lattice fashion.

Bake at 450° F. for 10 minutes; reduce heat to 350° F. and bake for another 20 minutes or until pastry is done.

FRESH BLUEBERRY PIE

   Pastry
¼ **cup CREAM OF THE WEST Flour**
1 **cup granulated sugar**
⅛ **teaspoon salt**
4 **cups fresh blueberries**
1 **teaspoon lemon juice**
1 **tablespoon butter or margarine**

Line 9-inch pie plate with pastry. Sift flour, sugar and salt together and sprinkle ¼ of it over uncooked bottom crust. Add the blueberries and remaining sugar mixture. Sprinkle with lemon juice and dot with butter or margarine. Add top crust—seal edges and flute.

Bake at 450° F. for 15 minutes and reduce heat to 350° F. and continue baking until berries are tender (about 30 minutes).

RHUBARB PIE

4 **cups fresh rhubarb, cut in**
   ½-inch pieces
1½ **cups granulated sugar**
3 **tablespoons quick-cooking**
   tapioca
¼ **teaspoon salt**
1 **tablespoon butter**

Combine rhubarb, sugar, tapioca and salt. Place in a pastry lined 9-inch pie plate; dot with butter. Top with ½ inch wide strips of pastry to make a lattice effect. Flute edge.

Bake at 450° F. for 10 minutes; reduce temperature to 375° F. and continue baking for another 25 to 30 minutes or until rhubarb is tender.

LEMON MERINGUE PIE

3 tablespoons cornstarch
3 tablespoons
  CREAM OF THE WEST Flour
1 cup granulated sugar
¼ teaspoon salt
1½ cups boiling water
2 egg yolks
6 tablespoons lemon juice
2 teaspoons grated lemon rind
2 teaspoons butter

Mix cornstarch, flour, sugar and salt in top of a double boiler, add boiling water slowly; cook over **direct heat** until thick and smooth, stirring constantly. Cover and cook over boiling water for another 10 minutes. Beat egg yolks and add a little hot mixture to them; stir, then add to hot mixture and blend well. Still stirring, cook 2 minutes over hot water. Add butter, lemon juice and rind; remove from heat and cool. Pour into baked shell. Cover with this meringue.

Meringue:

Beat 2 egg whites to peaks; gradually beat in 3 tablespoons granulated sugar and one teaspoon cornstarch.

Bake until delicately brown in a 350° F. oven.

LEMON CAKE PIE

Pastry:
½ cup softened butter
¼ cup boiling water
1 cup sifted
  CREAM OF THE WEST Flour
¼ teaspoon baking powder
  Few grains salt

Put softened butter into a bowl; add boiling water and stir. Then gradually blend in sifted dry ingredients to form a soft, moist dough.

Lightly flour board and roll out dough until very thin.

Line a 9-inch or 10-inch ungreased pie plate.

Filling:
2 tablespoons
  CREAM OF THE WEST Flour
1 cup granulated sugar
½ teaspoon salt
  Grated rind of one lemon
2 tablespoons butter
  Juice of one lemon
2 egg yolks, slightly beaten
1 cup milk
2 egg whites, stiffly beaten

Combine flour, sugar, salt and lemon rind. Blend in the butter; add lemon juice and slightly beaten egg yolks. Gradually add milk and combine well. Fold in stiffly beaten egg whites.

Pour into prepared pie crust. Bake at 425° F. for 10 minutes; lower temperature to 350° F. and bake for 20 to 25 minutes.

RHUBARB CREAM PIE

4 cups finely cut fresh rhubarb
1½ cups granulated sugar
⅓ cup sifted
  CREAM OF THE WEST Flour
¼ teaspoon salt
¾ cup cream

Put rhubarb in a pastry lined pie plate.

Mix the sugar, flour, salt and cream together. Pour this mixture over the rhubarb.

Bake at 425° F. for 10 minutes; reduce temperature to 350° F. and bake until pastry is nicely browned and the rhubarb is tender.

This is equally delicious with any kind of raw fruit.

BANANA CREAM PIE

3 eggs, separated
¾ cup granulated sugar
¾ cup potato flour
1 teaspoon baking powder
¼ teaspoon salt
½ teaspoon vanilla or lemon
  flavouring

Beat egg whites until stiff. Then beat yolks and add sugar; beat well. Fold in egg whites. Sift flour, baking powder and salt together; fold into the first mixture.

Bake in two 8-inch layer pans at 400° F. for 10 to 12 minutes.

Put bananas between the layers and top with whipped cream.

RAISIN BUTTERMILK PIE

1½ cups seedless raisins
1⅓ cups buttermilk
½ cup granulated sugar
1½ teaspoons cornstarch
⅛ teaspoon salt
1 teaspoon grated lemon rind
1 tablespoon lemon juice
Pastry for single 8-inch crust
Cinnamon

Rinse raisins and drain; add the buttermilk, sugar, cornstarch, salt, lemon rind and juice. Blend well. Pour into pastry lined pie plate. Sprinkle with cinnamon.
Bake in a 450° F. oven for 10 minutes. Reduce heat to 350° F. and bake an additional 35 minutes.

PUMPKIN PIE

1½ cups cooked pumpkin or squash (sieved)
1 cup granulated sugar
½ teaspoon each of ginger, nutmeg, cinnamon, salt
¼ teaspoon cloves
2 eggs, beaten
2 cups milk

Combine sugar and spices. Add them to the pumpkin or squash, then blend in beaten eggs and milk.
Pour into an unbaked 9-inch pie shell. Bake at 450° F. for 10 minutes, then reduce temperature to 350° F. and bake for an additional 30 to 35 minutes or until a silver knife inserted in the centre comes out clean. (Do not let the pie boil.)

SPICE CRUMB APPLE PIE

2 cups sifted
CREAM OF THE WEST Flour
1 teaspoon salt
⅔ cup shortening

Sift flour and salt together; cut in the shortening with a pastry blender or two knives until mixture resembles coarse crumbs. Divide in two.
To one-half, add 3 tablespoons ice water and mix lightly to form a dough. Chill for 10 minutes and then roll out. Line 10-inch deep pie plate with this pastry; flute the edges.
To other half of crumb mixture, add:
¼ cup granulated sugar
½ teaspoon cinnamon
¼ teaspoon nutmeg

Work in until well blended; set aside.
Combine:
½ cup granulated sugar
½ cup light brown sugar
¼ teaspoon cinnamon
¼ teaspoon nutmeg
2 tablespoons
CREAM OF THE WEST Flour
Add to 6 cups of peeled and sliced cooking apples; toss lightly. Now, arrange the apple mixture in the lined pie plate.
Top with the spiced crumb mixture.
Bake at 425° F. for 20 minutes; reduce temperature to 350° F. and bake an additional 20 minutes or until apples are tender.

LASSY TART

Prepare your favourite pastry; line an 8-inch pie shell and prepare pastry strips for the top.

Filling:
1 egg
1 cup molasses
1 cup soft bread crumbs

Beat the egg; add molasses and beat until combined. Stir in the bread crumbs.
Pour into uncooked pie shell. Top with strips of pastry and bake in a 400° F. oven for about 20 minutes or until pastry is lightly browned and the filling is firm.

BUTTER TARTS

½ cup brown sugar
¼ cup corn syrup
3 tablespoons soft butter
1 egg, well beaten
Few grains salt
½ teaspoon vanilla
1½ teaspoons vinegar
⅓ cup currants (washed and dried)
¼ cup chopped walnuts
12 unbaked tart shells

Combine sugar, corn syrup and soft butter. Add the well beaten egg and blend. Stir in remaining ingredients.
Fill unbaked tart shells ⅔ full. Bake at 375° F. for 10 to 12 minutes or until filling has set.

EGG TARTS

Make pastry; cut in circles and line muffin tins.

Blend together:

2   cups brown sugar
2   eggs
2   tablespoons vinegar
2   tablespoons melted butter
     Few grains salt
1   teaspoon vanilla

Beat filling well and put about 3 table-spoons of it in each tart shell.

Bake at 400° F. for 15 minutes.

CRUNCHY PARTRIDGEBERRY APPLE TARTS

Line muffin tins with your favourite pastry.

2   cups apples, finely chopped
1   cup partridgeberry sauce
2   tablespoons
     CREAM OF THE WEST Flour
1/4 teaspoon nutmeg
1/4 teaspoon cinnamon

Gently mix apples and partridgeberry sauce. Stir flour and spices together and mix with the partridgeberry mixture. Spoon into unbaked tart shells.

Topping:

1/2 cup sifted
     CREAM OF THE WEST Flour
1/2 cup brown sugar
1/4 cup butter

Sift flour and sugar together. Cut in butter until mixture is crumbly. Sprinkle over tarts. Bake 10 minutes in a 425° F. oven and then lower oven to 350° F. and continue baking until pastry is nicely browned.

Partridgeberry Sauce:

Combine:

4   cups partridgeberries
2   cups granulated sugar

Cook together slowly without adding water.

NOTES:

FISH DISHES

Folks with a love of the sea are always noted for their excellent fish dishes, and here's where Newfoundland cooking comes into its own. I hope your favourite is among our selections.

FISHERMEN'S "FISH AND BREWIS"
FISH AND BREWIS
NEWFOUNDLAND FLIPPERS
BAKED FLIPPERS WITH VEGETABLES
DRESSED COD FILLETS
FISH AND TOMATO SCALLOP
BAKED CODFISH
CODFISH AU GRATIN CASSEROLE
SALT FISH BALLS AND FRITTERS
CODFISH CAKES
SALT CODFISH PIE
INDIVIDUAL SALT FISH LOAVES
BAKED COD TONGUES
FRIED COD HEADS
FRIED COD TONGUES
STEAMED SALMON LOAF
BAKED SALMON IN A BLANKET
SALMON IN POTATO SHELLS
SALMON RICE CASSEROLE
STEWED GRILSE
TROUTERS' SALMON
SPICED NEWFOUNDLAND HERRING
STUFFED BAKED HERRING
POTTED HERRING
ROASTED HERRING
HERRING FRIED IN OATMEAL

FRIED SQUID
BAKED SQUID
BAKED TURBOT
FISH SOUNDS
MATELOTE OF EEL
FRIED CAPLIN
FRIED SMELT
FRIED CLAMS IN BATTER
FRIED MUSSELS
BAKED SMOKED FILLETS
CODFISH SOUP
COD SOUP
FISHERMAN'S FRESH FISH STEW
FISH CHOWDER
OYSTER STEW
STUFFED MACKEREL
BAKED HALIBUT WITH TOMATO SAUCE
FISH SOUFFLE
BAKED FISH LOAF
FISH CRISPIES
FISH BAKED IN CUSTARD
KEDGAREE
LOBSTER CUTLETS
LOBSTER SOUFFLE
NEWFOUNDLAND LOBSTER SALAD

FISHERMEN'S "FISH AND BREWIS"

As made by Newfoundland fishermen when on board schooners, particularly on the East Coast.

Cut a quarter of a pound of fat back pork into very small pieces and put in an iron bake-pot over medium heat and cook until all the fat is rendered out of pork, leaving the fat and "scrunchions" in the bottom of the pot.

While pork is cooking, go on deck with a cod-jigger and catch a medium size codfish and remove head, tail, skin and guts. Wash in clean water from the side of the boat, then cut in three or four pieces and place in bake-pot with the fat and scrunchions and cook from fifteen to twenty minutes, or until it is cooked, then remove all bones with your fingers, or a fork if preferred, and you are ready for the hard bread.

Take a half-pound of Harvey's or PURITY Hard bread. Place in a piece of ship's canvas or heavy calico and beat with a hammer or head of small axe until it becomes very small and powdery. Then throw it in the bake-pot with the fish, scrunchions and fat, and mix through and through until all the vitamins from the juice of the fish have been mixed with the bread crumbs. Serve piping hot for three or four people, and you have some meal ....yum.......yum.

"Our contributor goes on to say: 'You can have this at home as well as on a schooner but make sure the fish is fresh. It can be made with salt cod just as well, but all the salt must be soaked out before cooking. Any kind of fish and brewis is a good meal, but the fresh fish as described beats them all.'" SALLY WEST.

FISH AND BREWIS

(As made from salt fish)

Remove bones and skin from the dried salt fish; cut fish into pieces.

Cover fish with cold water and soak overnight.

Split cakes of hard bread; soak overnight in cold water.

In the morning: Change water on the fish and bring to a boil. Boil for 20 minutes or until the fish is tender. Remove from the heat, drain and remove any bones.

Bring hard bread to boil in same water in which it has been soaked. Remove from heat and drain immediately. Keep hot.

Combine the cooked fish and hard bread. Serve with "Scrunchions". These are small cubes of fat pork or fat back fried to a golden brown and poured over the fish and brewis like a gravy.

Or, the fish and brewis can be added to the nicely browned fat back and chopped up with the scrunchions.

"Newfoundland families in all income brackets, and in all geographical locations serve fish and brewis with varying frequency, especially for Sunday morning breakfast. Sometimes the brewis is served with bacon or ham instead of fish. The fish, of course, is the salt fish and the brewis is made from the hard bread which can now be bought in grocery stores.". SALLY WEST.

Brewis

A hard tack, hard bread or hard biscuit that has been soaked over-night and brought to a boil. It is usually eaten with salt or fresh fish and served with pork scrunchions. It is also good with bacon and eggs, a poached egg or beef-steak and gravy. Hard biscuit was used as a bread substitute when men were at sea or away from home in the woods for a long time. Children like it with but-ter and sugar or molasses.

Before being put to soak the bread is usually broken and one story says that the cookee on a schooner would be told to break up the bread or "Bruise the bread", hence the name bruise or brewis.

NEWFOUNDLAND FLIPPERS

Do not parboil. Take flippers and soak in cold water with 1 tablespoon baking soda for about 1/2 hour. The soda makes the fat show white—then take a sharp knife and remove all traces of fat. Render out fat back pork—dip flippers lightly in salted CREAM OF THE WEST Flour and fry until brown in the pork fat. Onions are optional —if you like them fry them with the flippers. Take from frying pan when brown and put in a covered roaster. Add onions, make gravy to which has been added Worcestershire sauce to taste, pour over flippers and allow to bake at 350° F. until tender.

They may then be put in a pastry or served as they are.

Garnish with parsley and wedges of lemon, and you have a dish fit for a king.

Flipper—the forepaw of a seal.

BAKED FLIPPERS WITH VEGETABLES

2 flippers
3 slices salt fat pork
2 onions
1 turnip
2 carrots
1 parsnip
5 or 6 potatoes
Salt and pepper to taste

Remove all fat from the flippers. Wash and cut in serving pieces. Do not parboil.

Fry out the salt pork; remove "Scrunchions". Brown flippers in this fat. Then add a little water and simmer on the back of the stove until partly tender.

Add chopped onions and cut up vegetables, except potatoes. Season and add about 1 cup of water. Cook about 30 minutes and then add the potatoes. Cook another 15 minutes, adding a little more water, if needed.

Meanwhile, make this topping:

2 cups sifted
CREAM OF THE WEST Flour
2 teaspoons baking powder
1/2 teaspoon salt
1/2 cup shortening
Water to make a stiff dough

Roll this pastry out to fit your bake pot. When the flippers and vegetables are sufficiently cooked, top with this pastry and bake at 425° F. for 20 minutes, or until nicely browned.

"The contributor of this recipe tells us it has been passed on from one generation to another in her family". SALLY WEST.

DRESSED COD FILLETS

1 pound cod fillets
1 1/2 cups soft bread crumbs
1 teaspoon savory
2 teaspoons grated onion
1 teaspoon salt
1/8 teaspoon pepper
2 tablespoons butter
1 egg, beaten

Wipe thinly cut fillets with a damp cloth. Mix together the bread crumbs, savory, onion, salt and pepper; rub in the butter and then add beaten egg.

Place a thin layer of the dressing on each fillet; roll up like a jelly roll; secure with a toothpick. Coat fish rolls with CREAM OF THE WEST Flour and brown in hot fat.

Arrange browned fish rolls in a 1 1/2-quart casserole.

Sauce:

2 tablespoons shortening
2 tablespoons
CREAM OF THE WEST Flour
1/2 teaspoon salt
Few grains pepper
1/2 teaspoon savory
2 1/2 cups milk

Melt shortening, blend in flour and seasonings; add milk and cook until thickened and smooth.

Pour this sauce over the fish rolls. Then add:

3/4 cup drained canned tomatoes

Bake covered at 350° F. for 40 minutes. Then sprinkle with:

1/2 cup dry bread crumbs
2 tablespoons grated
cheddar cheese

Return to the oven, uncovered, until slightly brown (about 10 to 12 minutes).

To a Newfoundlander "fish" means cod. If you go to market and say "Have you any fish today?" The reply might well be—"No, but I have a nice piece of salmon."

FISH AND TOMATO SCALLOP

1 cup bread crumbs
1 cup canned tomatoes
2½ cups fresh codfish, cooked and flaked
2 onions, sliced
2 tablespoons butter
Salt
Pepper
1 egg, beaten
1 cup milk

Line bottom of 2-quart casserole with half of the bread crumbs. Add tomatoes, fish and onions. Dot with butter and season. Top with remaining bread crumbs. Combine beaten egg and milk; pour over the fish mixture.

Bake at 350° F. until sauce bubbles (about 1 hour).

BAKED CODFISH

Choose a firm fish for baking. Remove head, tail, fins and sound bone. Wash thoroughly and wipe dry.

Fry out salt pork in roasting pan. Meanwhile, make this bread dressing:

3 cups soft bread crumbs
1 tablespoon grated onion
1 tablespoon savory
1 teaspoon salt
⅛ teaspoon pepper
3 tablespoons butter or margarine
1 egg, beaten

Stuff the fish; tie or skewer securely.

Put fish in fried out pork. Bake at 450° F. for 10 minutes and then 400° F. for one hour for a medium-sized fish. Baste occasionally and add a sliced onion during the last 20 minutes.

> Rounders or tom-cods—small, salted unsplit codfish.

CODFISH AU GRATIN CASSEROLE

4 tablespoons butter
2 tablespoons CREAM OF THE WEST Flour
1 teaspoon salt
½ teaspoon pepper
2 cups milk
2½ cups fresh codfish (cooked, flaked and cooled)
1 cup grated cheese

Melt butter, add flour, salt and pepper; stir to make a paste. Add milk and cook until it thickens, stirring constantly.

Grease a 2-quart casserole; pour a little of the sauce over the bottom. Add a layer of codfish; sprinkle with cheese. Repeat these layers until all ingredients are used, ending with a layer of cheese.

Bake at 350° F. until nicely browned (about ½ hour).

SALT FISH BALLS AND FRITTERS

⅓ cup sifted CREAM OF THE WEST Flour
3 teaspoons baking powder
1 cup finely shredded salt codfish
½ cup water

Mix together the dry ingredients and codfish. Add water to form a batter.

Drop by spoonfuls into hot deep fat (390° F.) and fry until golden brown.

For a cocktail savory, use ½ teaspoon of the mixture for each ball; use 1 tablespoon of the mixture for fish fritters.

> To smert—to pain or hurt
> "Be careful when frying fat, if it splatters on your hand it smerts."

CODFISH CAKES

2 onions, chopped
2 cups cooked salt codfish, boned and shredded
6 to 8 cooked potatoes
3 to 4 cooked parsnips
¼ teaspoon pepper
1 egg, well beaten
½ cup fine bread crumbs

Cook onions in a very small amount of water. Mash together the fish, potatoes and parsnips. Add the onions and water in which they were cooked. Season. Add the beaten egg and combine well. Form into cakes; roll in bread crumbs. Fry in rendered pork fat.

SALT CODFISH PIE

Line a 1½-quart baking dish with mashed potatoes, well covering the bottom. Nearly fill the dish with boiled salt cod which has been minced or finely shredded. Add about 1 cup drawn butter sauce made with a little chopped onion. Spread a thick layer of mashed potatoes over the fish. Bake at 350° F. for 30 to 40 minutes.

INDIVIDUAL SALT FISH LOAVES

¾ **pound salt fish (cod or haddock)**
5 or 6 **medium sized potatoes, cubed**
1 **tablespoon minced onion**
1 **tablespoon finely chopped parsley**
1 **tablespoon butter**
⅛ **teaspoon pepper**
⅛ **teaspoon grated nutmeg**
Scalded milk
Crisp cereal flakes, crushed

Soak salt fish for 1 hour; drain. Remove any bones and cut in small pieces. Place fish and potatoes in a saucepan; cover with boiling water and cook until potatoes are tender (about 15 minutes). Drain well and then mash. Add the onion, parsley, butter and seasonings, and blend in enough hot milk to make the mixture creamy. Add salt if needed. Beat until very light.

Grease 12 muffin tins well; coat with crushed cereal flakes. Fill with mixture and bake at 350° F. for 20 minutes.

Turn out and serve with a well seasoned white sauce or tomato sauce.

BAKED COD TONGUES

1 **pound cod tongues**
Cracker crumbs
½ **teaspoon salt**
1 **teaspoon savory**
2 or 3 **small onions**
Pepper to taste
3 **tablespoons butter or margarine**
Milk to cover

Wash and dry cod tongues. Put a layer of tongues in a buttered 8-inch casserole; cover with cracker crumbs, sliced onions, salt, pepper and savory; dot with butter. Add another layer of tongues and continue until all are used. Have a layer of crumbs on top, dotted with butter. Cover with milk.

Bake at 350° F. until tongues are cooked (about 1¼ hours).

FRIED COD HEADS

Obtain 4 medium size cod heads. More for a large family.

After they have been sculped. (To sculp heads—With sharp knife, cut head down through to the eyes. Grip back of head firmly and pull.) Prepare to cook as follows: Cut heads in two, skin and remove lips. Wash well and dry. Dip both sides of head in CREAM OF THE WEST Flour, sprinkle with salt and pepper to taste.

Fry in fat until golden brown on both sides. Serve with potatoes and green peas, or any vegetable preferred.

Serves: 4 to 6.

FRIED COD TONGUES

Carefully wash fresh Cod Tongues and dry in a towel. Allow 6 or 7 per person. Put 1½ cups CREAM OF THE WEST Flour, 1 teaspoon salt, ½ teaspoon pepper together in a paper bag. Put tongues in and shake them until evenly floured. Cut up ½ pound salt pork and fry until golden brown. Remove pork cubes and fry tongues until nicely browned on both sides. Serve with potato and turnip fluff.

STEAMED SALMON LOAF

1 **large can salmon**
1 **cup stale bread crumbs**
1 **cup scalded milk**
1 **teaspoon salt**
½ **teaspoon onion juice**
1 **teaspoon lemon juice**
1 **tablespoon butter**
½ **cup fresh parsley, chopped**
2 **egg yolks**
2 **egg whites, stiffly beaten**

Flake salmon and remove bones. Soak bread crumbs in hot milk and add to the salmon. Blend in all ingredients, except the egg whites; combine well. Now fold in the stiffly beaten egg whites.

Pour into a greased mould; cover, and steam for 1 hour.

Serve hot or cold.

A "Scoff"—a meal, especially one hastily served up aboard a vessel. Now it has come to mean a "boiled dinner" or party late at night.

BAKED SALMON IN A BLANKET

1½ pound piece of salmon
¼ cup margarine
¾ cup sifted
   CREAM OF THE WEST Flour
¼ teaspoon dry mustard
¼ teaspoon salt
   Few grains pepper

Scale and wash salmon. Place cut side down in a greased baking dish.

Cream margarine and blend in sifted dry ingredients.

Spread this mixture over the salmon.

Bake in a 375° F. oven for about 50 minutes.

Note: The salmon may be stuffed with your favourite dressing.

SALMON IN POTATO SHELLS

6 or 8 large baked potatoes
1 tablespoon butter or margarine
½ cup milk
1 large can salmon (15 ounces)
   Salt and pepper

Cut baked potatoes in half; remove all of the potato from the shells being careful to keep shells intact. Mash the potatoes with the butter and milk, season to taste; add flaked salmon. Return mixture to the potato shells; dot with butter. Brown in 400° F. oven.

SALMON RICE CASSEROLE

3 cups cooked rice
2 tablespoons melted butter
1 cup cooked or canned salmon, flaked
1 tablespoon chopped parsley
1 tablespoon minced onion
   Dash curry powder (optional)
1 cup medium white sauce
1 egg, slightly beaten
½ teaspoon Worcestershire Sauce
   Salt and pepper to taste

Grease a 1½-quart casserole or loaf pan. Combine cooked rice and melted butter and line the baking dish with it, saving ½ cup to use on top.

Blend other ingredients together and fill the rice mould. Spread remaining rice on top.

Place in a pan of hot water and bake in a 350° F. oven for 40 minutes.

Serve with tomato or parsley sauce.

STEWED GRILSE

1 freshly caught grilse
3 or 4 generous slices of bacon
1 medium onion
1 tablespoon
   CREAM OF THE WEST Flour
¼ teaspoon pepper
¼ teaspoon chili powder
   Salt

Clean and fin the grilse; cut crosswise in 1½-inch pieces. Roll up thin parts of fish and fasten with a toothpick.

Fry out bacon in a deep 8-inch or 9-inch frying pan. Remove bacon and fry chopped onion in the fat until soft and tender. Remove cooked onion and set aside.

Place pieces of fish in hot fat and slightly brown the cut edges. Just cover fish with hot water and cook until water evaporates. Combine flour, pepper, chili powder and salt to taste; add water to make ½ cup. Add this to the fish and cook another 10 minutes.

TROUTERS' SALMON

Wash the salmon well, then cut down the back by the side of the bone. Clean and remove entrails. The cut bone may or may not be removed. A small fish can be opened out flat and placed on a toaster. A woodsman would split a stick and improvise a wooden rack as big as a snow-shoe to hold a whole, large salmon opened flat in this manner, or a large salmon could be cut into steaks and cooked the same way.

Cook out-of-doors over a clear fire. Cook skin side down to fire first and then the other side. While cooking brush with butter, add salt and pepper.

Serve with a lump of butter on each piece.

Really delicious - recommended by sportsmen.

SPICED NEWFOUNDLAND HERRING

4 fresh herring, filleted
2 teaspoons salt
2 tablespoons vinegar
2 tablespoons water
1½ tablespoons granulated sugar
¼ teaspoon pepper
   Pinch of ground cloves
2 tablespoons browned bread crumbs

Rub the filleted herring with salt and place them in a flat baking dish so that they overlap slightly.

Mix together the vinegar, water, sugar, pepper and cloves. Pour over the herring. Sprinkle with bread crumbs if you wish.

Bake at 350° F. for 25 to 30 minutes.

Serve with Newfoundland baked potatoes and carrots, cut lengthwise, wrapped in tinfoil and baked with the potatoes.

STUFFED BAKED HERRING

3   or 4 fresh herring
     Roe from the herring
1/2 cup bread crumbs
1   teaspoon chopped parsley
1   small onion, chopped
     Salt and pepper
1   tablespoon margarine

Clean herring and wipe with a damp cloth. Combine roe, crumbs, parsley, onion, salt and pepper. Mix well.

Sprinkle the inside of each herring with salt and pepper. Spread with a portion of the stuffing and fold fish back in shape. Dot with margarine.

Place in a greased baking dish. Cover and bake at 375° F. for 15 minutes, then uncover and cook until brown.

POTTED HERRING

Split herring and remove backbone. Rub with a little salt and pepper; sprinkle both sides of fish with oatmeal. Roll up and fasten with a toothpick or skewer; place in a baking dish. Mix 1/2 cup water and 1/2 cup vinegar; pour over fish.

Bake in a 350° F. oven for 1 1/4 hours. Baste often. (Add more vinegar and water if needed.)

Serve cold.

ROASTED HERRING

Herring should be cleaned, sprinkled with salt and allowed to stand overnight. Then wash in warm water, drain and dry with a cloth.

Cut three notches across the back of each herring; place in a well greased pan. Put a slice of fat pork over each notch. Season with salt and pepper.

Bake at 375° F. until golden brown. Serve with lemon sections and potatoes cooked in their jackets.

HERRING FRIED IN OATMEAL

Clean herring, removing heads, tails and fins. Wipe with a damp cloth.

Mix 1/2 teaspoon salt with 1/2 cup oatmeal. Coat herring with oatmeal and fry in hot fat until golden brown. Garnish with lemon or parsley.

FRIED SQUID

Clean fresh caught squid and wash well in cold water. Drop in salted boiling water and boil for 5 minutes. Remove and drain.

Meanwhile, fry out several slices of salt fat pork; remove the "Scrunchions" and keep hot.

Cut the fish in pieces; fry in the rendered fat, adding salt, pepper and a little chopped onion. When squid is done, serve with the pork scraps.

> *"You can't tell the mind of a squid."*
> This refers to an unreliable person. A squid can move backward or forward.

BAKED SQUID

To prepare squid for cooking remove the head thereby removing the inside of the fish. Wash well. Remove tail, peel off reddish skin, pull out the one bone and turn the cone-shaped fish inside out to remove the fat. Wash well. Boil for 45 minues.

Remove from water, drain and let cool.

Stuffing for 1 dozen Squid:
3   cups bread crumbs
1/2 cup soft butter
1 1/2 tablespoons savory
1/2 teaspoon salt
2   medium onions
     Dash of pepper

Combine all ingredients and fill squid. Place squid in a baking pan with a little fat (from fried salt pork). Sprinkle with salt, cover, and bake in a moderate oven 1 to 1 1/2 hours. A little water may be added to prevent burning.

BAKED TURBOT

     Turbot
1 1/2 cups crushed corn flakes
1   teaspoon salt
1   tablespoon savory

Clean turbot and cut into fillets. Combine crushed corn flakes, salt and savory; spread half of this over the bottom of a greased shallow baking pan. Lay fillets in the pan; sprinkle remaining corn flake mixture over the fish. Bake in a 400° F. oven for 35 to 40 minutes. Serve with lemon wedges or fish sauce.

FISH SOUNDS

Clean and wash sounds. Simmer for 30 minutes; drain and dry. Cut up the sounds until they are fine and place in a casserole. Cut up two slices of fat pork; chop two medium-sized onions. Fry these together slowly until brown. Sprinkle over sounds in the casserole. Season with salt and pepper.

Bake at 375° F. until piping hot. Serve hot with riced potatoes and green peas.

MATELOTE OF EEL

2   pounds eel, dressed
1   quart very cold water
2   tablespoons salt
½   cup chopped onions
2   tablespoons butter
2   cups sliced raw potatoes
1   cup diced raw carrots
½   cup chopped celery
¼   cup raw white rice
2   teaspoons salt
¼   teaspoon pepper
     Boiling water

Clean and skin eel; remove back bone and cut eel in 1½-inch pieces. Soak for 5 minutes in a quart of very cold water to which 2 tablespoons salt has been added. Drain.

Cook onions in melted butter until transparent, not brown.

Combine eel, cooked onion, raw vegetables, rice and seasonings. Add boiling water to cover. Cover and simmer gently until vegetables are tender.

FRIED CAPLIN

The fish should be fresh. Wash them well in salted water. Pinch head off and pull out as much of the entrails as possible. Force out remainder by pressing the stomach from tail to head. Again wash in salted water. Dry on a clean cloth. Dip in CREAM OF THE WEST Flour and fry in hot fat.

Season and serve with lemon slices.

> *"He's deaf as a haddock and she's foolish as a caplin."*

FRIED SMELT

To clean smelt, spread open outer gills and with the forefinger take hold of the inner gills and pull gently. The parts unfit for food are all attached to the inner gills and come away together, leaving the smelt in perfect shape.

Rinse fish thoroughly and wipe dry. Dip in milk or egg and roll in CREAM OF THE WEST Flour or bread crumbs.

Fry in deep fat heated to 375° F.

2   eggs, separated
½   cup milk
1   teaspoon olive or salad oil
1   cup sifted
     CREAM OF THE WEST Flour
¼   teaspoon salt
1   tablespoon lemon juice
1   pint small clams

Beat yolks of eggs until thick and lemon coloured. Add milk, olive oil, sifted flour, salt and lemon juice. Fold in stiffly beaten egg whites and add 1 pint small clams. Let stand in the refrigerator or other cold place for at least 2 hours. Fry by spoonfuls in hot deep fat (365° F.) a few at a time. Clams should be done in 4 to 5 minutes.

Makes 5 servings.

FRIED MUSSELS

Boil mussels in a large pot until shells open. Then remove meat from the shells and set aside.

Fry onions slightly in salt fat. Then add mussels, salt and pepper. Cook for about 10 minutes and serve hot.

BAKED SMOKED FILLETS

Cover 1 pound smoked fillets with cold water and soak for 2 hours. Drain and dry. Place it in a 2-quart greased casserole. Pour 1¼ cups medium white sauce over the fish. Combine 1 cup coarse bread crumbs and 2 tablespoons melted butter. Sprinkle over top of the fish. Bake at 375° F. for 30 minutes or until mixture is brown.

> *Yaffle—an armful of dried fish.*

CODFISH SOUP

Prepare 6 medium sized codfish heads and place in a saucepan. Cover with cold water and add 1 teaspoon salt. Bring slowly to the boil and then simmer for 40 minutes. Remove from the heat and let stand overnight. Next morning empty contents into a large basin and remove all bones. Return the bone-free mixture to the saucepan and add 1 large, finely chopped onion, 2 tablespoons butter, salt and pepper to taste and 1 tablespoon CREAM OF THE WEST Flour which has been blended with a little water. Cook until the onion is tender and your soup is ready to serve.

COD SOUP

This soup can be made with a cod's head, with tom cods or with 2 pounds of fresh cod fish. Wash the head well in salt water, remove the eyes and then cover with water and boil until well broken up. Strain through a collander and put the liquid back into a clean pot. (The soup will stick if the same one is used.)

Add a finely chopped onion, two diced carrots and 1/2 cup rice.

When well cooked, add 2 tablespoons butter. If it is too thick, thin out with 1 cup of milk. A little finely cut parsley makes this a delicious soup. (It is really best made with cod's head.)

FISHERMAN'S FRESH FISH STEW

4 slices fat back (pork)
5 pounds fresh codfish
1 medium onion or chives
  Potatoes
  Pepper
  Water

Place fat pork in a pot; let fry out well. Clean fish thoroughly, wash and remove skin; cut in squares about 2-inches. Add fish to fat and then add sliced onion or chives. Slice potatoes 1/4-inch thick and cover fish with the potato slices; season. Add 3/4 cup boiling water (more if needed). Cook slowly until potatoes and fish are tender (about 1/2 hour).

Serves 6.

> *"Fish in summer and fun in winter."*
> —*everything in its place.*

FISH CHOWDER

3 slices of salt pork, diced
1/3 cup sliced onions
1 1/2 cups sliced potatoes
1/2 teaspoon salt
1/8 teaspoon pepper
1/2 cup water
1 pound fish fillets
3 cups milk
2 tablespoons butter
  Soda biscuits

Fry salt pork until golden brown; add onions and cook slowly until tender. Add potatoes, salt, pepper and water. Cover and cook for 10 minutes. Add fish and cook for 15 minutes, adding more water if necessary. Add milk and butter and heat (do not boil). Serve, sprinkling crushed soda biscuits over the top.

> *Scroopy—squeaking boots—which because they are new indicate a degree of prosperity. After a big haul of seals you "couldn't hear your ears in church with scroopy boots."*

OYSTER STEW

2 cups milk
2 slices of onion
3 tablespoons butter
1/2 pint fresh oysters with liquor
  Salt and pepper to taste
15 soda biscuits, crushed finely

Heat milk and onions over low heat, until almost to the boiling point. Remove the onion. Add the butter; when it is melted, put in the oysters and liquor. Cook at just below the boiling point for 4 minutes or until the oysters begin to curl. Remove from the heat and season to taste. Serve immediately, sprinkled with finely crushed soda biscuits.

STUFFED MACKEREL

3 mackerel, about 1 pound each
6 tablespoons olive oil
1 onion, finely chopped
1 cup bread crumbs
1/4 cup grated cheese
1 tablespoon parsley, chopped
1 teaspoon dry mustard
  Salt
  Pepper
1 lemon, sliced

Have the mackerel cleaned; slit down the centre and boned. Sprinkle the inside with salt and pepper.

Make stuffing by combining half of the olive oil, onion, bread crumbs, cheese, parsley, dry mustard, salt and pepper.

Stuff the fish and skewer the edges together. Place in a flat baking dish with remaining olive oil. Bake at 400° F. for 15 minutes; reduce heat to 350° F. and bake an additional 30 minutes or until fish is tender. Baste frequently.

Serve with lemon slices.

BAKED HALIBUT WITH TOMATO SAUCE

2 cups canned tomatoes
1 cup water
1 slice of onion
3 cloves
2 teaspoons granulated sugar
3 tablespoons butter
3 tablespoons
   CREAM OF THE WEST Flour
3/4 teaspoon salt
1/8 teaspoon pepper
2 pounds halibut, fillets or steak

Combine tomatoes, water, onions, cloves and sugar in a saucepan. Simmer for 20 minutes. Strain.

Melt butter; add flour, salt and pepper; blend to a smooth paste. Add strained tomato mixture and cook until thickened, stirring constantly.

Arrange fish in a baking pan. Pour half of the sauce over the fish. Bake at 375° F. for 35 minutes or until fish is done.

Place fish on a hot platter. Pour second half of the hot tomato sauce over the fish.

FISH SOUFFLE

2 cups boiled salt cod
2 tablespoons butter
2 tablespoons
   CREAM OF THE WEST Flour
1 1/2 cups milk
1 tablespoon chopped parsley
1 teaspoon grated onion
3 eggs, separated
   Salt and pepper to taste

Flake the cooked cod. Make a white sauce by melting the butter and adding the flour to form a paste. Add the milk, chopped parsley and grated onion. Cook until thickened.

Add cod to the white sauce and stir in 3 well beaten egg yolks. Season to taste. Beat whites until stiff and fold into the fish mixture.

Pour into a buttered 8-inch casserole Place casserole in a pan of warm water and bake at 325° F. for 40 minutes or until firm.

Serve with tomato sauce.

BAKED FISH LOAF

1/2 cup rolled oats
1/2 cup milk
2 tablespoons mayonnaise
2 tablespoons chopped fresh
   parsley or 2 teaspoons parsley
   flakes
1 1/2 teaspoons minced onion
1 1/4 teaspoons salt
1/8 teaspoon pepper
2 tablespoons lemon juice
2 eggs, beaten
2 cups flaked cooked cod or salmon

Combine rolled oats and milk. Add mayonnaise, parsley, onion, salt, pepper and lemon juice; combine well. Blend in beaten eggs and fish.

Grease an 8-inch x 5-inch loaf pan or a mould.

Press fish mixture into this and bake at 375° F. for 50 to 55 minutes.

Unmould on a hot platter and pour egg sauce over the top just before serving.

FISH CRISPIES

2 pounds fish fillets
1/2 teaspoon salt
1 1/2 cups soft bread crumbs
1 tablespoon finely minced onion
1 teaspoon poultry seasoning
1/4 teaspoon pepper
1 tablespoon melted butter
1/2 cup milk
4 slices bacon

Wipe fish with a damp cloth and cut in individual pieces; sprinkle with salt. Place in a greased baking dish.

Mix together the bread crumbs, minced onion, seasonings, melted butter and milk. Place this dressing in small mounds on the fish.

Sprinkle with chopped bacon.

Bake in a 425° F. oven until fish is cooked (about 25 minutes).

FISH BAKED IN CUSTARD

1 **pound fresh fillets**
1 **cup milk**
   Salt and pepper to taste
1 **tablespoon margarine**
2 **eggs**

Cook fillets in the milk until tender; add salt and pepper to taste. Remove from stove and add margarine. Beat eggs slightly and add hot milk to them. Place fish in a casserole; pour egg mixture over it.

Place casserole in a pan of hot water; bake at 350° F. for 45 minutes or until custard is firm.

> *"You are making a nice kettle of fish."*
> *Making a mess of affairs.*

KEDGAREE

⅔ **cup raw rice**
2 **cups cooked fish, boned and flaked**
¼ **cup melted butter**
2 **egg yolks, slightly beaten**
1 **teaspoon finely chopped parsley**
½ **teaspoon salt**
   Pepper

Cook rice in boiling salted water until tender; drain. Add flaked fish to the cooked rice and place in top of a double boiler to heat over boiling water. Add melted butter to the slightly beaten yolks; blend in parsley, salt and pepper. Add to the fish and rice. Cook for 2 minutes, stirring gently. Serve.

LOBSTER CUTLETS

2 **tablespoons butter**
¼ **cup CREAM OF THE WEST Flour**
½ **cup milk**
½ **pound cooked lobster meat, cut up**
1 **teaspoon lemon juice or vinegar**
   Cayenne pepper and salt to taste
1 **egg**
   Fine bread crumbs

Melt butter; add flour and stir to a smooth paste. Add milk and cook until sauce is thick, stirring constantly. Blend in lobster, lemon juice or vinegar and seasonings. Turn onto a plate and leave until cool and quite firm. Then shape into cutlets; dip in beaten egg; roll in bread crumbs. Fry until golden brown.

LOBSTER SOUFFLE

2 **tablespoons butter**
2 **tablespoons CREAM OF THE WEST Flour**
½ **teaspoon salt**
1 **cup milk**
½ **cup mayonnaise**
3 **egg yolks**
1 **cup lobster meat**
3 **egg whites**

Melt butter; add flour and salt, stir to a smooth paste. Add milk and cook until thickened, stirring constantly. Remove from heat and blend in the mayonnaise and well beaten egg yolks. Add finely broken lobster meat. Beat egg whites until stiff but not dry; fold them into the lobster mixture. Pour into an ungreased 2-quart casserole. Place in a pan of hot water and oven poach at 350° F. for 45 minutes or until set and lightly browned.

> *"You are like a fish out of water."*
> *—Not at home in your environment.*

NEWFOUNDLAND LOBSTER SALAD

3 **freshly boiled lobsters, shelled**
3 **hard-cooked eggs, chopped**
½ **cup mayonnaise**
½ **cup sweet pickles, chopped**
1 **small onion, finely minced**
½ **teaspoon salt**
   Few grains pepper

Cut lobster into bite size pieces; add other ingredients and toss together. Serve on lettuce leaves.

NOTES:

_____

_____

_____

_____

_____

_____

_____

The Typical

The typical Newfoundlander
   (And I'm proud that I am one)
Besides the King's good English
   Has a language all his own;
For instance if you meet one
   And enquire about his health—
He's not "just fine" nor "like the bird"
   He's "First rate b'y, how's yerself".

Such sayings as "I bound you will"
   "Sove up" and "hard afore"
And "most to rights" and "straightened up"
   And "dunch" and "dout the fire"
Those need no definitions
   We heard them in our cradles,
We know how much a "yafful" is
   Though it wasn't in our "tables".

We all know what a "grapple" is
   A "haul-off" and a "killock"
I spent my time around the punts
   Although I was a "twillick".
There's "slewed around" and "went to work"
   "Turned to" and "took a spell";
While of "clever-lookin'" boys and girls
   I'm sure you've all "heard tell".

We go round the "bally ca'ters"
   When there's "swatches" in the ice,
And only a Newfoundlander
   Can "fall down" and "get a h'ist".
You'd never guess a "bedlamer"
   Is an adolescent lad,
While intermittent snowflurries
   Are "dwighs" or "just a scad".

Now other people say "down South"
   This I dont understand—
For everybody always says
   "Down North" in Newfoundland.
"Bide where you're at", or "leff en bide"
   You'll hear the old folks say;
And if you're drinking "switchel"
   That's black, unsweetened tea.

Newfoundlander

Some think we live on "fish and spuds"
    This fairly makes me boil,
Yet 'tis a treat when spring comes round
    To get a meal of "swile".
A local dish is "fish and brewis"—
    The youngsters like the "scrunchions"
And they love the "lassy sugar"
    From the bottom of the "puncheons".

Besides the reg'lar meal-time
    You'll see all hands "knock off"
For their "lev'ner" or their "fourer"
    A "mug-up" or a "skoff".
We used to have such hearty grub
    As "toutons", "duffs" and "tarts",
But the maids have gone romantic
    With their cookies shaped like hearts.

Poor Grampa—he's "all crippled up"
    With "rheumatiz"—not gout;
He "keels out" on the "settle"
    And says he's "fair wore out".
Sometimes he gets his "dander up"
    Because he "lost his spring",
He frets and grumbles when he thinks
    How his work is "all in slings".

Does your clock be sometimes "random"?
    Were you ever "in a tear"?
Does your house be "in a ree raw"?
    Do you find things "shockin' dear"?
Or were you ever "real put out"?
    Did you ever "notch a beam"?
If you're not a Newfoundlander
    You dont know what I mean.

But times bring alterations—
    And soon we'll hear no more
Those quaint old local sayings
    As in the days of yore.
Yet in my heart I treasure them,
    They always seem to be
A precious part of Home Sweet Home
    To simple folk like me.

            —Rose M. Sullivan.
            (Mrs. William Sullivan
             Trinity, T.B., Nfld.)

MEAT, POULTRY AND GAME

There are so many appetizing ways to cook and serve meat. We have tried to include a number of recipes that will also help to stretch your food budget.

POT ROAST

HEART STEW

SPICE MEAT CASSEROLE

BEEF TONGUE

APPLE BEEF BALLS

LIVER WISH

MOCK DUCK AND PEAS

STEAK AND KIDNEY PUDDING

MEAT AND BISCUIT ROLL

MINER'S CHOWDER

STEAK AND ONION PIE

CORNED BEEF PATTIES

BEEFSTEAK AND KIDNEY PIE

CORNED BEEF AND CABBAGE DINNER

POOR MAN'S GOOSE

YORKSHIRE PUDDING

BAKED LIVER WITH APPLES

THRIMBLE

BAKED BEANS WITH PORK CHOPS

PORK AND TURNIP PIE

HAM OR BACON AND EGG PIE

PORK PIE

BRAWN

HAM CASSEROLE

CANDIED HAM LOAF

SAUSAGES WITH BISCUIT CRUST

BAKED LAMB WITH RICE

RABBIT STEW

RABBIT PIE

RABBIT BRAWN

BAKED STUFFED RABBIT

CHICKEN STEW WITH DUMPLINGS   BREADED CHICKEN

MOOSE POT PIE

MOOSE STEW

ROAST PARTRIDGE

POTATO DUMPLINGS

MOOSE OR CARIBOU AND BREWIS   BAKED TURR

PREPARING MOOSE OR CARIBOU

POT ROAST

1/4 cup shortening
4 to 5 pound roast, rump or chuck
2 medium-sized onions, sliced
2 cups tomato juice, soup or sauce
2 cups water
1 teaspoon salt
1/4 teaspoon pepper
1/4 teaspoon ginger
8 whole cloves

Melt shortening in a deep, heavy pan. Brown meat on all sides. Add the remaining ingredients, cover tightly and simmer over low heat for 3 to 3½ hours or until tender.

Then add:

6 medium-sized potatoes, pared and halved
6 carrots, cut lengthwise
1 teaspoon salt

Cook for another 30 minutes or until vegetables are tender.

"*Tis not every day that Morris kills a cow.*"

Good opportunities are rare.

SPICE MEAT CASSEROLE

1 pound ground beef
1/4 teaspoon salt
1/4 teaspoon curry powder
1½ teaspoons Worcestershire Sauce
3 tablespoons
    CREAM OF THE WEST Flour
1 (10 ounce) can tomato soup
1 tablespoon prepared mustard
1 cup hot water
    Tea Biscuit topping

Fry beef only until it has lost its pink colour. Add salt, curry powder, Worcestershire Sauce and flour; mix well. Stir in tomato soup, mustard and water. Cook over medium heat until mixture thickens; stir to prevent sticking. Turn down the heat and allow to simmer for 10 minutes while you prepare your favourite tea biscuits.

Pour meat mixture into a 2-quart casserole; top with tea biscuits cut in 2-inch rounds. Bake at 425° F. for 15 minutes.

Note: The meat mixture is also delicious served with spaghetti.

APPLE BEEF BALLS

1 pound ground beef
1 cup grated fresh apple
1 cup dry bread crumbs
2 eggs, beaten
1½ teaspoons salt
1/2 teaspoon pepper
1 cup tomato juice

Mix together the ground beef, grated apple, bread crumbs, beaten eggs and seasonings. Form into 1½-inch balls and place in a 2-quart casserole. Pour tomato juice over the meat balls. Bake for one hour at 375° F. Add more tomato juice if necessary.

Cream of celery soup or tomato soup may be used in place of the tomato juice.

MOCK DUCK AND PEAS

1/2 loaf bread
1½ pounds hamburg
3 large onions, chopped
1 teaspoon salt
    Sage, thyme and pepper to taste
1 vegetable marrow or squash
    Rendered bacon fat or strips salt pork

Soak bread in water until moist; squeeze out the water. Add hamburg, chopped onions and seasonings to the bread and blend well.

Peel the vegetable marrow or squash, cut in half, remove seeds. Place meat mixture inside the vegetable and put the halves together. Place in a pan, with fat on the top. Baste; cook for 1 hour or until tender. Slice and serve hot or cold with brown gravy.

PEAS

Soak dried peas overnight. Drain and simmer in fresh water until tender. Serve with mock duck.

MEAT AND BISCUIT ROLL

1 cup sifted
    CREAM OF THE WEST Flour
2 teaspoons baking powder
1/4 teaspoon salt
2 tablespoons shortening
2 tablespoons butter
1/4 cup milk
1½ cups minced cooked meat
1/4 teaspoon salt
1 egg, well beaten
1 tablespoon catsup

Sift dry ingredients, cut in shortening and butter; add milk to make a soft dough. Roll out on a lightly floured board to form a rectangle 1/4-inch thick.

Combine meat, salt, egg and catsup. Spread over the dough and roll up like a jelly roll. Bake at 375° F. for 25 minutes. Serve with tomato sauce.

> *"May his whiskers grow green, when he eats a crubeen."*
> (Crubeens—pickled pig's feet.)

STEAK AND ONION PIE

5   **tablespoons**
    CREAM OF THE WEST Flour
1/2 **teaspoon paprika**
1   **teaspoon salt**
    Few grains ground ginger
    Few grains ground nutmeg
1   **pound stewing beef, cut in 1-inch cubes**
1/4 **cup shortening or drippings**
1   **cup thinly sliced onion**
2 1/2 **cups tomato juice or beef stock**
1 1/2 **cups diced potatoes**

Sufficient pastry to top an 8-inch x 12-inch pan.

Combine the dry ingredients and roll the meat in them until well coated.

Brown the meat in the hot fat; add onions and cook for a few minutes. Add tomato juice or stock; simmer gently until meat is tender (30 to 40 minutes). Add potatoes and cook for 12 to 15 minutes.

Grease an 8-inch x 12-inch pan; pour in meat mixture. Top with your favourite pastry; brush with a little cold milk.

Bake at 425° F. for 18 to 20 minutes or until pastry is done.

BEEFSTEAK AND KIDNEY PIE

2   **pounds round steak**
2   **pounds beef kidney**
2   **onions, sliced**
4   **medium potatoes, thinly sliced**
2   **tablespoons butter**
2   **tablespoons**
    CREAM OF THE WEST Flour
    Salt and pepper to taste

Soak kidney 1 hour in salted water (4 cups water to 1 tablespoon salt).

Cut the steak and kidneys into small pieces; place in a saucepan and add the onion.

Cover with boiling salted water and simmer until the meat is tender. Remove the meat and onions from the water; set them aside. Cook the potatoes in the same water for 6 minutes; remove the potatoes.

Measure the liquid and add boiling water to make one pint. Melt the butter, add the flour to make a smooth paste. Add the liquid and cook until it thickens, stirring constantly. Season to taste.

Line a baking dish with half of the potatoes. Add the meat and top with remaining potatoes. Cover with the gravy.

Cover with pastry or tea biscuit dough and bake at 425° F. for 25 to 30 minutes.

POOR MAN'S GOOSE

1 1/4 **pounds beef or pork liver**
2   **tablespoons bacon fat**
    Salt and pepper
5   **medium onions, sliced**
5   **medium potatoes, sliced**
5   **slices bacon**

Remove skin and veins from liver; cut in serving pieces. Brown slightly in hot fat (about 1/2 minute for each side). Sprinkle with salt and pepper. Put liver and drippings in bottom of a casserole; add onions and then potatoes. Sprinkle with salt and pepper; top with bacon slices.

Cover casserole and bake at 350° F. for 1 hour; remove cover and bake for another 15 minutes.

Serve hot.

BAKED LIVER WITH APPLES

1   **pound beef liver (sliced 1/4 inch thick)**
2   **large apples (peeled, cored and chopped coarsely)**
1   **medium onion (chopped)**
1 1/2 **teaspoons salt**
1/8 **teaspoon pepper**
6   **slices bacon (cut in pieces)**
1/4 **cup water, beef stock or left-over vegetable juice**

Place liver in a shallow casserole or baking dish. Cover with apples and onion. Add salt and pepper. Top with bacon; add liquid.

Cover pan and bake in a 325° F. oven for 1 1/2 hours. Remove cover during last 20 minutes of baking.

Serve with carrots and fluffy mashed potatoes.

HEART STEW

1½ pounds beef heart
2 tablespoons
   CREAM OF THE WEST Flour
1 teaspoon salt
   Few grains pepper
1 tablespoon shortening
2 onions, sliced

Remove tough membrane from the heart; cut in thin slices. Dredge in flour, salt and pepper. Brown in the hot shortening. Add onions and a little water; cover and cook over low heat, until tender (about 45 minutes).

BEEF TONGUE

3 or 4 pound fresh beef tongue
1 tablespoon vinegar
6 whole cloves
6 peppercorns

Wash tongue; place it in a deep kettle and cover with boiling water. Add vinegar, cloves and peppercorns. Simmer until fork easily penetrates centre of the tongue (from 3 to 4 hours). Let cool in the water in which it was cooked. Then remove and peel off the skin. Serve cold or with sauce.

Note: A smoked tongue may be prepared in the same way, but soak it over-night before cooking.

LIVER WISH

1½ to 2 pounds beef liver
1½ to 2 pounds fresh pork
2 or 3 medium onions
3 cups oatmeal
1½ tablespoon salt
1 tablespoon savory
1 teaspoon allspice
1 teaspoon pepper
1 cup cold water

Boil liver until tender.

Mince boiled liver, fresh pork and onions. Add dry ingredients and mix well. Add the cold water.

Pack into greased vegetable or fruit cans from which the tops have been completely removed. Cover with tin foil or waxed paper; secure with string or elastic bands. Place upright in boiling water; boil for 1 hour.

Remove from cans when partly cool. Store in a cold place. Slice and fry as required.

> "Nofty was forty when he lost the pork."
>
> Never be sure of anything; the man Nofty was playing the card-game of forty-fives, he was forty on game and held the best trump but lost to an opponent.

STEAK AND KIDNEY PUDDING

½ pound kidney
1 pound steak
1½ cups sifted
   CREAM OF THE WEST Flour
½ pound shredded suet
1 teaspoon salt
   Few grains pepper
   Water
¾ cup meat stock

Wash kidney. Remove outer membrane. Split through centre lengthwise. Remove fat and white tissue. Soak 1 hour in salted water (4 cups water to 1 tablespoon salt). Mix the flour and suet; add salt. Add enough water to form a dough. Roll out dough to desired thickness on a floured board. Line a greased pudding mould with this pastry and save the extra pastry to cover the top.

Cut kidney and steak into cubes; roll both in flour. Put them in the prepared mould; add a few grains of salt and pepper, and the meat stock. Cover top with the pastry trimmings.

Cover and steam for 3 hours.

MINER'S CHOWDER

This recipe is sort of a Miner's Special. It originated during the Depression of the 30's. On pay day the pantry would be quite empty so as soon as the miner came home with his pay-cheque, one of his children would be sent off to the store for the necessary ingredients:

4 or 5 slices fat back pork
1 large onion, chopped
1 large can of tomatoes (28 oz.)
1 can cooked corned beef
2 or 3 large potatoes, diced

Fry pork and onions until golden brown. Then put about one quart of water in a pot and add all the ingredients to it. Cook until the potatoes are done.

CORNED BEEF PATTIES

2 cups sifted
   CREAM OF THE WEST Flour
1 teaspoon baking powder
½ teaspoon salt
6 tablespoons shortening
1 egg, beaten
⅓ cup milk

Sift dry ingredients; cut in shortening. Combine beaten egg and milk; add these to the dry mixture to make a soft dough. Roll out until thin, cut dough into 4-inch squares. Put in muffin tins; fill with Corned Beef Filling and fold over edges of pastry; seal by pinching together.
Bake in a 400° F. oven for 20 minutes.

CORNED BEEF FILLING

2 tablespoons butter
¼ cup chopped onion
2 tablespoons
   CREAM OF THE WEST Flour
1½ cups corned beef (or 1 can corned beef)
1½ cups canned tomatoes
   Few grains salt
   Few grains pepper

Melt butter, add onion and cook slowly until soft. Add flour and stir until well blended. Add remaining ingredients and boil until thick and smooth - stirring constantly. Let simmer for 10 minutes. Use for patties.

CORNED BEEF AND CABBAGE DINNER

2 pounds corned beef
6 potatoes
6 carrots
6 parsnips
1 medium-sized turnip
1 head cabbage (3 pounds)

Cover corned beef with cold water and let soak overnight. Next morning, drain and add fresh cold water to cover the meat. Bring to a boil and then reduce heat and simmer until the meat is tender (about 2 hours).
Scrape the carrots and parsnips; cut in halves lengthwise. Cut pared potatoes into halves and turnip into thick slices. Cut cabbage into quite large wedges. Wash all vegetables well in cold water.
Add vegetables to the meat about 30 minutes before meat is cooked.
Serves 6.

Lashins—plenty
"Have another cut of pork, John?"
"No, M'am, thank-ye, I've got lashins on my plate."

YORKSHIRE PUDDING

Pour ¼ cup beef drippings into a 9-inch square pan. Heat to sizzling in oven while mixing batter.

Place together in a bowl:

2 eggs
1 cup sifted
   CREAM OF THE WEST Flour
1 cup milk
1 teaspoon salt

Beat until well blended. Pour over hot fat. Bake at 450°F. for 20 to 25 minutes.

THRIMBLE

6 double pork chops
   Salt and pepper
2 cups fresh cranberries
¼ cup bacon drippings or butter
2 cups chopped apples
1 cup brown sugar
1 cup fresh bread crumbs
1 tablespoon minced onion

Have butcher make a slit-pocket in each double loin pork chop. Sprinkle chops with salt and pepper.

Chop cranberries and sauté them for 3 minutes in drippings or butter. Add remaining ingredients and combine well. Spoon this mixture into the slit-pockets made in the chops.

Arrange stuffed chops in a greased roasting pan. Cover and bake for 1½ hours at 350° F.
Serve hot.

PORK AND TURNIP PIE

1½ pounds pork shoulder, cut in serving pieces
1½ cups boiling water
1½ cups raw turnip, cut in thin finger strips
2 cups raw potatoes, cut in slices
2 teaspoons salt
   Few grains pepper
1½ cups sifted
   CREAM OF THE WEST Flour
½ teaspoon salt
3 teaspoons baking powder

¼ cup shortening
¾ cup milk

Arrange cut up pork shoulder in a heavy baking dish; add boiling water and let simmer for ½ hour.

Arrange turnip over the meat and then the potatoes. Add salt and pepper. Cover and cook until vegetables are nearly done (about 20 minutes). Thicken with 2 tablespoons CREAM OF THE WEST Flour if you wish.

Meanwhile, make the biscuit topping:

Sift dry ingredients together; cut in the shortening. Add the milk to make a soft dough. Turn on a lightly floured board and roll to ½ inch thickness.

Place as one piece over the vegetables or cut in biscuits and arrange over the pie.

Bake at 450° F. until brown (about 15 minutes).

PORK PIE

1½ pounds pork butt (cubed)
6 stalks celery
2 onions
1 teaspoon salt
Few grains pepper
1½ cups water
Pastry shell

Combine meat, celery, onions, seasonings and water. Simmer for 1½ hours. Cool and remove celery and onions. Put meat and liquid into a pastry shell; cover with pastry.

Bake at 450° F. until brown (about 20 minutes). Serve while very hot.

Note: They are excellent when made in muffin pan pastry shells.

HAM CASSEROLE

Sliced ham
For each slice use:

1 teaspoon dry mustard
1 teaspoon vinegar
1 apple
1 tablespoon brown sugar

Place ham slice in a greased casserole dish. Sprinkle with dry mustard and vinegar. Add sliced apple and sugar. Repeat with as many layers as needed.

Bake at 300° F. for 45 minutes. Serve with potato or corn scallop.

SAUSAGES WITH BISCUIT CRUST

1 pound sausages
3 apples
2 tablespoons sugar
Biscuit dough for topping

Prick sausages and place in a frying pan. Cover with boiling water and parboil for 10 minutes. Pour off the water and allow sausages to brown.

Arrange browned sausages in bottom of a greased baking pan. Slice apples over them; sprinkle with sugar.

Make your favourite biscuit dough topping and place over the apples. Bake in a 400° F. oven for 35 minutes. Serve with tomato sauce.

BAKED BEANS WITH PORK CHOPS

2 cups white beans
1 medium onion
⅛ pound salt pork
1 teaspoon salt
½ teaspoon dry mustard
2 tablespoons tomato catsup
2 tablespoons dark molasses
Boiling water
Pork chops

Soak beans overnight. Then bring them to a boil in this same water, and cook until the skins begin to burst. Now, turn beans and cooking water into bean pot or covered baking dish. Add the coarsely chopped onion and sliced salt pork.

Put salt, mustard, catsup and molasses in a cup; fill cup with boiling water and mix well. Add to the beans.

Cover and bake slowly at 300° F. for 6 to 8 hours. Add additional water if necessary. One hour before serving time, add the required number of pork chops and continue baking until the chops are well cooked.

Duff—any kind of pudding, usually of flour, fat pork and molasses. Pork and duff was the fisherman's favorite meal.

82

HAM OR BACON AND EGG PIE

Pastry
Eggs
Sliced Back Bacon or Cooked Ham
Salt
Pepper

Line a pie plate with uncooked pastry.

Place overlapping slices of either back bacon or cooked ham on the pastry; drop in 1 egg for each person. Sprinkle with salt and pepper. Add a second layer of overlapping meat slices. Top with pastry, sealing the edges.

Bake at 425° F. for 10 minutes, then reduce heat to 350° F. and bake another 20 minutes.

Serve hot or cold.

BRAWN

Wash a pig's head and feet, and a shin of beef weighing about 1½ pounds. Cover these with boiling water and allow to boil for 2½ hours.

Lift meat from the stock, remove all bones and chop meat into pieces. Return meat to stock. Add 1 tablespoon salt, 1 teaspoon white pepper, 1 teaspoon mixed spices and a dash of cayenne. Mix thoroughly.

Rinse a mould with cold water. Press in the brawn and place a weight on top. Turn out when solid.

CANDIED HAM LOAF

2 **cups coarse whole wheat bread crumbs**
1 **cup milk**
2 **eggs, slightly beaten**
2 **pounds ground ham**
1 **pound ground beef**
1 **teaspoon dry mustard**
½ **teaspoon salt**
½ **cup brown sugar**
½ **teaspoon ground cloves**

Soak bread crumbs in the milk. Add slightly beaten eggs, ground meat, mustard and salt. Combine well.

Mix sugar and cloves, spread over bottom of a 9-inch x 5-inch loaf pan. Pack meat mixture in the pan.

Bake at 350° F. for 1½ hours.

Serves 8 to 10.

BAKED LAMB WITH RICE

¼ **cup salad oil or meat drippings**
2 **medium onions, minced**
1 **small clove of garlic, minced**
1 **pound shoulder of lamb, cut in individual pieces**
1 **cup uncooked rice**
1 **can tomato juice (20 oz.)**
1 **teaspoon sugar**
½ **teaspoon sage**
½ **teaspoon salt**
Few grains pepper

Fry minced onion and garlic in the salad oil or drippings. Remove them from the fat when golden brown. Now, brown the cut up lamb in the same fat.

Put the browned meat in a baking dish. Add the cooked onions and garlic; sprinkle with rice and then add the tomato juice, sugar and seasonings.

Bake at 375° F. for 45 minutes.

Serve with potatoes and green peas.

RABBIT STEW

Skin and clean a rabbit of any size. Cut into sections, that is, 4 legs and body in 3 sections. Wash and dry thoroughly; then flour. Fry out 4 or 5 medium slices of fat pork in a frying pan. Fry rabbit in this fat until it is golden brown.

Place browned rabbit in a large stew pot. Add water to the frying pan to remove all browning, then add this to the stew pot. Add enough water to just cover the rabbit. Add a medium onion which has been cut into pieces and salt to taste. **Simmer** for 2 to 2½ hours (do not boil).

Then add 2 carrots which have been cut into ½-inch slices and a small turnip which has been cubed. Now bring the stew to a slow boil until vegetables are cooked. Make flour thickening and add it to the stew to make gravy.

Potatoes may be added if desired, but they are better if boiled in a separate pot; drained and placed on plates and the stew poured over them.

Newfoundland Dumplings may be added.

"Eat up. The boy's is workin'."

DUMPLINGS

2¼ cups sifted CREAM OF THE WEST Flour
1 teaspoon salt
3 teaspoons baking powder
2 teaspoons butter
1 cup milk

Sift together flour, salt and baking powder. Cut in butter; add milk. Mix until smooth. Drop by spoonfuls on hot stew. Cover tightly. Cook 10 to 12 minutes without removing cover.

"*Our contributor adds: 'This is one of the many strictly Newfoundland dishes that my family are really delighted with. Of course it is a bit of a delicacy in the past few years as rabbits have been very scarce if not impossible to obain.'*" SALLY WEST.

RABBIT BRAWN

Clean rabbit and cut into pieces. Cover with lightly salted water and boil until the meat drops from the bones.

Remove all bones.

Add to the meat and liquid:
1 medium onion, finely chopped
Few grains salt
5 or 6 soda crackers
1 egg, beaten

Beat until well blended. Boil together until mixture thickens. Pour into mould and allow to stand until it gels.

RABBIT PIE

Skin and dress a brace of fresh rabbits and cut in sections. Fry out several rashers of fatback pork, making sure it is of good quality as the least trace of rustiness will ruin the flavour of the dish. Fry legs and thick back sections of rabbits until nicely browned. (The ribs and lower back section - and head if desired - may be used for soup.) When meat is browned remove from fire and add:
1 large onion, chopped
1 medium carrot and 1 very small parsnip, sliced
½ medium-sized turnip, diced

Add water to just cover and continue cooking in 350° F. oven, adding a little water now and again as necessary. Allow ample time for cooking, especially if rabbit is large and possibly tough, as the meat is most delicious when it comes readily from the bone.

Cover with a not-too-rich pastry - using CREAM OF THE WEST Flour, of course - and serve with potatoes, green peas or other vegetables, according to family preference.

Note: Flipper is also delicious prepared as above. Every vestige of fat should be removed from the flipper before cooking. Baking soda added to the water used in washing the meat facilitates this job.

BAKED STUFFED RABBIT

Clean rabbit thoroughly. Prepare this dressing:

4 cups fine bread crumbs
¼ cup soft butter
2 tablespoons savory
2 tablespoons onions
Salt
Pepper

Fill rabbit with dressing and sew together or fasten with skewers. Place in a roasting pan and lay four or five slices of fat pork across its back. Add a little water; cover the pan.

Bake at 350° F. until meat is tender (about 25 to 30 minutes per pound).

Remove from the oven and thicken the drippings for gravy. Top with your favourite pastry and return to the oven. Bake at 450° F. until pastry is nicely browned. Serve at once.

CHICKEN STEW WITH DUMPLINGS

5 to 6 pounds stewing hen
1 cup sifted CREAM OF THE WEST Flour
2 teaspoons salt
¼ teaspoon pepper

Disjoint the fowl; remove the excess fat and melt it in a heavy pot. Mix flour and seasonings in a bag; dredge the pieces of the fowl by shaking them in the bag. Brown in the melted fat. When all pieces are nicely brown, add water to cover. Simmer, covered, for 2½ hours.

Dumplings
2 cups sifted CREAM OF THE WEST Flour
4 teaspoons baking powder
1 teaspoon salt
¾ cup milk

Sift the dry ingredients together; add the milk and mix well. Bring stew to a boil, drop batter by spoonfuls over the liquid. Cover tightly and cook for 20 minutes. Arrange chicken and dumplings on a deep platter. Pour gravy over all. Serve with vegetables which have been cooked separately.

> *Dunch—a dumpling made with flour and water only.*
>
> *Expression still used for a heavy cake or soggy bread—"pure dunch."*
>
> *Dough-boy—a hard dumpling.*

BREADED CHICKEN

1   **roasting chicken**
1   **egg, slightly beaten**
1   **tablespoon cold water**
9   **cream crackers**
½   **onion**
    Salt and pepper
    Shortening or margarine for frying

Cut chicken into serving size portions. Combine beaten egg and cold water. Dip chicken in this mixture and then roll in cracker crumbs, which have been rolled to the fineness of cornmeal.

Fry chicken in hot fat until golden brown, adding salt and pepper. Then, arrange it in a roasting pan. Rinse frying pan with hot water; pour this over the chicken. Add chopped onion and season. Cover and roast for 1½ to 2 hours or until meat is tender (350° F. oven). Add more water to roaster if necessary to prevent sticking.

When done, remove chicken to a hot platter and make gravy.

MOOSE POT PIE

Cut 2 pounds moose meat into small cubes; roll in ½ cup CREAM OF THE WEST Flour and 2 teaspoons salt, until the cubes are well coated. Place in a dutch oven with a little shortening or pork and brown. Then add 4 cups water and simmer for 2 hours.

Now add (in this order):

6   **medium carrots, sliced**
2   **onions, chopped**
1   **small turnip, cubed**
3   **parsnips, sliced**
8   **medium potatoes, cut in small pieces**

Potatoes are added last because they require less cooking.

Now cook for about 25 minutes or until the vegetables are just tender. Add more water if needed but keep the juice thick enough for gravy.

Cover the meat and vegetables with pastry and bake at 425° F. until pastry is ready (about 15 minutes).

ROAST PARTRIDGE

Clean and dress one brace of partridge. Stuff with this bread and savory dressing:

1½   **cups bread crumbs**
1½   **teaspoons dried savory**
1½   **tablespoons butter**
1   **teaspoon chopped onion**
    Salt
    Pepper

Arrange stuffed partridge in a baking pan; season with salt and pepper.

Lay three strips of bacon over each partridge; bake at 350° F. until tender.

> *Rames—the bare bones—remains.*

MOOSE OR CARIBOU AND BREWIS

Soak hard bread in cold water overnight, breaking each cake into 4 pieces. (3 cakes of hard bread will serve 6 people.)

In the morning, add salt and bring to a boil. Drain at once.

Choose tender moose or caribou steaks which are about ½-inch thick. Fry in bacon dripping or salt pork; season with salt and pepper.

Serve meat, pouring the juice over the brewis.

PREPARING MOOSE OR CARIBOU

The basic rule is to treat Moose or Caribou as you would any other piece of beef. Since steaks and roasts are the most popular of the meat class, the prime ingredient for these dishes is a properly aged (7 to 10 days) and dressed-out piece of meat.

STEAKS: Peel off the membrane around the muscles which cause the gamey odour and taste. Then, in a heavy iron skillet over a high heat, sear both sides of the steak in light fat. Turn the heat down to medium and cook to the desired rareness.

ROASTS: Marinate a roast in a beef barbecue sauce, using a covered crockery or other non-metal dish, for 24 hours. Then, pour the remaining sauce over the roast. Roast in a low oven for the same time as you would a similar weight beef roast.

MOOSE STEW

3   pounds moose, cut in small pieces
1/4 pound butter
6   cups water
**   Salt and pepper**

Brown moose meat in hot butter; add water, salt and pepper. Let simmer, adding a chopped onion after about an hour of cooking. Cook for another hour. Then cut up and add:

2   carrots
2   parsnips
1   small turnip
10   potatoes

Cook for another 30 minutes or until vegetables are tender. Make dumplings if you wish.

POTATO DUMPLINGS

1/2 cup CREAM OF THE WEST Flour
1½   teaspoons baking powder
1/2 teaspoon salt
**   Few grains pepper**
1   cup mashed potatoes
1   egg, well-beaten
1   teaspoon minced parsley
1   teaspoon onion juice
2   tablespoons milk

Sift dry ingredients. Add mashed potato, beaten egg, seasonings and milk to make an easily handled dough. Drop by spoonfuls into hot stock or stew and boil, covered, for 15 to 20 minutes.

BAKED TURR
(Sea Bird)

Clean the birds, and drain well, then dress. Following is dressing enough for one turr:

2   cups bread crumbs
1   small onion (chopped)
1/2 teaspoon savory
1/2 teaspoon salt
1/4 teaspoon pepper
1   tablespoon shortening

Put dressed bird in roaster. Sprinkle lightly with salt. Bake for about one hour. Prick

skin of bird with fork, to drain off fat. Remove bird and throw all fat from roaster. Return bird to oven placing 1/4 pound salt pork around and over bird, and bake until pork is brown. Add four or five cups of hot water, one large onion and one teaspoon salt. Bake until brown and tender. Baste or turn occasionally.

If you prefer gravy, mix two or three tablespoons CREAM OF THE WEST Flour with five tablespoons cold water and stir well and add to liquid after bird is cooked. Boil for two minutes.

Some people like a light pastry baked over the turr before making the gravy. Any plain pastry recipe is good.

"Turrs are native to Newfoundland, and especially in the old days were eaten as a change from fish." SALLY WEST.

NOTES:

_____
_____
_____
_____
_____
_____
_____
_____
_____
_____
_____
_____
_____
_____
_____
_____

OTHER MAIN DISHES

Soups and hashes are a good way to dress=up leftovers and they add variety to your meal=planning. You can work wonders with a few recipes like these.

SOUPS:

SCOTCH BROTH
CORN CHOWDER
GRANDMA'S OLD FASHIONED SOUP
BEET AND CABBAGE SOUP

CREAM OF POTATO SOUP
HAM AND PEA SOUP
NEWFOUNDLAND PEA SOUP

SALADS:

CORNED BEEF SALAD SANDWICHES   PINEAPPLE COLE SLAW

MEAT DISHES:

BUBBLEM SQUEAK
LOB SCOUSE
POTATO PORK CAKES
CORNISH PASTRIES
CHEESEBURGER LOAF
SHIP WRECK OR SEVEN LAYER DINNER

HOMEMADE BLOOD PUDDING
LIVER LOAF
TASTY BAKED HASH
FISHERMAN'S TREAT
HAM AND POTATO BALLS
CABBAGE ROLLS

VEGETABLE DISHES:

STUFFED VEGETABLE MARROW
HUSH PUPPIES
FRENCH FRIED PARSNIPS
IRISH CAULCANNON
SCALLOPED POTATOES
FRENCH FRIED POTATO PUFFS
POTATO PUFF
SAVORY POTATOES

LIMA BEAN LOAF
POTATO AND CHEESE SOUFFLE
BAKED BEANS
BOSTON BROWN BREAD
SUPPER DISH
CORN AND CHEESE CASSEROLE
ONION SQUARES

SUPPER DISHES: FRENCH TOAST

SCOTCH BROTH

¼ pound Scotch barley
½ pound dried peas
1 pound mutton (best end of neck)
1 tablespoon salt
1 medium turnip
1 medium head of cabbage
3 medium onions
2 carrots, grated

Soak barley and peas (separately) overnight. In the morning, cover mutton with cold water; add the salt and bring to a boil. Boil for 1 hour, then add barley and peas, and finely chopped vegetables (except carrots). Stir. Let boil for ¾ hour, then add grated carrot. Boil for an additional 15 minutes.

Note: Do not skim off the fat.

CORN CHOWDER

2 slices salt pork, cubed
1 onion, sliced
2 cups potatoes, cubed
3 cups boiling water
1 can cream style corn
2 cups milk
  Salt and pepper to taste
1 tablespoon butter

Fry out the pork and add sliced onion to it. Cook for 5 minutes.

Add potatoes and boiling water; simmer slowly until potatoes are tender. Then add corn and milk; season to taste. Add butter.

GRANDMA'S OLD FASHIONED SOUP

Get marrow bone with some beef on it and a veal shank which has been broken in two. Cover these bones with cold water; add a little salt and cook for a couple of hours. Then add:

5 carrots, diced
2 onions, diced
5 potatoes, diced
2 or more stalks of celery, cut up
1 20-ounce can tomatoes
1 green pepper, diced
⅛ teaspoon summer savory
  Salt and pepper to taste

Cook until meat and vegetables are tender. If a more hearty soup is wanted, add some macaroni or noodles, or a tablespoon of barley.

BEET AND CABBAGE SOUP

1 pound fresh meat
1 slice salt beef
2 onions, chopped
3½ cups chopped white cabbage
  Juice of one lemon
1 tablespoon vinegar
2 cups finely chopped cooked beets
  Salt and pepper to taste

Boil meat and onions in 2½ quarts salted water for 30 minutes. Add cabbage and continue to cook until meat is well done. Then remove fresh meat from the soup and add lemon juice, vinegar and beets; season to taste. Boil for about 10 minutes.

CREAM OF POTATO SOUP

2 cups raw potatoes, chopped
1 small onion, chopped
4 cups boiling water
2 teaspoons salt
1 tablespoon butter
1½ tablespoons
  CREAM OF THE WEST Flour
3 cups milk (fresh or half evaporated milk and half water)

Cook potatoes and onion in the boiling, salted water until done. Drain, saving the cooking water to use in the soup. Mash hot potatoes and onion with butter; blend in the flour. Gradually stir in the milk and then the water in which the potatoes and onion were cooked. Bring soup to a boil and cook until slightly thickened, stirring constantly. Season to taste.

HAM AND PEA SOUP

½ pound dried peas
1 foreknuckle of ham (about 1 pound)
4 pints water
4 onions
1 pound potatoes
  Salt and pepper
½ teaspoon granulated sugar
1 tablespoon chopped parsley

Wash peas; pour boiling water over them and soak for 12 hours.

Wash foreknuckle of ham and put in a large saucepan; cover with water. Bring to a boil and simmer for 2 hours or longer, with lid on.

Drain peas and rinse in cold water. Add them to the soup and simmer for 30 minutes. Peel onions and potatoes; cut in slices and add to the soup with the seasonings and sugar. Simmer until vegetables are tender. Add chopped parsley and more seasonings; if needed.

Just before serving, remove ham knuckle from the soup; cut off all lean meat and return it to the soup in convenient pieces for serving.

NEWFOUNDLAND PEA SOUP

Soak a piece of salt beef or ham bone overnight. Soak dried peas overnight as well. In the morning cook both together in fresh water. Add chopped carrots, turnips and onions. Boil together. 20 minutes before serving put in whole potatoes. Serve with dumplings.

CORNED BEEF SALAD SANDWICHES

1½ cups cooked or canned corned beef, finely chopped
2   cups shredded cabbage
1   tablespoon grated onion
1   tablespoon pickle relish
1   teaspoon vinegar
½   teaspoon granulated sugar
1   tablespoon cream
½   cup mayonnaise

Combine corned beef, cabbage, onion and pickle relish. Blend vinegar, sugar and cream into the mayonnaise. Add this to the corned beef mixture; toss lightly. Chill.

Serve in rolls which have been hollowed out or use as sandwich filling.

PINEAPPLE COLE SLAW

4   cups shredded raw cabbage
2   or 3 cups grated raw carrot
1   or 2 teaspoons granulated sugar
1   cup crushed pineapple, well drained
1   cup dressing of your choice

Combine all ingredients in a bowl and toss lightly.

BUBLEM SQUEAK

Fry diced salt pork in a bake pot (do not brown). Add sliced onion and cook a little. Then add left-over carrots and turnips which have been cut in slices or cubes. Add enough water to simmer then add sliced potato and cabbage. Salt to taste if necessary.

> *Solomon Gosse's Birthday*
> *—Usually Thursday, when bublem squeak and figged-duff would be the order of the day.*

LOB-SCAUCE

1   pound salt meat, cut in cubes
1   cup each of diced carrots, turnip and potatoes
1   parsnip, diced
1   medium onion, diced
1   cup chopped cabbage
2   tablespoons rice

Soak meat overnight to remove the salt. Drain. Add 6 or 7 cups of fresh cold water and cook for one hour.

Then add the vegetables and rice. Cook until vegetables are tender.

Note: Spareribs may be used instead of salt meat and Newfoundland hard tack may be substituted for the rice.

> *Lob-scauce*
> *—A very thick soup or stew of vegetables and saltmeat. A native of Liverpool, England, to this day is often called a "lob-scaucer."*

POTATO PORK CAKES

8   large potatoes
1   pound fat back pork (salted)
2½ cups sifted
      CREAM OF THE WEST Flour
3   teaspoons baking powder

Boil and mash the potatoes.

Cut pork into pieces and fry out. Add the scrunchions to the mashed potatoes. Then mix in sifted flour and baking powder. Form into cakes and bake at 350° F. for 30 minutes.

Serve with boiled fish.

CORNISH PASTIES

For six pasties
6   potatoes
1   turnip
2   carrots
1   pound frying beef or steak
1   onion
      Salt and pepper to taste
      Pastry

Prepare vegetables, cube and cook in boiling salted water until they are tender. Fry cubed meat and chopped onion until done. While these are cooking, use your favourite recipe to make sufficient pastry for six pasties.

Drain the cooked vegetables; add the meat, onion and any gravy. Add salt and pepper to taste.

Roll out pastry in 8-inch circles. Spoon vegetables and meat on centre of the pastry; fold over and press edges together (seal with water). Make a slit in the top and pour 2 tablespoons water through the slit.

Repeat for each pasty.

Place on a cookie sheet. Bake at 425° F. for 10 minutes, then lower the temperature to 375° F. for an additional 15 to 20 minutes.

CHEESEBURGER LOAF

1½ pounds ground beef
1 cup soda biscuit crumbs
2 tablespoons chopped onion
1½ teaspoon dry mustard
1 teaspoon salt
  Few grains pepper
1 tablespoon catsup
1 egg, beaten
½ cup evaporated milk (undiluted)
1 cup grated cheese

Thoroughly combine all ingredients except the cheese. Grease a 9-inch x 5-inch x 3-inch loaf pan and spread ½ cup grated cheese over the bottom. Press half of the meat mixture over the cheese; then add remaining cheese and second layer of meat.

Bake at 350° F. for 1 hour.

Allow loaf to stand for about 10 minutes before turning out on a platter. Slice for serving.

SHIP WRECK OR SEVEN LAYER DINNER

Slice 2 onions and fry until tender, but not brown. Spread over the bottom of a 2-quart casserole. Add a layer each of sliced potatoes, sliced carrots and peas (including the liquid). Sprinkle with ¼ cup raw rice.

Arrange sausage, ground beef or pork, or fish fillets on the top. Dilute 1 can tomato soup with a can of water. Pour this over the entire mixture.

Bake, covered, at 350° F. for one hour; remove cover and continue baking until done (about 30 minutes).

Note: Season each layer with salt and pepper.

HOMEMADE BLOOD PUDDING

½ pound chopped onions
1 loaf bread made into crumbs
1 pound rice, boiled
1 cup ground suet
2 teaspoons pepper
1 pint milk
  Salt to taste

Combine the above ingredients and add one gallon of blood. Mix thoroughly. Steam for three hours in a large double boiler or pudding bag.

When cooked, allow to cool. Then slice and fry in a little fat.

LIVER LOAF

1 pound liver (beef, pork or lamb)
1 cup bread crumbs
1 medium onion
¼ cup chopped parsley
1 egg
1 teaspoon salt
⅛ teaspoon pepper

Grind the liver or chop it until very fine. Add the remaining ingredients and combine well. Press into a greased 9-inch x 5-inch x 3-inch loaf pan.

Bake at 350° F. for 1 hour.

TASTY BAKED HASH

2 cups cooked meat, ground or finely chopped
3 cups cooked potatoes, chopped
1 small onion, chopped
1 teaspoon salt
1 tablespoon pickle relish
1 tablespoon catsup
1 to 2 tablespoons milk
¼ cup grated cheese
¼ cup cracker crumbs
2 tablespoons butter

Combine meat, potatoes, onion, salt, relish and catsup; mix well together. Blend in 1 to 2 tablespoons milk. Spread mixture 1 inch thick in a buttered 8-inch baking dish. Cover with grated cheese and cracker crumbs; dot with butter.

Bake at 400° F. for 40 minutes.

FISHERMAN'S TREAT

8　large cabbage leaves
2　teaspoons pork fat
½　pound sausage meat
1　medium onion (chopped)
2　cups tomatoes (chopped)
½　teaspoon salt
　　Dash of pepper
1　tablespoon granulated sugar
1½　cups cooked spaghetti

Cook cabbage leaves in boiling water for 5 minutes; drain. Heat fat and fry sausage meat and chopped onion until deliciously brown.

Add 1 cup chopped tomatoes, salt, pepper, sugar and cooked spaghetti.

Simmer and stir until hot and well blended. Put a heaping spoonful on each cabbage leaf; roll up and fasten with a toothpick. Put in a baking dish. Pour second cup of chopped tomatoes over the rolls; cover and cook at 400° F. for 30 minutes or until tender.

Remove cover and let brown.

Serve with hashed potatoes.

HAM AND POTATO BALLS

Mash 6 boiled potatoes and add few grains of salt, 1 tablespoon melted butter and 1 cup evaporated milk. Mix well. Add 2 well beaten eggs and 1 cup finely chopped cooked ham.

Mould into egg shaped balls; roll in flour. Fry in hot deep fat (385° F.) until nicely browned.

Serve with your favourite cream sauce.

CABBAGE ROLLS

1　head cabbage
1　pound uncooked rice
1　pound hamburg
1　teaspoon salt
¼　teaspoon pepper
1　large can tomatoes
2　cups cold water
　　Salt

Separate cabbage leaves; place in hot water for a few minutes, then drain and dry the leaves.

Combine the uncooked rice, hamburg, 1 teaspoon salt and pepper. Place about 2 tablespoons mixture in each cabbage leaf and roll up. Lay in a saucepan, placing the rolls close together.

Sprinkle with salt; add tomatoes and water. Boil for 2 hours.

STUFFED VEGETABLE MARROW

1　vegetable marrow (about 2 pounds)
1　pound minced meat
1　onion, chopped
　　Salt
　　Pepper

Wash and dry marrow; cut in half length-wise and take out the seeds.

Combine minced meat, onion, salt and pepper. Put in centre of the marrow; tie together.

Bake in a covered roaster for 1½ hours at 350° F. Slice and serve hot.

HUSH PUPPIES

1　cup cornmeal
⅓　cup sifted
　　CREAM OF THE WEST Flour
1　teaspoon baking powder
½　teaspoon salt
1　onion (minced)
1　egg
⅓　cup milk

Sift dry ingredients together, then add the minced onion. Blend in the unbeaten egg and milk, until well combined.

Drop by spoonfuls into hot fat (350° F.) and fry for 10 to 15 minutes or until golden brown.

These are especially good with with fried clams, shrimp or chicken.

FRENCH FRIED PARSNIPS

3　medium parsnips
1　egg
⅓　cup milk
　　Fine bread crumbs or salted
　　CREAM OF THE WEST Flour

Scrape parsnips and cut in quarters, lengthwise; then cut once across. Cover with boiling salted water and cook until tender. Drain. (Be careful not to over-cook.)

Add milk to the beaten egg. Dip the parsnip strips in this mixture and then roll in either bread crumbs or salted flour. Fry in hot deep fat (390° F.) until golden brown. Drain and serve hot.

"You'll do it in the long run."
Eventually you will succeed.

IRISH CAULCANNON

Caulcannon can be made from any vegetables. Prepare those of your choice (potatoes, onions, parsnips and cabbage are good, plus carrots, turnip and leeks for colour), and boil in the usual way. Mash all of the cooked vegetables through a ricer while they are still hot.

Next, mix the riced vegetables together and put them in a saucepan. Add 1 tablespoon of butter for every cup of vegetables. Heat until piping hot; stir constantly to prevent sticking. Press the hot vegetables into a well buttered mould.

Bake at 400° F. for 20 minutes.

SCALLOPED POTATOES

Peel 6 large potatoes. Slice thinly and place in a buttered 2-quart baking dish in layers. Cover each layer with a sprinkle of CREAM OF THE WEST Flour; dot with butter, and season with salt and pepper. Fill the dish with hot milk up to the top layer of potatoes and sprinkle with grated cheese.

Bake slowly until tender (about 1¼ hours) at 350° F.

FRENCH FRIED POTATO PUFFS

4   **slices bacon**
4   **cups left-over mashed potatoes**
2   **eggs, well beaten**
1   **cup sifted**
      CREAM OF THE WEST Flour
2   **teaspoons baking powder**
1   **teaspoon salt**

Fry bacon until crisp; crumble into small pieces. Combine with potatoes and beaten eggs.

Sift dry ingredients into potato mixture. Blend well.

Heat fat to 385° F. in a deep pan (you need about 2 inches of fat). Drop potato mixture by tablespoons into hot fat.

Fry 3 to 5 minutes or until brown.

Excellent with roast beef.

POTATO PUFF

2   **cups mashed potatoes**
2   **tablespoons shortening or**
      butter, melted
2   **eggs**
 ½ **cup milk**
    Salt and pepper

Combine mashed potatoes and melted shortening or butter and beat until creamy.

Add well beaten eggs, milk and seasonings. Place in greased baking dish (1½-quart casserole) and bake at 375° F. until brown (about 20 minutes).

SAVORY POTATOES

To 4 cups of well-mashed hot potatoes, add one small onion which has been finely chopped and a few grains of pepper. Add 2 tablespoons butter and 1 to 2 tablespoons savory; blend well. Press into a 1-quart bake pan; dot with butter and brown in a 400° F. oven.

LIMA BEAN LOAF

1   **tablespoon margarine**
2   **tablespoons minced onion**
 ½ **teaspoon sage**
 ½ **teaspoon salt**
1   **cup tomato puree**
2   **cups lima bean puree**
1   **cup whole wheat bread crumbs**
2   **eggs, beaten**

Melt the margarine in a saucepan; add onion, sage and salt; simmer until the onions are tender but not brown. Add the tomato puree and blend.

Combine the bean puree and bread crumbs. Add the tomato mixture and beaten eggs. Mix lightly and turn into a greased 9-inch x 5-inch x 3-inch loaf pan. Bake at 350° F. for 30 to 40 minutes. Unmould on a platter and garnish with parsley. Serve with tomato sauce.

POTATO AND CHEESE SOUFFLE

2   **cups boiled potatoes**
 ½ **cup hot milk**
2   **eggs**
 ¾ **cup grated cheese**
    Salt and pepper

Boil enough potatoes to make two cups. Mash them and beat in milk. Then add well beaten egg yolks and seasonings, also ½ cup of grated cheese. Fold in stiffly beaten egg whites. Put mixture in a greased 1½ quart baking dish. Sprinkle remaining cheese on top.

Place dish in pan of hot water and bake in moderate oven (350° F.) for 25 to 30 minutes.

Serves 6.

BAKED BEANS

4 cups navy beans
1 medium onion, finely chopped
½ cup molasses
½ cup catsup
2 teaspoons salt
2 teaspoons dry mustard
¼ teaspoon ginger
½ pound salt pork, cut in thick slices

Cover beans with cold water and soak overnight. Drain and place beans in a large saucepan. Add 2½ quarts fresh water and onion. Bring to a boil, lower heat and simmer gently until skins burst. Drain beans and reserve liquid.

Combine molasses, catsup, salt, mustard and ginger. Add 2 cups of the water drained from beans.

Arrange half of pork in bottom of large bean crock or casserole with a tight fitting cover. Add beans and top with remaining pork. Pour molasses mixture over all. Add enough water to cover (use that drained from beans).

Cover and bake in a 300° F. oven for 5 hours. Remove cover for last 30 minutes of cooking time. Add more water if necessary during the cooking.

BOSTON BROWN BREAD

1 cup cornmeal
1 cup graham flour
1 teaspoon baking soda
½ teaspoon salt
½ cup molasses
2 cups sour milk
1 cup seeded raisins

Combine dry ingredients and then stir in the liquids and raisins. Pour into a greased one quart mould. Steam for 3 hours.
Excellent with baked beans.

SUPPER DISH

4½ cups hot mashed potatoes
5 teaspoons catsup
5 eggs
½ cup grated cheese
Salt
Pepper

Spread hot mashed potatoes in greased shallow baking dish. Make five nests and put 1 teaspoon catsup in each. Drop an egg in each nest and season with salt and pepper.

Bake in a 300° F. oven until eggs are almost done (about 10 minutes).
Sprinkle grated cheese over the eggs. Return to oven to melt the cheese.
Serve hot.

> *A gommil—a foolish person.*
> *—"Even a gommil can make dumplings."*

CORN AND CHEESE CASSEROLE

1 cup cream style corn
1 cup grated cheese
1 cup bread or cracker crumbs
½ teaspoon salt
1 tablespoon melted butter
1 teaspoon Worcestershire Sauce
2 tablespoons chopped pimiento or parsley (optional)
2 eggs, separated
2 cups milk

Combine all ingredients except the eggs and milk. Beat the egg yolks; add the milk and pour over corn mixture; stir well. Fold in stiffly beaten egg whites. Pour into ungreased 2-quart casserole.
Oven poach at 350° F. for 40 minutes or until firm.

ONION SQUARES

6 medium size onions
3 tablespoons shortening
1¾ cups sifted
   CREAM OF THE WEST Flour
4 teaspoons baking powder
1 teaspoon salt
1 teaspoon curry powder
5 tablespoons chilled shortening
½ cup drained kernel corn
⅔ cup milk
1 egg, slightly beaten
½ cup milk
   Few grains salt
   Few grains pepper

Peel onions and cut in ¼-inch slices; separate into rings. Sauté the onion rings in the 3 tablespoons of shortening until they are tender and very lightly browned. Drain off excess fat.

Sift the dry ingredients; cut in the shortening. Add the corn. Make a well in the centre and add ⅔ cup milk. Mix lightly to make a soft dough. Knead gently for a few seconds, and then pat into a greased 8-inch or 9-inch square pan.

Arrange cooked onions over the dough. Combine slightly beaten egg, ½ cup milk, salt and pepper. Pour over the onions.

Bake at 425° F. for 30 to 35 minutes.

Cut in 9 squares. Serve hot.

FRENCH TOAST

1   **egg**
¼ **cup milk**
   Few grains salt
4   **slices of bread**
   Butter or margarine

Beat egg slightly; add milk and salt. Dip bread slices in egg mixture and brown in hot butter or margarine, turning once.

Serve hot with jam, maple syrup or honey.

NOTES:

PRESERVED FOODS

Nothing beats home-preserving when it comes to jams, jellies and pickles. Preserving is a ritual in our home, as it probably is in yours.

JAMS AND JELLIES:
PARTRIDGEBERRY JAM
BLUEBERRY JAM
BAKEAPPLE JAM
DOGBERRY AND APPLE JELLY
MARSH BERRY JELLY

RHUBARB MARMALADE
PRUNE MARMALADE
BLUEBERRY AND APPLE CONSERVE
PARTRIDGE WALNUT CONSERVE

PICKLES AND CHUTNIES:
CRANBERRY-PINEAPPLE RELISH
APPLE AND RAISIN RELISH
SWEET RELISH
RHUBARB RELISH
CHUTNEY
TOMATO CHUTNEY
APPLE CHUTNEY
SPICED BLUEBERRIES
SPICED CRANBERRIES
PICKLED CABBAGE

PICKLED BEETS
PICKLED ONIONS
PICKLED CRAB APPLES
TOMATO PICKLES
VEGETABLE MARROW PICKLES
CABBAGE PICKLES
GOOSEBERRY PICKLES
DRIED APPLE PICKLES
RHUBARB CATSUP
MUSTARD PICKLES

MINCEMEAT:
OLD FASHIONED MINCEMEAT

MINCEMEAT

CANNED FOODS:
BOTTLED TURR

PRESERVED MOOSE

94

PARTRIDGEBERRY JAM
5½ cups prepared fruit
7 cups granulated sugar
½ bottle Certo

Put 1½ pounds fully ripe partridgeberries in a saucepan and add 3 cups water. Bring to a boil and simmer in a covered saucepan 10 minutes. Measure 5½ cups of this fruit into a large saucepan to make jam. Add 7 cups sugar to fruit in saucepan and mix well. Place over high heat, bring to a full boil. Boil hard for 1 minute, stirring constantly. Remove from heat; at once stir in ½ bottle Certo. Stir 5 minutes. If Certo is not available or if apples are plentiful, the pectin may be extracted and used instead of Certo in the recipe.

APPLE PECTIN
4 pounds apples
4 quarts water

Select firm sour apples a little under ripe. Scrub thoroughly and slice apples thinly. Bring to a boil quickly; cover and boil rapidly for 20 minutes. Strain until juice ceases to drip. Remove fruit from bag. Measure and add equal amount of water. Boil 20 minutes and strain. Mix first and second extractions (about 3 quarts) together. Mix in a wide pan, liquid 2 inches deep or less. Heat rapidly about 30 to 45 minutes to ¼ of original volume. Pour while boiling hot in jars and seal.

BLUEBERRY JAM
6 cooking apples (sour)
½ cup water
22 cups blueberries
10 cups granulated sugar

Peel and core apples; chop. Put them in a preserving kettle and add water. Stew until well cooked and then mash. Add blueberries and sugar; blend well and let boil for 30 minutes or until jam drops from spoon in sheets. Bottle in hot sterilized jars and seal with hot parafin. Store in a cool place.

BAKEAPPLE JAM
Wash and weigh berries. Add ¾ pound granulated sugar to each pound of berries. Place both together in a container and let stand overnight. Next morning put berries on to cook, bringing the jam slowly to a boil.

Boil slowly for 20 minutes or a little longer. Pour at once into hot sterilized jars and seal.

Bake-Apples
Yellow berries of delicious flavour, shaped like black berries. They grow low down in bogs. In Scandinavian countries they are called cloud berries.
They are often confused by the stranger with baked apples but, of course, they are not at all the same. It is said that when the French first landed on the shores of Newfoundland and found this unknown berry they said "what is this berry called?" or "Baie qu' appelle?"

DOGBERRY AND APPLE JELLY
Add two dozen crab apples to one quart of dogberries. Cover with cold water and simmer until tender. Strain through cheese cloth or a jelly bag.
Add ¾ cup granulated sugar for each cup of juice. Boil until a drop of juice will jell on a cold plate. Pour into sterilized jars and seal. This is very good with chicken.

MARSH BERRY JELLY
Pick over and wash 4 cups of marsh berries. Put in saucepan with 2 cups of boiling water and boil 20 minutes. Put through sieve pressing all juice from the boiled berries. Cook juice for 3 minutes; add ¾ cup granulated sugar for each cup of juice and cook for another 2 minutes. Pour into sterilized jars and seal.

"This is an old recipe which was given to our contributor many years ago by a lady who operated a very successful hotel." SALLY WEST.

A sign—a small portion.
At dinner a person is asked if he will have a little more. He replies "Just a sign"—meaning half a plateful.

RHUBARB MARMALADE

12 cups rhubarb
    Juice and rind of 2 oranges and
    1 lemon
3 cups seedless raisins
6 cups granulated sugar

Cut rhubarb in small pieces. Add fruit juices, chopped rind of lemon and oranges, finely chopped raisins and sugar. Mix well. Let stand overnight.

Then simmer for 1 hour, stirring frequently. Pour into hot sterilized jars and seal.

Raisins may be omitted if you wish.

PRUNE MARMALADE

4 cups rhubarb
6 cups prunes
10 cups granulated sugar
    Juice and peel of 2 oranges
    Juice of 1 lemon

Cut rhubarb in ½ inch pieces and soak overnight. Soak prunes overnight and then cook them in the same water, removing the pits as they cook. Add the drained rhubarb, sugar and fruit juice and chopped peel. Simmer until thick and clear.

BLUEBERRY AND APPLE CONSERVE

4 cups diced apples
4 cups blueberries
5 cups granulated sugar
4 tablespoons lemon juice
½ cup raisins

Simmer apples and blueberries for 20 minutes. Add sugar, lemon juice and raisins. Boil until thickened. Pour into hot, sterilized jars; seal.

PARTRIDGE WALNUT CONSERVE

4 cups raw partridge berries
2½ cups granulated sugar
1 cup coarsely broken walnuts, toasted
1 cup orange marmalade
    Juice of one lemon

Combine partridge berries and sugar and place in a tightly covered baking dish. Bake at 350° F. for 1 hour. Spread walnuts in a shallow pan and toast in the 350° F. oven for about 12 to 15 minutes.

Stir together the baked partridge berries, walnuts, marmalade and lemon juice. Chill.

CRANBERRY-PINEAPPLE RELISH

4 cups fresh cranberries
1 cup crushed pineapple, drained
1 teaspoon lemon juice
1 cup granulated sugar

Put cranberries through a food grinder. Combine them with other ingredients. Chill before serving.

APPLE AND RAISIN RELISH

½ cup bleached raisins
½ orange
1 cup finely chopped, peeled apples
1 tablespoon lemon juice
½ cup chopped nuts
2 tablespoons honey

Put raisins and orange (cut in pieces) through the fine blade of a food chopper. Add remaining ingredients and chill overnight in the refrigerator.

This keeps for a week and is nice to serve with hot or cold meat.

SWEET RELISH

10 pounds green tomatoes
5 pounds onions
4 cups granulated sugar
1 quart vinegar
2 tablespoons salt
2 tablespoons pickling spices (in a small bag)

Put tomatoes and onions through the mincer. Add sugar, vinegar, salt and spice bag. Cook until tender, not mushy.

Put in a large jar or crock. Leave the spice bag in for a few days as this improves the flavour.

RHUBARB RELISH

2 quarts cut rhubarb
1 quart thinly sliced onions
1 pint vinegar
2 cups granulated sugar
1 tablespoon salt
1 teaspoon each of cloves, allspice, cinnamon and pepper

Cook together slowly until tender (about one hour).

Pour into hot, sterilized jars; seal.

CHUTNEY

2 quarts cider vinegar
12 cups brown sugar

12 cups gooseberries, green or acid apples
3 cups raisins (Valencia—stoned and sliced)
6 cups sultana raisins, finely minced
1 cup salt
1 cup whole ginger (broken into 1/2 inch pieces)
1/4 cup garlic, finely minced
1 tablespoon cayenne pepper
1/4 cup mustard seed (husked)

Make syrup by boiling vinegar and sugar together. Let it cool.

Add other ingredients to the cooled syrup and then boil for 5 minutes.

Bottle when cold.

Note: This is very good with cold meat.

TOMATO CHUTNEY

2 dozen red or green tomatoes
6 to 8 apples
4 medium onions
3 tablespoons pickling spice
1 teaspoon salt
1/2 teaspoon black pepper
1/8 teaspoon red pepper
1 1/2 cups vinegar
1 1/4 cups brown sugar (packed)

Wash tomatoes and cut in quarters; peel and chop the apples and onions. Put all ingredients except the sugar in a large saucepan or kettle. Bring to a boil and cook until soft. Add the sugar and cook for another 10 minutes.

Put in hot, sterilized jars and seal.

APPLE CHUTNEY

12 cups unpeeled, chopped apples
1 large onion, chopped
3 cups chopped celery
1 cup raisins
2 cups cider vinegar
1/2 teaspoon pepper
2 cups granulated sugar
1 tablespoon salt
1 teaspoon ground ginger
1 teaspoon cinnamon
1/8 teaspoon ground cloves

Combine apples, onion, celery and raisins. Add vinegar and pepper. Cook slowly for 1 hour, stirring often. Add other ingredients. Cook until very thick. Seal in sterilized jars.

SPICED BLUEBERRIES

6 cups granulated sugar
1 pint cider vinegar
5 pints blueberries
2 tablespoons cinnamon
1 teaspoon cloves

Dissolve sugar in vinegar; add other ingredients.

Boil for one hour.

Seal in hot, sterilized jars.

SPICED CRANBERRIES

16 cups cranberries
9 cups brown sugar
2 cups vinegar
2 tablespoons cinnamon
2 tablespoons allspice
1 tablespoon cloves

Combine these ingredients and simmer together for 2 hours.

Serve with meat.

PICKLED CABBAGE

2 cups granulated sugar
1 tablespoon cinnamon
1 teaspoon allspice
1 teaspoon cloves
1 tablespoon salt
2 cups cider vinegar
1 lemon, thinly sliced
2 quarts white cabbage, chopped
2 quarts small beets, cooked and peeled

Combine sugar, spices and salt. Add vinegar and sliced lemon and cook to make a syrup. Pour hot syrup over the cabbage and beets; let simmer for 15 minutes.

Pour into hot sterilized jars and seal.

PICKLED BEETS

Boil young beets until tender; skin them. For each quart of beets, allow 1 1/2 cups brown sugar, 1 teaspoon salt, 3/4 cup vinegar and 3/4 cup water in which beets were boiled.

Heat beets in this mixture until it boils and then fill hot sterilized jars and seal them.

"Don't make strange." Said to make a guest feel at home.

PICKLED ONIONS

4   quarts small white onions
3   pints boiling water
1   cup salt
3   pints cold water
 1/4 cup mixed pickling spices
2   cups granulated sugar
2   quarts white vinegar

Cover onions with boiling water; let stand for 5 minutes. Drain and then peel.

Dissolve salt in cold water; add onions and let stand for 12 to 24 hours. Drain and then rinse with cold water.

Tie spices in a cheese cloth bag and add to the sugar and vinegar; heat to boiling and then remove spice bag. Add onions and simmer for 2 or 3 minutes.

Pack onions in hot, sterilized jars; fill with the hot vinegar; seal. Makes about 6 pints.

PICKLED CRAB APPLES

5   pounds crab apples
1   quart cider vinegar
4   cups granulated sugar
2   teaspoons ginger
2   teaspoons ground cloves

Wash crab apples, but do not remove the stems. Add them to the heated vinegar to which has been added the sugar, ginger and cloves.

Cook until the crab apples are tender and start to break the skins.

Put in hot sterilized jars; seal.

TOMATO PICKLES

2   apples
2   or 3 onions
1   can tomatoes (20 ounces)
1   cup vinegar
1   cup granulated sugar
1   teaspoon allspice
1   teaspoon salt

Peel and cut apples into small pieces; slice onions. Combine all ingredients and boil for 1/2 hour.

Fill sterilized bottles and seal immediately.

VEGETABLE MARROW PICKLES

Cut up about 5 pounds each of vegetable marrow and onions. Sprinkle with about 1/2 cup fine salt. Let stand overnight. In the morning, pour off any water which has formed.

Add 6 cups brown sugar, 1—28 ounce can tomatoes and 3 or 4 cups vinegar (white or cider) and 1/4 cup pickling spices, tied up in a gauze bag.

Let the pickles boil slowly for 1 hour or until soft. Bottle in sterilized jars.

CABBAGE PICKLES

1   quart cabbage
1   quart onions
1   quart vinegar
1   cup granulated sugar
1   teaspoon salt
1   tablespoon curry powder
1   tablespoon turmeric powder
1   tablespoon dry mustard
 1/2 cup CREAM OF THE WEST Flour
 1/2 cup water

Chop cabbage and onion until very fine; add vinegar and boil for 10 minutes. Add the sugar and salt. Mix seasonings with the flour; add water to make a paste. Stir flour paste into the boiling pickles and boil for 20 minutes. Bottle while hot.

GOOSEBERRY PICKLES

6   cups gooseberries
6   cups onions
4   cups granulated sugar
 1/2 pint vinegar
1   teaspoon salt
1   teaspoon pepper
1   teaspoon cinnamon
2   teaspoons pickling spices

Put gooseberries, onions and sugar in vinegar to soak overnight.

Add other ingredients and boil until berries are soft. Put in sterilized bottles and seal. These pickles will keep for years.

DRIED APPLE PICKLES

1   pound dried apples
     Water enough to make soft
1 1/2 pounds onions
3   cups sugar (white or brown)
1   teaspoon each of cinnamon, all-
     spice, salt, pepper
1   cup vinegar

Boil dried apples and water until like jam. Add the finely chopped onions and boil for a few minutes. Then add the sugar and spices. Simmer for about 30 minutes. Remove from the stove and stir in the vinegar. Bottle in sterilized jars.

RHUBARB CATSUP

12 cups rhubarb
6   cups brown sugar
3   cups chopped onions
1¼ cups white vinegar
1   teaspoon salt
1   teaspoon cinnamon
1   teaspoon ground cloves
½   teaspoon pepper

Cut rhubarb into small pieces; wash and drain. Add sugar to the rhubarb and let stand for 2 hours. Then add the chopped onions, vinegar and seasonings. Boil for 30 minutes or until thick. Stir occasionally to keep from sticking.

Delicious with cold meat.

MUSTARD PICKLES

1   pound pickling onions
1   large head cauliflower
    (2 pounds)
3   large cucumbers
1   sweet red pepper
½   cup salt
1   quart white vinegar
1½ cups granulated sugar
½   cup sifted
    CREAM OF THE WEST Flour
2   tablespoons dry mustard
1   tablespoon turmeric
½   cup water

Skin the onions and separate the cauliflower into small flowerlets. Cut unpeeled cucumbers and red pepper into wedges. Cover with water; sprinkle with salt and let stand overnight. Boil 10 minutes in water in which it has been soaked. Drain. Heat vinegar and sugar. Make a smooth paste with flour, mustard, turmeric and ½ cup water; add to vinegar and boil until thick. Pour over vegetables while still hot. Seal in hot, sterilized jars.

OLD FASHIONED MINCE MEAT

2   cups chopped lean meat
2   cups ground beef suet
3   quarts sour apples, chopped
1   cup grape or apple jam
2   cups peach jam or marmalade
1   pint grape juice
3   cups brown sugar
3   cups seeded raisins
3   cups seedless raisins
3   cups dried currants

4   cups mixed peel, minced
    Juice and grated rind of 2 oranges
    and 2 lemons
1   tablespoon salt
1   tablespoon cinnamon
½   teaspoon mace
    Few grains ground cloves

Cook the chopped meat until very tender; drain and put through a food chopper.

Prepare all the ingredients. Combine everything in a large pot and simmer gently for 1½ hours. Seal in hot, sterilized jars.

MINCE MEAT

6   cups raisins
6   cups currants
2   cups dark molasses
2   oranges, grated
2   lemons, grated
2   cups mixed peel
2   teaspoons ginger
6   cups brown sugar
2   cups shredded suet
4   cups sliced apples
2   tablespoons salt

Combine the raisins, currants and molasses; boil for 15 minutes (add a little water if necessary). Blend in the grated orange and lemon, mixed peel and ginger. Cook for a few minutes and then add the brown sugar and suet. Continue to simmer. Lastly, add the apple slices and salt. Continue to simmer for ¾ of an hour, stirring occasionally to keep from sticking. Cool slightly and then jar.

BOTTLED TURR

Clean the turrs; skin; and cut off back and rib bones where there is not much meat. Pack the legs and breasts in wide mouth mason jars. Add two slices fat pork, one chopped onion and one teaspoon salt to each jar. Fill the jars to one inch of top with boiling water. Screw on tops; loosen slightly.

Process in a pressure cooker for 90 minutes at 10 pounds pressure or in boiling water for 3 hours.

A quart jar will hold about 2 birds. If small mouth jars are used the meat will have to be cut in smaller pieces. Do not pack the giblets.

100

PRESERVED MOOSE

Wash moose meat and cut in small pieces. Place meat in jars; add 2 teaspoons salt and enough boiling water to fill jars to within one inch of top. Seal jars and then loosen slightly.

Process in boiling water for 4 hours or in a pressure cooker for 1¾ hours at 10 pounds pressure.

Seal jars as soon as possible.

NOTES:

MISCELLANEOUS

Last but not least! We hope you'll find a favourite sauce or candy recipe here—or perhaps a new idea for a frosting or beverage.

SAUCES:

MEAT AND FISH

EGG SAUCE

SWEET AND SOUR SAUCE

BARBECUE SAUCE

MILD MUSTARD SAUCE

HOT MUSTARD SAUCE

LEMON PARSLEY SAUCE

HOT TARTAR SAUCE

DRAWN BUTTER

TOMATO SAUCE

GREAT-GRANDMOTHER'S
    SALAD DRESSING

ONE EGG BOILED DRESSING

DESSERT

LEMON SAUCE

GRANDMOTHER'S SAUCE

SUNSHINE SAUCE

CANDY:

BROWN SUGAR FUDGE

FUDGE

COCOANUT FUDGE

PENUCHE

MOLASSES TAFFY

FROSTINGS AND FILLINGS:

CHOCOLATE CREAM FROSTING

SNOW FROSTING

SEVEN MINUTE FROSTING

COFFEE SHORT CUT ICING

CHOCOLATE FROSTING

COMFORT FROSTING

BEVERAGES:

RASPBERRY VINEGAR

PARTRIDGEBERRY COCKTAIL

BLUEBERRY SYRUP

BLUEBERRY WINE

EGG SAUCE

4   tablespoons butter
4   tablespoons
     CREAM OF THE WEST Flour
     Salt
     Pepper
2   cups milk
1   chopped hard-cooked egg

Melt butter in a saucepan. Add flour and seasonings; allow to bubble for 2 or 3 minutes, stirring constantly. Add milk gradually and stir until sauce is thick. Add the chopped egg.

SWEET AND SOUR SAUCE

1   cup pineapple juice
2   tablespoons granulated sugar
2   tablespoons vinegar
1/8 teaspoon garlic salt
1/2 teaspoon soy sauce
1/2 cup pineapple chunks
1/2 of a green pepper, chopped
1 1/2 tablespoons cornstarch
2   tablespoons cold water

Combine pineapple juice, sugar, vinegar, garlic salt and soy sauce in a saucepan; bring to a boil.

Add pineapple chunks and chopped pepper. (Dill pickles may be substituted for the pepper.)

Blend cornstarch and cold water; stir into the hot sauce mixture. Cook until sauce thickens, stirring constantly.

Pour over fish or spareribs.

BARBECUE SAUCE

2   tablespoons butter
1   onion, diced
3/4 cup celery, diced
3/4 teaspoon dry mustard
2   tablespoons brown sugar
1 1/2 teaspoons salt
3/4 teaspoon chili powder
3   tablespoons vinegar
1 1/2 cups tomato juice
1/2 cup water

Cook diced onion and celery in the hot butter for 2 minutes. Add dry ingredients and then the liquids. Simmer for 20 minutes.

Use it for basting meat.

MILD MUSTARD SAUCE

1   egg, slightly beaten
1/2 cup granulated sugar
1/3 cup vinegar
1   tablespoon dry mustard

Combine these ingredients in a saucepan and cook until thick, stirring constantly.

This is delicious with ham, hot dogs or hamburgers.

HOT MUSTARD SAUCE

2   tablespoons butter
1   tablespoon
     CREAM OF THE WEST Flour
2   tablespoons dry mustard
2   teaspoons granulated sugar
1/3 cup milk or cream
1/4 cup vinegar

Melt butter; add flour and stir until smooth. Remove from the heat and blend in the mustard and sugar; then gradually add the milk. Cook over hot water until thickened, stirring constantly. Cool slightly and add the vinegar. Serve cold with steak, chops, ham or cold meats.

LEMON PARSLEY SAUCE

Melt 1/4 cup margarine. Add 1 tablespoon lemon juice, 1/4 teaspoon Worcestershire sauce and 1 tablespoon chopped parsley; blend.

Serve with fish or vegetables.

HOT TARTAR SAUCE

2   tablespoons butter
2   tablespoons
     CREAM OF THE WEST Flour
1/2 teaspoon salt
1   cup milk or 1/2 cup milk and 1/2
     cup vegetable water
2   egg yolks
1/8 teaspoon pepper
     Few grains cayenne
1   teaspoon lemon juice
2   tablespoons butter
2   egg whites

Melt 2 tablespoons butter; stir in the flour and salt; cook for 3 minutes. Add the liquid gradually and cook over direct heat until thick and smooth (stir constantly). Beat egg yolks and add a little of the hot mixture and beat well. Return to thickened mixture and cook for 1 minute. Add seasoning, lemon juice and remaining butter.

Remove from heat and fold in stiffly beaten egg whites before serving.

DRAWN BUTTER

1/4 cup butter
2 small onions, chopped
2½ tablespoons
　　CREAM OF THE WEST Flour
1½ cup hot water
　　Salt and pepper

Melt butter in a small saucepan; add onions and cook for a few minutes over low heat. Then add the flour and blend thoroughly. Add hot water and cook until thickened, stirring constantly. Add salt and pepper to taste.

TOMATO SAUCE

1 28-ounce can tomatoes
1 bay leaf
2 small onions, chopped
1 stalk celery, sliced
1 tablespoon vinegar
2 tablespoons brown sugar
1/4 teaspoon salt
1/8 teaspoon pepper
1/4 teaspoon thyme
1/4 teaspoon oregano
　　Few grains cayenne pepper

Simmer the ingredients together for 30 minutes, removing the bay leaf after the first five minutes. Remove from heat and press through a sieve.

To thicken, melt 2 tablespoons butter in a saucepan; add 3 tablespoons CREAM OF THE WEST Flour and stir to a smooth paste. Add pureed tomato mixture and cook until thickened, stirring constantly.

A roasting—abuse or ridicule
"Did I ever get a roasting!"

GREAT-GRANDMOTHER'S SALAD DRESSING

1 tablespoon butter
2 teaspoons
　　CREAM OF THE WEST Flour
1½ tablespoons granulated sugar
1 teaspoon dry mustard
1/2 teaspoon salt
1 egg yolk
1/2 cup vinegar
1/2 cup milk

Melt butter; add flour and stir to a paste. Put on the stove until it bubbles. Mix the sugar, mustard, salt and slightly beaten egg yolk. Add this to the flour mixture, then mix in the vinegar and milk.

Put in a double boiler and stir until it thickens.

ONE EGG BOILED DRESSING

1 egg
3/4 cup granulated sugar
2 teaspoons dry mustard
2 tablespoons
　　CREAM OF THE WEST Flour
1 teaspoon salt
1/4 teaspoon pepper
1 cup milk
1 cup water
1 cup vinegar
1 tablespoon butter

Beat egg. Stir in sugar, mustard, flour, salt and pepper. Place in top part of double boiler and add the liquids gradually. Cook until thick, stirring constantly. Remove from heat and stir in the butter.

LEMON SAUCE

2 tablespoons
　　CREAM OF THE WEST Flour
3/4 cup granulated sugar
3/4 cup boiling water
1 teaspoon grated lemon rind
1 egg (if desired)
1 tablespoon butter
2 tablespoons lemon juice

Combine flour and sugar; add the boiling water and lemon rind. Cook until thickened, stirring constantly. If the egg is to be added, beat it slightly and add the hot mixture to it. Cook over very low heat for 2 minutes, stirring constantly.

Remove from heat and stir in the butter and lemon juice.

GRANDMOTHER'S SAUCE

1 cup scalded milk
1/2 cup butter
1 cup granulated sugar
1 egg, well beaten
1/2 teaspoon vanilla
　　Shake of nutmeg

Scald milk. Cream butter and sugar; beat in the egg. Add to the hot milk and cook for 2 minutes, stirring constantly. Remove from the stove and add vanilla and nutmeg. Serve over cake or with fruit pudding.

SUNSHINE SAUCE

½ cup butter or margarine
1 cup icing sugar
1 egg
½ teaspoon vanilla

Cream butter or margarine in top part of a double boiler; blend in the sugar. Add the egg and place over hot water. Beat constantly with a rotary beater until foamy. Add vanilla. Serve hot with a steamed or fruit pudding.

BROWN SUGAR FUDGE

2 cups light brown sugar
1 tablespoon cornstarch
Few grains salt
1 tablespoon butter
⅓ cup sweet cream or evaporated milk
1 teaspoon vanilla

Combine all ingredients except the vanilla. Boil to the soft ball stage. Take from the fire; add vanilla and beat until creamy.

Pour into a buttered 8-inch square pan. Mark into squares when still warm.

Note: ½ cup cocoanut, chopped nuts, raisins or cherries may be added.

FUDGE

2 squares unsweetened chocolate
2 cups granulated sugar
1 cup milk
1 teaspoon corn syrup
¼ teaspoon salt
2 tablespoons butter
1 teaspoon vanilla
½ cup chopped nuts

Grate the chocolate. Combine it with the sugar, milk, corn syrup and salt in a saucepan. Cook quickly to a soft ball stage, stirring occasionally. Remove from heat; add butter and vanilla. Cool without stirring, then beat until it stiffens and loses its shine. Stir in nuts. Pour into a buttered 8-inch pan and spread evenly.

COCOANUT FUDGE

3 cups brown sugar
¾ cup evaporated milk
¼ cup butter

Combine these ingredients and boil until mixture reaches the soft ball stage. Remove from the stove; add:

2 cups cocoanut

2 teaspoons vanilla

Beat for 1 minute. Pour into a greased 9-inch square pan. Cut when cool.

PENUCHE

2 cups light brown sugar
⅓ cup milk or cream
1 tablespoon butter
⅛ teaspoon cream of tartar
¾ cup chopped nuts
1 teaspoon vanilla

Combine sugar, milk, butter and cream of tartar in a saucepan. Boil until it reaches the soft ball stage, stirring as little as possible. Remove from fire; add nuts and vanilla. Beat until thick. Pour into a buttered 8-inch square pan. When cool, cut into squares.

"Long may your big jib draw."
A good wish for the future—in other words, mayt here always be wind for your sail.

MOLASSES TAFFY

1 cup brown sugar
1 cup molasses
2 tablespoons butter
1 tablespoon lemon juice

Cook all together, without stirring, until brittle when tested in cold water. Pour into a buttered pan and cool sufficiently to pull.

Pull the taffy until light; cut in serving pieces.

CHOCOLATE CREAM FROSTING

1 cup brown sugar
½ cup water
3 squares unsweetened chocolate
3 tablespoons butter
½ teaspoon salt
3 cups (approximately) icing sugar
1 teaspoon vanilla
1 cup chopped nuts

Combine sugar, water, chocolate, butter and salt in a saucepan. Bring to boiling point and cook for 3 minutes. Remove from heat and cool slightly. Add enough sifted icing sugar to spread. Stir in vanilla and chopped nuts.

Enough for a 2-layer cake.

SNOW FROSTING

1   egg white
¾ cup granulated sugar
    Few grains salt
3   tablespoons water
1   teaspoon light corn syrup

Blend these ingredients in top of a double boiler and place over boiling water. Beat constantly for 4 minutes or until frosting stands in peaks.
Remove from heat and beat in ½ teaspoon vanilla.
Simmer ½ cup raisins in water for 5 minutes. Drain and cut up.
Add these to ⅓ of the snow frosting and use for a filling between layers. Spread remaining frosting on cake. Use red and green cherries for decoration.

SEVEN MINUTE FROSTING

2   egg whites
1½ cups brown sugar
⅓ cup cold water
1   teaspoon flavouring

Combine egg whites, sugar and water in top of double boiler. Cook over rapidly boiling water, beating constantly, until it stands in stiff peaks (about 7 minutes). Remove from heat and beat in 1 teaspoon flavouring.

COFFEE SHORT CUT ICING

1   cup granulated sugar
½ teaspoon cream of tartar
½ teaspoon salt
1   egg white
3   tablespoons cold coffee

Put all ingredients in top of a double boiler. Place over rapidly boiling water and beat with a rotary beater until mixture stands in stiff peaks. (About 5 to 7 minutes.)
Use at once.

CHOCOLATE FROSTING

2   squares unsweetened chocolate
2   tablespoons butter
1   cup icing sugar
2   tablespoons milk
1   egg
1   teaspoon vanilla
    Few grains salt

Melt chocolate and butter together. Add other ingredients and place bowl in a pan of ice water. Beat until light and stiff enough to spread.

COMFORT FROSTING

2   cups light brown sugar
½ cup boiling water
1   egg white
    Few grains salt

Combine sugar and boiling water; cook to the soft ball stage.
Beat egg whites until stiff, adding salt when partly beaten. Gradually add the syrup to the beaten egg white, and continue beating until it holds its shape and is thick enough to spread.

RASPBERRY VINEGAR

Pick over, wash and drain 1½ quarts raspberries. Cover with 1 pint cider vinegar and let stand overnight. Strain through double thickness of cheese cloth. Boil 15 minutes. To each pint of juice, add 1 pound granulated sugar and bring to a boiling point. Boil 5 minutes. Pour into hot sterilized bottles. Cool and seal.
Delicious drink in hot weather.

PARTRIDGE BERRY COCKTAIL

1   quart partridge berries
6   cups water
2   cups granulated sugar
1   cup orange juice
3   tablespoons lemon juice
1   quart ginger ale

Cook berries in 4 cups of water until they are soft. Crush berries and force through cheese cloth. Boil sugar and 2 cups of water for 5 minutes. Add to the partridge berry juice; chill. Add fruit juices. Just before serving, add ginger ale.

BLUEBERRY SYRUP

Dissolve 4 ounces Tartaric Acid in 2 quarts cold water. Pour this on 2 gallons of blueberries and let stand 24 hours. Strain without pressing berries. Add 1½ pounds granulated sugar for each pint of syrup and stir until dissolved. Bottle and tie muslin over top of bottles.

BLUEBERRY WINE

To 2 quarts of berries add 4 quarts of boiling water. Let simmer on back of stove until it begins to boil. Strain and add 6 cups granulated sugar to a gallon of juice. Boil 5 minutes. When cool, add 3 cups prunes. Put in a crock or jar; cover with cheese cloth and let stand 2 months. Then strain; bottle and cork.
Note: This wine is strong and will keep from year to year.

NOTES:

NOTES:

NOTES:

NOTES:

AN ACKNOWLEDGEMENT
TO OUR
CONTRIBUTORS

The Treasury of Newfoundland Dishes is in large part the work of the 3297 Newfoundlanders whose names appear below. This is their book, for it was from their contributions that the recipes to be published were chosen.

In dedicating this book to Newfoundland and its people the publishers do so on behalf of these contributors, and extend to them their warmest thanks.

ADAM'S COVE B.D.V.
Mrs. Arch Baggs
Mrs. Viola Baggs

ADEYTOWN T.B.
Mrs. Anderson Adey

ADMIRAL'S COVE Cape Broyle
Mrs. Patrick Mackey

ANGEL'S COVE P.B. Cape Shore
Mrs. John Follett

APSEY T.B.
Mrs. C. Smith

APSEY BROOK Random Island
Mrs. David Phillips
Mrs. Roy D. Smith
Mrs. William C. Smith

AQUAFORTE S.S.
Mrs. Carrie Croft
Mrs. Joseph Croft
Mrs. Rupert Croft
Mrs. Dorothy Keough
Mrs. Ernest Keough
Mrs. James Maher
Mrs. Margaret Ryan

AQUATHUNA
Mrs. Bert Hynes

ARGENTIA P.B. (U.S.N.B.)
Mrs. C. Flynn
Mrs. Merle E. Strunk

ARBNOLD'S COVE P.B.
Miss Daphne Hollett
Mrs. Manuel Hollett
Mrs. Samuel Hollett
Mrs. Hedley Peach
Mrs. Wallace Peddle

AVONDALE C.B.
Mrs. M. F. Devereux
Mrs. M. Doyle
Mrs. Beatrice McGee
Mrs. Cyril Hennessey
Mrs. John Hicks
Mrs. Michael Moore
Mrs. Regina Murray

BACON COVE, C.B.
Mrs. John Gushue

BAR HAVEN, P.B.
Mrs. Rita Collier
Mrs. Thomas Farrell
Mrs. Philip Flynn
Mrs. Lucy Gaulton
Mrs. Catherine Murray
Mrs. Frank Shea

BARENEED, C.B.
Mrs. Pearl Batten
Mrs. Arthur Boone
Miss Effie Boone
Mrs. Robert Boone

BARR'D ISLAND, Fogo Dist.
Mrs. Levi Blake

BARRETT'S SIDING, B.B.
Mrs. C. Whiffen

BAULINE, St. John's East
Mrs. Ambrose King
Mrs. Solomon LeGrow (Sr.)

BAY BULLS, S.S.
Mrs. Bertha Coady
Mrs. Maude Coady
Miss M. Dunphy
Mrs. Betty Glynn
Mrs. Wm. Glynn
Mrs. Basil Maloney
Mrs. Vincent Mullowney
Mrs. Gerald O'Driscoll
Mrs. Hannah Ryan
Mrs. Genevieve St. Croix
Mrs. Gerard Williams
Mrs. M. Williams (North Side)

BAY DE VERDE, C.B.
Mrs. Enias Blundon
Mrs. Mary Noonan (Jr.)
Mrs. D. B. Riggs
Mrs. Wm. C. Riggs
Mrs. Edward Walsh

BAY L'ARGENT, F.B.
Mrs. J. Good
Mrs. James Hardiman
Mrs. Elizabeth West
Miss Eileen West

BAY ROBERTS, C.B.
Mrs. H. S. Atkinson
Mrs. Isaac Badcock
Mrs. Roland Bagga
Mrs. Fred Bennett
Mrs. Isaac Bishop
Mrs. G. Boone
Mrs. Fred Bowering
Mrs. Thomas Brown, Water St.
Mrs. J. L. Burke
Mrs. G. Bursey, Box 19
Mrs. Alice Butler
Mrs. Julia Butler
Mrs. Wallace Cave
Mrs. Betty Churchill, Box 75
Mrs. Arthur Cluett
Miss Jessie Crane
Mrs. W. K. Elms
Mrs. Mary Fitzpatrick
Mrs. Cecil Gosse
Mrs. W. Gosse
Mrs. W. F. Guy, Box 88
Mrs. T. Hillyard
Mrs. James House
Mrs. B. Jones
Mrs. Fannie King
Mrs. Wallace Menchions
Mrs. Wilfred Menchions
Mrs. Chesley Mercer
Mrs. Edsel Mercer
Mrs. Edmond Mercer
Mrs. Eugene Mercer
Mrs Eva Mercer
Mrs. G. S. Mercer
Mrs. Snowden Mercer
Mrs. Cecily Morgan
Mrs. J. North
Mrs. Norman Noseworthy
Mrs. L. Parsons

Mrs. Edward Roach
Mrs. Dorothy Russell
Mrs. Edgar Russell
Mrs. R. Russell
Mrs. Robert Saunders (Jr.)
Mrs. Clayton Snow
Mrs. Florence Snow, Country Road
Mrs. Philip Snow
Mrs. Reuben Snow
Mrs. V. C. Sparkes
Mrs. Alan Stoodley
Mrs. Marcella Williams
Mrs. K. M. Winsor
Mrs. Eric Wood
Mrs. Dorothy Young

BEAR COVE, W.B.
Mrs. Edward Davis
Miss Rowena Blanchard

BELLEORAM, F.B.
Mrs. Hubert Coombs
Mrs. J. Parsons
Mrs. Amelia Rose
Mrs. Charlotte Savory

BELLEVUE, T.B.
Mr. James Heffernan
Mrs. Vincent Walsh

BELL ISLAND C.B.
Mrs. Ernest Ballard
Mrs. F. Bickford
Mrs. Lynn Bickford
Mrs. Michael Boland
Mrs. Charles Bown
Mrs. Sydney Bown
Mrs. R. B. Butler
Mrs. William Cantwell
Mrs. William Clarke
Mrs. Gus Coombs
Mrs. Hayward Crane
Mrs. Harold Davis
Mrs. Elinor Fleming
Mrs. Helen Flight
Mrs. Elizabeth Fitzgerald
Mrs. A. Freake
Mrs. Joseph Frye
Mrs. William George
Mrs. W. Hammond
Mrs. Roy Harvey
Mrs. Frances Hedderson
Mrs. Mary Hickey
Mrs. Stanley Hoffe
Mrs. Roy Hookey
Mrs. Dorothy Hunt
Mrs. John J. Hunt
Mrs. Oswald Hunt
Mrs. Una Jefferies
Mrs. Rhoda Kent
Mrs. Eleanor Lamswood
Mrs. George Lilly
Mrs. Gordon Mercer
Mrs. L. Morgan
Mrs. P. T. Murphy
Mrs. Patrick Neary
Mrs. George O'Brien
Miss Agnes O'Dea
Mrs. Ben Parsons
Mrs. Roland Parsons
Mrs. Shenstone Parsons
Mrs. Harry Peddle
Mrs. R. D. Pepper

Mrs. Edwin Petrie
Mrs. W. Pike
Mrs. Herman Rees
Mrs. Florence Richards
Mrs. Nellie Robbins
Mrs. Dorothy Russell
Mrs. E. Shave
Miss Anita Simon
Mrs. Thomas Skanes
Mrs. Lloyd Snow
Mrs. William Snow
Mrs. R. Spudy
Miss Jean Spurrell
Mrs. J. C. Squires
Mrs. Richard Sutton
Mrs. A. Tucker
Mrs. W. Warren
Mrs. Oliver White

BEACH HILL, BELL ISLAND
Mrs. Hilda Churchill
Mrs. Clyde Junt

THE FRONT, BELL ISLAND
Mrs. Albert Butler
Mrs. Martin Cahill
Mrs. W. C. Case
Mrs. J. Fitzgerald
Mrs. Cecelia Hancock
Mrs. Edwards Hunt
Mrs. Fred Kearley
Mrs. R. Littlejohn
Mrs. Patrick Murphy
Mrs. Vincent Murphy
Mrs. Harold Parsons
Mrs. Harry Peach
Mrs. Dick Power
Mrs. Albert Sellars
Mrs. Ellen Shea
Mrs. Llewellyn Skanes
Miss Mary Skanes

LANCE POINT, BELL ISLAND
Mrs. William Bickford
Mrs. M. Dawe
Mrs. George Hammond
Mrs. George Hiscock
Mrs. John A. Kent
Mrs. Ted Kent, Sr.
Miss Terry Kent
Mrs. Stewart Rees
Mrs. N. Stoyles
Mrs. William Hiscock

MARTIN'S HILL, BELL ISLAND
Miss Anita Shea

QUIGLEY'S LINE, BELL ISLAND
Mrs. Marjorie Kavanagh

SCOTIA RIDGE, BELL ISLAND
Mrs. Vivian Butler
Mrs. Sadie Clarke
Mrs. William Clarke

WABANA, BELL ISLAND
Mrs. Edward Duggan
Miss Helen Duggan
Miss Shirley Duggan
Mrs. Walter Kienitz
Mrs. Peter King
Mrs. Peter Neary
Mrs. Mary Nolan
Miss Catherine O'Neill
Mrs. Mary Skanes
Mrs. W. P. Skanes
Mrs. B. Stares
Mrs. Gordon Woodland

WEST MINES, BELL ISLAND
Mrs. Caleb Anthony
Mrs. Frank Craig
Mrs. James Edmunds
Mrs. Leonard Gosse
Mrs. Harold Linthorne
Mrs. Walter Maloney
Mrs. Albert Miller, Jr.
Mrs. Douglas Mugford
Mrs. Clifford Noseworthy
Mrs. Minnie Rose
Mrs. Gerald Vokey

BENOIT'S Cove, Bay of Islands
Mrs. Doreen Jesso

BENTON, BB
Mrs. Stanley Simmons

BISCAY BAY, SS
Mrs. Wm. Baker

BISHOP'S COVE, CB
Mrs. Cavelle Barrett
Mrs. Nath Barrett

BISHOP'S FALLS
Mrs. Allan Bryne
Mrs. Lewis Greene
Mrs. Myrtle Hoffe
Mrs. Freemen King
Mrs. Ray LeValliant
Mrs. Calvin Linthorne
Mrs. Bernard McMahon
Mrs. Douglas Osbourne
Mrs. Leonard Stride
Mrs. Herbert Tuck
Mrs. Mabel Whalen

BLAKETOWN, TB
Mrs. Victor Kowalski
Mrs. Fred Osbourne
Mrs. Herbert Osbourne
Mrs. Eldred Russell
Mrs. Nathanial Smith

BLOOMFIELD, BB
Mrs. Minnie Hann
Mrs. Murdock Holloway
Mrs. Ford Little
Mrs. R. Parsons
Mrs. Ashwell Reader
Mrs. C. Wiseman
Mrs. John Wiseman

BOAT HARBOUR PB
Mrs. Charlie Denty
Mrs. F. Denty
Mrs. George Denty
Miss Rhoda Denty
Mrs. William Lockyer
Mrs. Oakley Matterface
Mrs. Max Thornhill

BONAVISTA BB
Mrs. Grace Abbott
Miss Debbie Abbott
Mrs. Joseph Abbott
Mrs. Lillian Abbott
Mrs. R. Abbott
Mrs. Alice Bartlett
Mrs. Percy Butler
Mrs. Fred Dominey
Mrs. J. Dunn
Mrs. Millicent Dunn
Mrs. Annie Durdle
Mrs. E. Dwyer
Mrs. Alex Fifield
Mrs. Joseph Fifield
Mrs. R. Ford
Mrs. Shirley Gibbs
Mrs. Gertie George
Mrs. Gerald Hennebury
Mrs. Wilfred Hicks
Mrs. Eric Hiscock
Mrs. George Lawrence
Mrs. Ron Mouland
Mrs. C. J. Paul
Mrs. Olive Paul
Mrs. Phoebe Ryder
Mrs. Albert Sharpe
Mrs. Edith Sharpe
Mrs. Harry Strathie
Mrs. C. Sweetland
Mrs. H. Frank Sweetland
Mrs. Myra White
Mrs. Hjordis Hiscock

BOTWOOD
Mrs. John Arklie
Mrs. Ambrose Ball
Mrs. Herbert Bartlett
Mrs. Mary Boone
Mrs. Joseph Butt
Mrs. George Coates
Mrs. F. Curlis

Mrs. Max Howell
Mrs. Jamse Jewer
Mrs. W. Lambert
Mrs. George Noseworthy
Mrs. T. W. Peyton
Mrs. Nathan Roberts
Mrs. John Ruth
Mrs. G. Seabright
Mrs. Juanita West
Mrs. Marshall West
Mrs. R. Woolridge
Mrs. James Wooridge
Mrs. E. W. Young

BOXEY FB
Mrs. H. Blagdon
Mrs. Jerry Blagdon
Mrs. S. Blagdon
Mrs. Nathan Cutler
Mrs. John Keiping
Mrs. Reginald Skinner
Mrs. W. Stoodley

BOYD'S COVE N.D.B.
Mr. Bertram Burry
Mrs. Audrey Freake

BRIGUS C.B.
Mrs. Brendan Bartlett
Mrs. Ethel Barlett
Mrs. Barton Gushue
Mrs. Leonard Gushue
Mrs. Ruth Gushue
Mrs. E. Leamon
Mrs. Murray Moores
Mrs. Fred Payne
Mrs. John Peddle
Mrs. Graham Percy
Mrs. Douglas Pinkston
Mrs. James Roberts
Mrs. Roger Tobin
Mrs. Marion Trickett
Mrs. James Tucker, (Roche's Line)

BRISTOL'S HOPE, via Harbour Grace
Mrs. Robert Taylor

BRITISH HARBOUR T.B.
Mrs. Eli Duffett

BRITANNIA T.B.
Mrs. Francis George
Mrs. Ivy George
Mrs. Amelia Granter
Mrs. Annie Hansford
Mrs. Marie Hodde
Mrs. Edward Hoskins
Mrs. A. Ivany
Mrs. Mary Leawood
Mrs. Mabel Rice

BROAD COVE B.D.V.
Mrs. Wm. Badcock
Mrs. Zena Burden
Mrs. Clarence Crowley
Miss Doreen Flight
Mrs. Lewis King
Mrs. Ada LeGrow
Mrs. Edward LeGrow
Mrs. Roy LeGrow
Mrs. Ralph Noftle
Mrs. Oscar Parsons
Mrs. Irene Robbins

BROAD COVE NORTH B.D.V.
Mrs. Hudson LeGrow
Mrs. Thomas LeGrow

BROOKFIELD B.B.
Mrs. Duncan Gates
Mrs. Philip Sturge

BROOKLYN B.B.
Mrs. Josephine Butt
Mrs. Maxwell Hancock
Mrs. Gilbert Russell
Mrs. Nettie Stares

BROWNSDALE T.B.
Mrs. S. George Austin
Mrs. Nelson Belbin
Mrs. Douglas Bursey
Mrs. A. H. Matthews

Mrs. Gerry Matthews
Mrs. Henry Matthews

BRYANT'S COVE C.B. via Harbour Grace
Mrs. Herbert Parsons

BUCHANS
Mrs. John Follett
Mrs. H. Lear
Mrs. Neil McIsaac

BUCHAN'S JUNCTION
Mrs. C. Jackson
Mrs. Robert Moss

BULL'S COVE, Burin North
Mrs. C. Martin

BURGEO S.C.
Mrs. Joyce Benoit, Box 85
Mrs. Charles Blagdon
Mrs. Cecil Buckland, Box 89
Mrs. Dinah Matthews

BURGOYNE'S COVE T.B.
Mrs. John Duffett

BURIN P.B.
Mrs. Howard Beasley
Mrs. Jack Beasley
Mrs. Ernest Brinton
Mrs. G. Brown
Mrs. Garland Collins
Mrs. Rod Dancey
Mrs. Austin Hollett
Mrs. Vivian Shave
Mrs. E. Matthews

BURIN BAY P.B.
Mrs. David Inkpen

BURIN BAY ARM P.B.
Mrs. George Moulton

BURIN NORTH P.B.
Mrs. Elizabeth Anderson
Mrs. J. J. Coady
Mrs. Walter Isaacs
Mrs. William Kelly
Mrs. Frank Moulton
Mrs. Clem Penney
Mrs. Joseph Penney

BURNSIDE B.B.
Mrs. Violet Hunter
Mrs. Henry Oldford, Jr.

BURNT COVE S.S. via Tor's Cove
Miss A. Tee

BURNT POINT C.B.
Mrs. William Bursey
Mrs. Eva Milley

BURNT POINT B.D.V.
Mrs. Douglas Milley
Mrs. Fanny Milley
Mrs. Otto Milley
Mrs. G. O'Flaherty

CALVERT S.S.
Mrs. Ronald Condon
Mrs. Martin Kavanagh
Mrs. James Keough
Mrs. Carmel Power
Mrs. John Sullivan
Mrs. Maude Sullivan
Mrs. Eileen Walsh
Mrs. Mary Walsh

CAMPBELL'S CREEK via Port au Port
Miss Theresa Duffy

CAMPBELLTON N.D.B.
Mrs. Annie Tilley
Mrs. Grace Wells

CANNING'S COVE B.B.
Miss Jessie Chatman
Mrs. Gordon Penney
Mrs. James Penney

CAPE BROYLE S.S.
Mrs. Elizabeth Aspell
Mrs. Bridget Duggan
Mrs. Joan Duggan
Mrs. Ambrose Hawkins
Mrs. Hilda Hawkins
Mrs. John Lahey
Mrs. John Maddox
Mrs. Mae Maddox
Mrs. Aloysius O'Brien
Mrs. Anna Marie O'Brien
Mrs. Jim O'Brien
Mrs. Louis O'Brien
Mrs. Rita O'Brien
Miss Theresa O'Brien
Mrs. John Shannahan, Jr.
Mrs. Sally Shannahan
Mrs. L. Shannon
Mrs. John Whelan

CAPE FREELS NORTH B.B.
Mrs. Leslie Fifield
Mrs. Inez Stagg
Mrs. Rita Stokes

CAPE FREELS SOUTH B.B.
Mrs. Cecil Hann
Mrs. Olive Hann
Mrs. Mary Hillier

CAPLIN COVE C.B.
Mrs. Esther Garland
Mrs. Stanley Power
Mrs. Harold Reynolds
Mrs. Ralph Reynolds

CAPPHAYDEN
Mrs. Maisie Rossiter

CARBONEAR C.B.
Mrs. Henry Ash
Mrs. C. D. Bishop
Mrs. Cecil Burgess
Mrs. Clara Burgess
Mrs. Wallace Burgess
Mrs. Gus Chubbs
Mrs. Fred Clarke
Mrs. Frank Clarke
Miss Carrie Colbourne
Mrs. Harry Cole
Mrs. Frank Davis
Mrs. John Forward
Mrs. Stewart Forward
Mrs. Joe Hiscock
Mrs. Chesley Horwood
Mrs. Cyril Horwood
Mrs. Walter Horwood
Mrs. Frederick Howell
Mrs. Herbert Marshall
Mrs. Roy Moores
Mrs. V. A. Moores
Mrs. Vera Moore
Mrs. Gladys Morrissey
Mrs. Fred Murphy
Mrs. Margaret Murphy
Mrs. George Osmond
Mrs. George Penney
Mrs. Mabel Penney
Mrs. Melba Penney
Mrs. Raymond Penney
Mrs. George Pike, Jr.
Mrs. Joseph Power
Mrs. Estelle Quinlan
Mrs. LeRoy Quinlan
Mrs. Blanche Rowe
Mrs. Harry Saunders
Mrs. Walter Snow
Mrs. Grace Soper
Mrs. Llewellyn Squibb
Mrs. Frank Thoms
Mrs. Rupert Tilley
Mrs. Lewis Trickett
Mrs. George White
Mrs. Reuben Whyte
Miss Sharon Whyte

CARBONEAR EAST C.B.
Mrs. Frank Forward

CARBONEAR Southside C.B.
Mrs. George Penney
Mrs. W. H. Penney
Mrs. James Thoms

CARMANVILLE Fogo District
Mrs. John Collins
Mrs. D. Snow

CATALINA T.B.
Mrs. Elizabeth Bartlett
Mrs. Davis Bursey
Mrs. Richard Bursey
Mrs. R. Butt
Mrs. R. Curtis
Mrs. Susie Duffett
Mrs. Melvin Freake
Mrs. Herman Gould
Mrs. Charles Haynes
Mrs. Joseph Haynes
Mrs. Trixie Haynes
Mrs. Stanley Hoffe
Mrs. Isaac Johnson
Mrs. Anna Joy
Mrs. B. Joy
Mrs. Leo Joy
Mrs. Jean King
Mrs. Victor King
Mrs. Arthur Ludlow
Mrs. Winnifred Ludlow
Mrs. Edward Maidment
Mrs. John Manuel
Mrs. V. P. Martin
Mrs. W. S. Norman
Mrs. R. Rogers
Mrs. Phyllis Simons
Mrs. John Tippett
Mrs. Sally Tippett
Miss H. Young

CAVENDISH T.B.
Mrs. Eli Critch
Mrs. Joseph Cull
Mrs. Douglas Jackson
Mrs. Gerald Jackson
Mrs. Stanley Jackson
Mrs. Richard Jerrett
Mrs. Clayton Vetcher
Miss Mabel Wright

CHAMBERLAINS C.B.
Mrs. Charles Adams
Mrs. J. W. Butler
Mrs. Phoebe Chaytor
Mrs. Cyril Mercer

CHAMPNEY'S EAST T.B.
Mrs. Walter Cole
Mrs. Alex Walters

CHAMPNEY'S WEST T.B.
Miss Evelyn Goldsworthy
Miss Mary Hiscock
Miss Mollie Hiscock

CHANCE COVE T.B.
Mrs. Wilmore Smith

CHANGE ISLANDS Fogo Dist
Mrs. Chester Bates
Mrs. J. C. Bates
Mrs. W. H. Earle
Mrs. Morley Hoffe
Mrs. Ernest Hyde
Mrs. Katherine Hynes
Mrs. Reginald Hynes
Mrs. Stanley Peckford
Mrs. Fred Porter
Mrs. Frank Waterman

CHANNEL S.W. Coast
Mrs. Eileen Blackmore
Mrs. Joseph Feltham
Mrs. Angus Mullins
Mrs. George Richards
Mrs. Cecil Strickland

CHAPEL ARM T.B.
Mrs. Elizabeth Newhook
Mrs. Gladys Newhook
Mrs. Willis Newhook
Mrs. William Piercey
Mrs. Norman Smith
Mrs. I. Warren
Mrs. Merrill Warren

CHAPEL'S COVE C.B.
Mrs. Frederick Fewer
Mrs. Michael Walsh
Mrs. Philip Whelan

CHARLESTON B.B.
Mrs. Rosstyn Pike
Mrs. F. Quinton
Mrs. Norman Tremblett

CLARENVILLE T.B.
Mrs. A. H. Baird
Mrs. Elsie Baird
Mrs. Effie Balsom
Mrs. Belle Barbour
Mrs. L. B. Barbour
Mrs. E. Barnes
Mrs. Walter Blackmore
Mrs. E. E. Brushett
Mrs. R. B. Burden
Mrs. Peter Cholock
Mrs. R. Clouter
Mrs. Samuel Cooper
Mrs. Lloyd Davis
Mrs. Wm. Easton
Mrs. Gordon Hiscock
Mrs. Wallace Hutchings
Mrs. Genevieve Hynes
Mrs. William Jillett
Mrs. Dulcie Long
Mrs. Arthur Newman
Mrs. S. Noseworthy
Mrs. Mary Pearce
Mrs. Charles Pitcher
Mrs. Harry Pitcher
Mrs. Shirley Pitcher
Mrs. Augustus Seaward
Mrs. Edgar Stanley
Mrs. A. Stanley
Mrs. H. J. Strong
Mrs. Wilfred Strong
Mrs. Frank Tilley
Mrs. Vida Trickett
Mrs. Josephine Webber
Mrs. Mabel West

CLARKE'S BEACH C.B.
Mrs. Wesley Bartlett
Mrs. A. M. Boone, South River
Mrs. Lester Burry
Mrs. Fannie Dawe, The Broads
Mrs. Walter French
Mrs. C. J. Hodgson-Robinson, (Ottebury)
Mrs. John Howe
Mrs. Nyrtle Mugford
Mrs. J. T. Richards
Mrs. Albert Snow
Mrs. Fred Snow
Mrs. Gerald Snow
Mrs. Issac Watson, South River

CLATTICE P.B. South West
Mrs. M. Leonard
Mrs. P. Pomer

CODROY West Coast
Mrs. George Reid

COLEY'S POINT via Bay Roberts C.B.
Mrs. K. M. Batten
Mrs. Ethel Boland
Mrs. Alice Butler
Mrs. George Dawe
Mrs. Gilbert Fradsham
Mrs. Ralph Gilbert
Mrs. Irving Keefe
Mrs. Margaret Mercer
Mrs. Harvey Russell
Mrs. Nellie Russell
Mrs. Isaac Samways

COLEY'S POINT South C.B.
via Bay Roberts
Mrs. Marion Parsons

COLLIERS C.B.
Mrs. Anna Conway
Mrs. Thomas Hearn
Mrs. Doreen Trahey
Mrs. Christine Whelan
Miss Margaret Walsh
Mrs. James Whelan

COLLIN'S COVE Burin
Mrs. N. Mayo

COME BY CHANCE P.B.
Mrs. Neil Best

CONCEPTION HARBOUR C.B.
Mrs. John Bishop
Mrs. George Dalton, Sr.
Mrs. Albert Fewes
Mrs. Mary Gushue
Mrs. Loretta Keating
Mrs. Elizabeth Rotchford
Miss Jean Rotchford
Mrs. John Rotchford

COOK'S HARBOUR Straits of Belle Isle
Miss Gladys Diamond

COOMB'S COVE F.B.
Mrs. A. Vallis

CORMACK
Mrs. Donald G. Dodds

CORNER BROOK
Mrs. L. F. Batstone, 99 Humber Road
Mrs. Raymond Bishop, 32 East Valley Road
Mrs. Frank Breen, 21 Armstrong Avenue
Mrs. George Bryant, 1 Batstone Road
Mrs. Lewis Bryant, 24 Greenings Hill
Mrs. P. Chaffey, 74 East Valley Road
Mrs. Ernest Chaulk, 120 Humber Road
Mrs. Mona Collins, 21 West Valley Road
Mrs. Alex Cooper, 75 West Valley Road
Mrs. W. Earle, 4 Coronation Street
Mrs. Edward J. Evans, 107 Reid Street
Mrs. G. Gamberg, 59 Park Street
Mrs. L. Garmier, 10 Victoria Avenue
Mrs. Harold Gibbons, 3 Gibbons Avenue
Mrs. N. Hollahan, 37 Pier Road
Mrs. H. M. Hollands, 49 West Street
Mrs. Harry House, 39 Queen Street
Mrs. E. Humber, 97 East Valley Road
Mrs. E. Martin, 49 East Valley Road
Mrs. E. L. Noseworthy, 25 Humber Park
Mrs. Brendan Perry, 12 Mount Bernard Ave.
Mrs. Frank Powell, 107 Reid Street Extension
Mrs. May Pynn, 14 Elserick Road
Mrs. Fred Rendell, 19 Armstrong Avenue
Mrs. Baxter Smith, 102-A Humber Road
Mrs. D. M. Soper, Drawer #158
Mrs. James Whalen, 34 Main Street

COTTRELL'S COVE N.D.B.
Mrs. Evangeline Boone
Mrs. Hedley Boone
Mrs. Theodore Budgell
Mrs. Harry Hustins
Mrs. William White

CRAWLEY'S ISLAND P.B.
Mrs. Alphonsus Nolan

CRESTON P.B. via Marystown
Mrs. Ray Hanham
Mrs. Vera Mayo

CUPIDS C.B.
Mrs. C. Ackerman
Mrs. Edward Ackerman
Mrs. George Anthony
Miss Angela Curran
Mrs. J. Curran
Mrs. John Hoyles
Mrs. Martha LeDrew
Mrs. Allan LeDrew
Mrs. Nath Morgan
Mrs. Harold Wells
Mrs. W. A. Wells

CUPID'S CROSSING Roche's Line
Mrs. Dorothy Butler
Mrs. Michael Edmunds

CURRENT ISLAND St. Barbe District
Mrs. Annie Gibbons

DANIEL'S POINT Trepassey
Mrs. George Tobin

DARK COVE GAMBO
Mrs. Lucy Genge
Mrs. William Pitcher

DEEP BAY via Fogo
Mrs. Rebecca Coles

DEEP BIGHT T.B.
Mrs. Wilfred Green

DEER HARBOUR Random Island
Mrs. Jemima Avery
Mrs. Austin King

DEER LAKE
Mrs. Harold Curleu, Box 151
Mrs. W. Wellon
Mrs. James White, Jr., Box 367
Mrs. Howard Wight, Box 83

DILDO T.B.
Mrs. Stephen Gosse
Mrs. Llewellyn Newhook
Mrs. E. Pretty

DONOVAN'S C.B. Topsail
Mrs. Lorraine Lynch
Miss Margaret Murphy
Mrs. Albert Parsons
Mrs. N. Stone

DOVER B.B.
Mrs. Clifford Mercer
Mrs. Gladys Mercer

DOYLES
Mrs. Duncan MacIssac
Mrs. M. S. Martin

DOYLES via Great Codroy
Mr. Bert O. Regan

DUNFIELD T.B.
Mrs. Arch King

DUNTARA B.B.
Miss Rosie Legge

DUNVILLE P.B.
Mrs. William Budden
Mrs. Charles Butler
Mrs. Raymond Jones
Mrs. Alfred Walsh

DURRELL Twillingate
Mrs. R. B. Smith

EASTPORT B.B.
Mrs. Wallace Cresby
Mrs. Ronald Lane
Mrs. Edwin Moore
Mrs. Abner Penny

ELLIOTT'S COVE T.B.
Mrs. Murley Berkshire
Mrs. Douglas Cooper
Mrs. William Copper
Mrs. George Patey
Mrs. Gilbert Patey
Mrs. Aaron Smith
Mrs. Alice Smith
Mrs. Clyde Smith
Mrs. Kevin Smith
Mrs. W. Smith
Mrs. W. Smith, Jr.

ELLISTON T.B.
Mrs. Lewis Cole
Mrs. M. Diamond
Mrs. Clarence Goodland
Miss Willamina Goodland
Mrs. F. Murphy
Mrs. Roy Tilley

EMBREE via Lewisporte
Mrs. Clarence Anstey
Mrs. Robert Anstey
Mrs. Woodrow Fess
Mrs. Arthur Hoddinott

ENGLISH HARBOUR T.B.
Mrs. Mary Batson
Mrs. Daniel Penny
Mrs. Gilbert Skiffington

ENGLISH HARBOUR WEST F.B.
Mrs. George Lane
Mrs. Meta Shirley

EPWORTH Burin
Mrs. Harry Beasley
Mrs. William Beasley
Mrs. William Brinston
Mrs. Harold Dale
Mrs. Flora Henning
Mrs. Jean Manning
Mrs. Fred Roberts
Mrs. Ralph Street

FELIX COVE Port au Port
Mrs. Ted Felix

FERMEUSE S.S.
Mrs. Eileen Fahey

FERRYLAND S.S.
Mrs. Anna Curran
Mr. Patrick J. Curran
Mrs. Thomas Keough

FLAT ISLAND B.B.
Mrs. James Chaytor

FLATROCK C.B. via Carboneer
Mrs. Vera Pottle

FOGO N.D.B.
Mrs. D. Cheeseman, Box 70
Mrs. H. C. Haines, South Side
Mrs. T. A. Jones
Mrs. Cora Keefe, Box 95
Mrs. Ivy Layman
Mrs. Grace Sibley, North Side
Mrs. William Willis, Box 1

FORTUNE Burin District
Mrs. Blanche Clouter
Mrs. Leah Day
Mrs. B. R. Foley
Mrs. Margaret Harris
Mrs. John Hillier
Mrs. Joseph Hillier
Mrs. Lena Hillier
Mrs. William Hillier
Mrs. T. Matthews
Mrs. Frank Patten
Mrs. Grace Piercey
Mrs. Clyde Warren
Mrs. Frank Wetherall

FOX COVE Burin North
Mrs. Hester Antle

FOX HARBOUR P.B.
Mrs. A. Darmody
Mrs. Cyril Duke

FOXTRAP C.B. via Kelligrews
Mrs. Julia Batten
Miss Ada Batten
Mrs. Sam Batten
Mrs. Patrick Bishop
Mrs. Beatrice Butler
Mrs. Peter Petten
Mrs. Belinda Rideout
Mrs. Florence Taylor
Miss Elsie Taylor
Mrs. Eric Rideout
Mrs. Grace Rideout

FRANCOIS Hermitage Bay
Mrs. E. Touchings

FREDERICKSON N.D.B. Fogo Dist
Mrs. Harvey Wheaton
Mrs. Ivanhoe Wheaton

FRENCHMAN'S COVE Garnish F.B.
Mrs. Arch Rideout
Ambrose Tapper (Mrs.)
Mrs. Doris Tibbo

FRESHWATER C.B.
Mrs. William Broderick
Mrs. G. Butt
Mrs. Mina Butt
Mrs. George Davis
Mrs. Vinetta Davis

Mrs. M. McIntyre
Mrs. Fred Snow
Mrs. G. Snow

FRESHWATER P.B.
Mrs. Monica Beresford
Mrs. Thomas Carroll
Mrs. Pat Coffey
Mrs. John Cleat
Mrs. M. Dakins
Mrs. Nicholas Hawes
Mrs. Pat Lambe
Mrs. Theresa Mahar
Mrs. Douglas Mercer
Mrs. Bernard Penney
Mrs. Lena Power
Mrs. John J. Roche
Mrs. Esau Thoms
Mrs. Trudy Thoms
Mrs. Kathleen Watson

GALLOW'S COVE Witless Bay, S.S.
Mrs. David Tobin

GAMBO B.B.
Mrs. Ambrose Blackwood
Mrs. John Brazil
Mrs. John Foley
Mrs. Patrick Kelly
Mrs. Gordon Paul
Mrs. Jesse Pritchett

GANDER
Mrs. Wesley Bath
Mrs. Frank Belbin, Box 45
Mrs. S. H. Blandford, Box 5
Mrs. Fred Chafe, 37 Chestnut Ave.
Mrs. Edna Chisholm, Box 187
Mrs. Ethel Goodyear, Box 385
Mrs. Max Hoddinott
Mrs. G. S. Hollett, Box 11
Mrs. Jacob Lehr, Box 45
Mrs. Gus Lewis
Mrs. Betty McMorran
Mrs. Lense Meyer
Mrs. S. Mabel Moss, Box 174
Mrs. Spencer Pritchett, 15 Fitzmorris Rd.
Mrs. Harold Saunders
Mrs. Donald Skiffington
Mrs. Fred Waterman, Box 359
Mrs. Winnie Wells
Mrs. Enid West, Box 336
Mrs. James White, Army Side

GARNISH F.B.
Mrs. Charles Anstey
Mrs. Florence Cluett
Mrs. L. Grandy
Mrs. Mildred Lorenzen

GEORGE'S BROOK T.B.
Mrs. B. Bailey
Mrs. Herbert Bailey
Mrs. Joshua Brook
Mrs. Baxter Pelley
Mrs. Roland Pelley

GEORGETOWN C.B. via Brigus
Mrs. Bert Newell
Mrs. Maud Newell

GIN COVE T.B. Smith Sound
Mrs. Richard Frampton

GLENDALE Mount Pearl Park
Mrs. Ethel Antle, 4 Pine Bud Avenue
Mrs. W. Bannister, 37 First Street
Mrs. Betty Bartlett, 20 St. Andrews Ave.
Mrs. A. B. Boyce, 190 Park Avenue
Mrs. Mack Chaulk, 6 Sunrise Avenue
Mrs. Reuben J. Cole, 148 Park Avenue
Mrs. Rex Collins, G.P.O.
Mrs. Baxter Dalley, 76 Park Avenue
Mrs. Valerie Dodd, 2 Churchill Avenue
Mrs. Frances Dunn, 218 Park Avenue
Mrs. Ivy Garland, 4 Jersey Avenue
Mrs. Edison Greening, Norman's Avenue
Mrs. Robert Hamlyn, 134 Park Avenue
Mrs. Patrick Hunt, 4 Ruth Avenue
Mrs. M. Kean
Mrs. Alex Lehr, 18 Glendale Avenue
Mrs. Florence Lester, Mt. Pearl Road
Mrs. John MacDonald, 15 Ruth Avenue

Mrs. James Major, 34 First Street
Mrs. B. Mercer, 22 Park Avenue
Mrs. Dorothy Newhook, 3 Teasdale St.
Mrs. R. C. Morris, 5 Edinburgh Drive
Mrs. W. J. Norman, 8 Ruth Avenue
Mrs. Elsie Norris, 23 Delaney Avenue
Miss Ena Norris, 23 Delaney Avenue
Mrs. Frank Phillips, 17 Valleyview Rd.
Mrs. Cyril Piccott, Mt. Pearl Road
Mrs. D. Pomeroy, 7 Glendale Avenue
Mrs. Lloyd Samson, 20 St. Andrews Ave.
Mrs. L. Samson, 33 Sunrise Avenue
Mrs. Belle Skanes, 31 First Street
Mrs. John Snow, 18 Park Avenue
Mrs. Gladys Squires, 7 Ruth Avenue
Mrs. J. Thistle, 75 Park Avenue
Mrs. S. Thistle, 20 Park Avenue
Mrs. Jessie Toope, 26 Jersey Avenue
Mrs. W. Walters, Mt. Pearl Road
Mrs. George White, 5 Norman's Avenue
Mrs. Alex Young, 8 Edinburgh Drive

GLENWOOD
Mrs. Howard Andrews
Mrs. Roland Richards
Mrs. Wilfred Richards
Mrs. Blanche Ryan
Mrs. Roy Stoles
Mrs. Harvey Waterman
Mrs. W. Wright, c/o Naval Radio Station

GLOVERTOWN B.B.
Mrs. F. Blackwood
Mrs. Jean Blackwood
Miss Geraldine Briffett
Mrs. Eva Brooking
Mrs. J. W. Butt
Mrs. Percy Collins
Mrs. John Davis, Box 242
Mrs. Hector Harris, Box 64
Mrs. Roland Lane
Mrs. Sarah Lane
Mrs. N. Wey

GOULDS, St. John's West
Mrs. Patricia Butler
Mrs. Weston Butler
Mrs. George Carnell, Forest Pond
Mrs. J. Finn
Mrs. John Hennessey
Mrs. Michael Joyce
Miss Elizabeth Noonan
Mrs. Val Noonan
Mrs. Timothy Raymond
Mrs. B. Stone
Mrs. Weston Williams, Forest Pond

GRAND BANK F.B.
Mrs. Anne Anstey, Edwin Street
Mrs. John Anstey, College Street
Mrs. Margaret Brooks, Box 397
Mrs. Wilson Crowley, Box 217
Mrs. Frances Douglas
Mrs. Walter Emberley, Box 447
Mrs. A. Forsey, Water Street
Mrs. Bertha Forsey ,Riverside West
Mrs. Azariah Grandy, Box 165
Mrs. Essie Grandy
Mrs. R. Hickman
Mrs. Hector Hillier
Mrs. Ben Hiscock, Box 53 College Street
Mrs. Freeman Johnson, Box 336
Mrs. William Kelland, Box 176
Mrs. Bertha Lee, Marine Drive
Mrs. George Morris, Elizabeth Avenue
Mrs. George Nurse, Fortune Road
Mrs. F. Oakley
Mrs. James Penwell, Box 266
Mrs. Janet Penwell, Box 266
Mrs. W. J. Penwell, Box 22
Mrs. Hannah Piercey
Mrs. Elsie Rose, Box 75
Mrs. James R. Rose, Seaview Road
Mrs. Hubert Skinner, Box 291
Mrs. L. Stewart, Hickman Street
Mrs. Allister Stone, West Street
Mrs. Philip Stoodley, Riverside West
Mrs. Beatrice Thornhill
Mrs. Jacob Thornhill, Hickman St.
Mrs. Margaret Thornhill, West Street
Mrs. Buff Tibbo
Mrs. Edwin Vallis, 93 Elizabeth Ave.

Mrs. Mary J. Welsh, Box 45
Mrs. Melinda Welsh, Fortune Road

GRAND BEACH F.B.
Mrs. Maxwell Rideout
Mrs. Stephen Tapper

GRAND FALLS
Mrs. E. Bannister
Mrs. Ellis Cashin, 34 Beaumont Avenue
Mrs. May Delaney, 12 Carmelite Road
Mrs. Cyril Down, Sr., 29 Circular Road
Mrs. Ronald Fewer, 15 Greenwood Ave.
Mrs. Jerry Foley, 46 Beau Street
Mrs. G. Forward, 12 Memorial Drive
Mrs. Charles Giles, 16 Junction Road
Mrs. Ronald Griffin, 6 Riverview Road
Mrs. F. Hayward, 13–A Carmelite Road
Mrs. Stephen Healey
Mrs. John Hollett, 9 Memorial Avenue
Mrs. W. J. Hollett, 48 Greenwood Ave.
Mrs. Patrick Kane, 16 Fourth Avenue
Mrs. Errol Knight, 77–A Botwood Road
Mrs. Stella Noel, 1 Carmelite Road
Mrs. F. Shapleigh, 12 Beaumont Avenue
Mrs. B. Skiffington
Mrs. G. S. Taylor, 2 Station Road
Mrs. William Thoms, Botwood Highway
Mrs. Victor Young, Box 192

GREAT PARADISE P.B.
Mrs. Martin J. Byrne
Mrs. Thomas Dunphy
Mrs. Frank Millrooney

GREAT SALMONIER via Epworth, Burin
Mrs. Fred Beasley
Mrs. Robie Beasley
Mrs. William Beasley

GRATE'S COVE B.D.V.
Mrs. Adolphus Benson
Mrs. Wesley Cooper
Mrs. Wilson Cooper
Mrs. Arthur Duggan
Mrs. Betty Jewer
Mrs. William Lambert
Mrs. Llewellyn Meadus
Mrs. Roy Snelgrove (T.B.)

GREELEYTOWN, via Kelligrews
Mrs. Roy Greeley

GREEN'S HARBOUR T.B.
Mrs. Bessie Bennett
Mrs. Fred Bennett
Mrs. Allan Bishop
Mrs. James Brace
Mrs. Selby Burt
Mrs. Lloyd Case
Mrs. Harold Drover
Miss Robin Drover
Mrs. Jane Hopkins
Mrs. Arthur March
Mrs. Victor March
Mrs. B. Penney
Mrs. W. Rodgers
Mrs. Bessie Rowe
Mrs. William Smith

GREENSPOND B.B.
Mrs. Arthur Burry
Mrs. M. Green
Mrs. Thomas Hunt, Box 43
Mrs. Maggie Parsons
Mrs. William Parsons
Mrs. Edna Way
Mrs. James Way
Mrs. Arnold Torraville

GRIGUET W.B.
Mrs. Harry Bartlett
Mrs. Leo Bartlett
Mrs. M. Bartlett

GULL ISLAND C.B.
Mrs. Ellen Oliver
Mrs. Jerry Oliver
Miss Rita Oliver

HAMPDEN W.B.
Mrs. George Colbourne
Mrs. Augustus Eveleigh

Mrs. George Eveleigh
Mrs. Walter Jenkins
Mrs. R. Manuel
Mrs. Augustus Oldford (Bayside)
Mrs. Colin Smith

HANT'S HARBOUR T.B.
Mrs. Fred Critch
Mrs. Robert Ellis
Mrs. Clyde King
Mrs. Don King
Mrs. Edwin Mitchell
Mrs. Bertram Price, Sr.
Mrs. Newman Shaw
Mrs. Newman Short
Mrs. Reuben Thomas
Mrs. Gordon Tuck

HAPPY ADVENTURE B.B.
Mrs. Newton Morgan
Mrs. Sidney Powell
Mrs. Phoebe Turner

HARBOUR BRETON F.B
Mrs. C. Elliott
Mrs. D. G. King
Mrs. James Piercey
Mrs. E. Snow

HARBOUR BUFFETT P.B.
Mrs. Cyril Best
Mrs. Percy Collett
Mrs. Loretta Collett
Mrs. Walter Dicks
Mrs. Malcolm Masters
Mrs. Neil Masters, Jr.
Mrs. Adelaide Shave

HARBOUR BUFFETT P.B. North East
Mrs. George Upshall

HARBOUR GRACE C.B.
Mrs. John Adams
Mrs. Harold Ash
Mrs. Theodore Ash
Miss Susie Barrett
Mrs. William Brickham
Mrs. Minnie Browne
Mrs. Gerald Butler
Mrs. Florence Cooper
Mrs. James Cooper
Mrs. Dorothy Cran
Mrs. L. C. Davis
Mrs. C. G. Dwyer
Mrs. William Dwyer
Mrs. A. Edwards
Mrs. Raymond Fitzgerald
Mrs. Evelyn French
Mrs. Morley Gillett
Miss L. Godden
Mrs. R. Goodwin
Mrs. John Horwood
Mrs. James Hunt
Mrs. Joyce Hunt
Mrs. Edna Janes
Mrs. W. Kennedy
Mrs. Frank Morris
Mrs. Harry Noseworthy
Mrs. Jessie Oke
Mrs. Harold Parsons
Mrs. Jennie Parsons
Mrs. Max Parsons
Mrs. William Peddle
Mrs. Gladys Pike
Mrs. George Pike
Mrs. Hettie Regular
Miss Elizabeth Rogers
Mrs. Azariah Sheppard
Mrs. Eldred Sheppard
Mrs. G. W. Simmons
Mrs. George Stevenson
Mrs. Ada Tapp
Mrs. Melinda Tobin
Mrs. Chesley Yetman

HARBOUR GRACE SOUTH C.B.
Mrs. Elsie Osborne
Mrs. Robert Peddle

HARBOUR MAIN C.B.
Mrs. Samuel Costigan
Miss Cecelia Dalton
Mrs. Gregory Dalton

Mrs. Luke Dalton
Miss Madelyn Dalton
Mrs. Helena Fewer
Mrs. Mary Garman

HARBOUR MILLE F.B.
Mrs. Harvey Bungay

HARCOURT T.B.
Miss Bernice Brown
Mrs. Cynthia Brown
Mrs. Newman Cooper
Mrs. E. Frampton
Mrs. Albert Freude
Mrs. Alfred Hyde
Mrs. A. E. Pelley
Mrs. N. C. Pelley
Mrs. Raymond Pelley
Mrs. Samuel Pelley
Mrs. Sidney Pelley
Miss Sylvia Pelley

HARE BAY B.B.
Mrs. Gordon Burry
Miss Beryl House
Miss Bride House
Mrs. J. House
Mrs. Hannah Parsons

HARMON FIELD Air Force Base St. G.B.
Mrs. J. C. Pearcey

HARRICOTT S.M.B.
Miss Mary Nolan
Miss Mary Wade

HARR'S HARBOUR N.D.B.
Mrs. Raymond King, Sr.

HARRY'S HARBOUR N.D.B.
Mrs. Lloyd Moss
Mrs. R. Norman
Mrs. Gordon Turner
Mrs. Betty M. Upward

HATCHET COVE T.B.
Mrs. Freeman Curtis

HEART'S CONTENT T.B.
Mrs. Arch Budden
Mrs. Jean George
Mrs. Absalom Hiscock
Mrs. Cecil Hobbs
Mrs. Margaret Peddle
Mrs. James Piercey

HEART'S DELIGHT T.B.
Mrs. Charles Chislett
Mrs. Charles Crocker
Mrs. Harriet Crocker
Mrs. Hayward Crocker
Mrs. Jean Crocker
Mrs. Cyril Ghent
Mrs. E. P. Legge
Mrs. Lewis Legge
Mrs. Nita Legge
Mrs. William Legge
Mrs. Lizzie Reid
Mrs. E. J. Sooley
Mrs. F. Sooley
Mrs. Pleamon Sooley
Mrs. Vincent Sooley
Mrs. Sam Worthman

HEART'S DESIRE T.B.
Mrs. Rita St. George

HERMITAGE Hermitage Bay
Mrs. Pearl Roberts

HERRING NECK N.D.B.
Mrs. Philip Blandford
Mrs. Julie Ginn
Mrs. H. Hussey
Mrs. Frank Kearley

HICKMAN'S HARBOUR T.B.
Mrs. Cyril Blundell
Mrs. Irene Butt
Mrs. Charles Critch
Mrs. John Martin
Mrs. James Piercey
Mrs. H. Vardy
Mrs. M. B. Vardy

HIGGIN'S LINE, St. John's
Mrs. Ronald Dawe

HIGHLANDS via St. Fintan's
St. George's Bay
Mrs. Donald MacPherson
Mrs. Honora MacPherson

HILLVIEW T.B. S.W.Arm
Mrs. Janet Churchill
Mrs. Margaret Churchill
Mrs. Woodrow Churchill
Mrs. Samuel Cooper
Mrs. Sarah Cooper
Mrs. Alma Loder
Mrs. Mary Pearce
Mrs. Alfred Stoyles
Mrs. Alfred J. Vey

HODGE'S COVE T.B.
Mrs. John Peddle
Mrs. Cyril Thomas

HOLYROOD C.B.
Mrs. Doris Hynes
Mrs. Angela Maloney
Mrs. Agnes Reynolds
Mrs. Elva Strong
Mrs. Marie Veitch
Mrs. Brian White

HOLYROOD SOUTH C.B.
Mrs. P. Hickey

HOPEALL T.B.
Mrs. Reginald Piercey

HOPEWELL Upper Gullies
Mrs. M. Dawe

HORSE ISLANDS W.B.
Mrs. G. Burton

HORWOOD NORTH N.D.B.
Mrs. Malcolm Bennett
Mrs. Lambert Hodder
Mrs. A. Benjamin Paynter
Mrs. Chesley Russell

HOWLEY
Mrs. John Barrett
Mrs. Lloyd Gillard
Mrs. Don Manuel
Mrs. Audrey Woolridge

HUMBERMOUTH
Mrs. Ethel Fifield
Mrs. Theresa Fifield
Mrs. A. Langley
Mrs. Alice Osmond
Mrs. Baxter Smith

INDIAN BAY B.B.
Mrs. Baxter Cook

INDIAN BURYING PLACE N.D.B. via
Nipper's Harbour
Mrs. Walter Stoodley

INDIAN ISLANDS Fogo
Mrs. Jethro Collins
Mrs. Marshall Collins
Mrs. Meta Collins
Mrs. Richard Collins
Mrs. Mary Perry
Mrs. Malachi Sheppard

IRELAND'S EYE T.B.
Mrs. Sylvia Toope

ISLE AU VALER P.B.
Mrs. William Lockyer

ISLAND COVE T.B.
Mrs. Beulah Spurrell

ISLAND HARBOUR Fogo
Mrs. Charles Bailey
Mrs. Patrick Thistle

ISLINGTON T.B.
Mrs. G. S. Chislett
Mrs. Florence Welsh

IVANHOE T.B.
Mrs. Nellie Cooper
Mrs. C. J. Miller
Mrs. Willis Miller
Mrs. Lawrence Watson

ISPREY BROOK T.B.
Mrs. R. Smith

JAMESTOWN B.B.
Mrs. Reginal Blundon
Mrs. G. Elliott
Mrs. Clarice Haines
Mrs. Robert Haines

JENNEX SIDING via Codroy Pond
Mrs. George Matchem

JERSEY SIDE P.B.
Mrs. Eva Ash
Mrs. John Blanche
Mrs. W. G. Berg
Mrs. Edward Bruce
Mrs. G. E. Clarke
Mrs. William Hynes
Mrs. Mary Mulrooney

JOE BATT'S ARM Fogo
Mrs. Austin Freake
Mrs. B. Freake
Mrs. L. Freake
Mrs. Jacob Newman

JOB'S COVE C.B.
Mrs. Maxwell Johnson
Mrs. M. Royal

KELLIGREWS C.B.
Mrs. Ida Batten
Mrs. Pat Dwyer
Mrs. Rosaline Dwyer
Mrs. Bob Haynes
Mrs. Elizabeth Haines
Mrs. Fred Haines
Mrs. E. Hatcher
Mrs. Lillian Hibbs
Mrs. L. A. Hoskins
Mrs. S. Knight
Mrs. Daisy LeDrew
Mrs. Vera Mercer
Mrs. Gerald Murphy
Mrs. Marion Murphy
Mrs. Jacob Petten
Mrs. Allan Tilley
Mrs. G. Tilley
Mrs. Ella Woodland

KETTLE COVE via Twillingate
Mrs. Ada Hicks
Mrs. Harry Hopkins
Mrs. M. Hopkins
Mrs. Rideout

KILBRIDE St. John's West
Mrs. Chafe, Box 1
Mrs. Jean Dillon, Box 4
Miss Hannah Connolly
Mrs. Edward Dooley, Kilbride Road
Mrs. E. P. Kavanagh
Mrs. C. R. Kelsey, Box 20
Mrs. Marion Morris
Mrs. Stan Murphy
Miss Janet Stanley

KINGSTON via Carbonear C.B.
Mrs. Tim Fahey

KINGUELS P.B.
Mrs. S. Boutcher

KINGWELL P.B.
Mrs. Llewellyn Boutcher
Mrs. Wallace Boutcher
Mrs. G. Rodway
Mrs. George Slade
Mrs. Charles Upshall

LADLE COVE Fogo
Mrs. Beaton Tulk

LADY COVE T.B. Random Islands
Mrs. Chesley March
Mrs. Harvey March

Mrs. Mayward March
Mrs. Hector March
Mrs. Vernon March
Mrs. Stephen Pelley
Mrs. Ernest Reid
Mrs. Wallace Reid

LAKE VIEW C.B. via Harbour Main
Mrs. Patrick Millmore

LALLY COVE F.B.
Miss Velma Drake

LAMALINE
Mrs. Bertram Bonnell
Mrs. J. B. Greene
Mrs. W. G. Pittman

LAWN P.B.
Mrs. Patricia Flanagan
Mrs. W. Kearney
Mrs. Joseph Manning

LAURENCETON via Lewisporte
Miss Reynetta Hutchings
Mrs. G. Purchase
Miss Muriel Purchase

LEAD COVE T.B.
Mrs. Edmund Button

LETHBRIDGE B.B.
Mrs. Daniel Diamond
Mrs. Eileen Diamond
Mrs. W. R. Diamond
Mrs. Edward Halloway
Mrs. Bruce Keats
Mrs. E. Pye
Mrs. John Strowbridge

LEWIN'S COVE Burin Bay Arm
Mrs. Samuel Harfitt
Mrs. Walter Hellett
Mrs. Donald Moulton
Mrs. Jessie Stone

LEWISPORTE
Mrs. Mark Burt
Mrs. Bramwell Clarke
Mrs. Lewis Janes
Mrs. Lila Janes
Mrs. Ross Noble
Mrs. Mary Peddle
Mrs. Henry Russell
Mrs. Beth Woolfrey

LITTLE BAY Green Bay
Mrs. A. Short

LITTLE BAY WEST F.B.
Mrs. C. Strowbridge

LITTLE BAY ISLANDS N.D.B.
Mrs. Peter Grimes
Mrs. R. Oxford
Mrs. Thomas Roberts

LITTLE BURNT BAY via Lewisporte
Mrs. Scott Clarke

LITTLE CATALINA T.B.
Mrs. V. Dalton
Mrs. D. Eddy
Mrs. Viola Eddy
Mrs. S. Jackson
Mrs. Emma Johnson
Mrs. Jabez Johnson
Mrs. John Johnson
Mrs. Marjorie Johnson
Mrs. Mark Johnson
Mrs. Millie Johnson
Mrs. Wesley Johnson

LITTLE HARBOUR T.B. Smith Sound
Mrs. Aubrey King

LITTLE HARBOUR EAST P.B.
Mrs. Jerry White

LITTLE HARBOUR WEST P.B.
Mrs. Andrew Murphy

LITTLE HEART'S EASE T.B.
Miss Joyce King
Mrs. Solomon Martin

LOGY BAY St. John's East
Mrs. Rosemarie Devereaux
Mrs. Margaret Ogon

LONG BEACH T.B.
Mrs. Baxter Peddle
Mrs. G. Very
Mrs. Reginald Vey

LONG HARBOUR Alexander Bay
Mrs. E. Murray

LONG HARBOUR P.B.
Mrs. Edward Bruce, Sr.

LONG ISLAND Beaumont South
Mrs. Chesley Rideout

LONG POND MANUELS C.B.
Mrs. Charles Greenslade
Mrs. Gladys Greenslade
Mrs. B. M. Kennedy
Mrs. Hugh Kennedy
Mrs. George Locke
Mrs. Stanley Porter
Mrs. Thomas Rideout
Mrs. Adam Smith

LONG RUN S.S. via Ferryland
Mrs. John Power

LOON BAY N.D.B.
Mrs. Wilson Elliott
Mrs. Samuel Luscombe
Mrs. Ronald White

LOWER COVE Port au Port via Ship Cove
Mrs. Stella Tucker

LOWER ISLAND COVE C.B.
Mrs. Bernice Bussey
Mrs. Fred LeShane
Mrs. Pearl LeShane
Mrs. William LeShane
Mrs. Allan Morris
Mrs. W. J. Morris
Mrs. George Rogers
Mrs. Elias Sparkes
Mrs. Harold Sparkes
Mrs. Mary Sparkes
Mrs. Arthur Wheeler

LOW POINT C.B.
Mrs. Gertrude Hannon

LUMSDEN NORTH
Mrs. Jack Gray

LUMSDEN SOUTH Fogo
Mrs. Jack Gray
Mrs. Naida Robbins
Mrs. S. Stagg

**MADDOX COVE Petty Harbour
St. John's West**
Mrs. William Doyle

MAKINSON'S C.B.
Mrs. Edward Abbott
Mrs. Stanley Bussey
Mrs. George Efford
Mrs. Arthur Loder
Mrs. Louise Lawrence
Mrs. Winnifred Reid

MANUELS C.B.
Mrs. Olga Andrews
Mrs. Ted Butler
Mrs. Roy Chaytor
Mrs. Nora Dooley
Mrs. George Earle
Mrs. Sylvia Earle
Mrs. Donald Evelly
Mrs. A. Frampton
Mrs. Walter Greenslade
Mrs. Hilda Grouchy
Mrs. C. Mercer
Mrs. James Metcalfe
Mrs. Lizzie Metcalfe

Mrs. Jim Rideout
Mrs. Bert Smith
Mrs. Florence Smith
Mrs. Phoebe Smith
Mrs. L. Squires
Mrs. Georgina Stone
Mrs. Hazel Taylor
Mrs. Harold Thistle
Mrs. Patricia Tilley
Mrs. Walter Tobin

MARKLAND via Whitbourne
Mrs. Walter Lundrigan, Jr.
Mrs. William Penney
Mrs. Kevin Smith

MARYSTOWN P.B.
Mrs. Augustine Baker
Mrs. Mercedes Brake
Mrs. Michael Brinton
Mrs. Sadie Brinton
Mrs. John Butler
Mrs. Cecil Evans
Mrs. Eileen Farrell
Mrs. T. Flaherty, Marystown South
Mrs. Richard Hannahan
Mrs. Mary Mills
Mrs. Eli Molley
Mrs. Patrick Murphy
Mrs. James O'Keefe Marystown South
Mrs. V. Pike
Mrs. Theresa Pittman
Mrs. W. A. Pittman
Mrs. James Power
Mrs. James Power, Jr.
Mrs. Michael Power
Mrs. Angela Walsh
Mrs. D. Walsh
Mrs. John Withero

MARYSVALE C.B.
Mrs. John Simms

McIVERS, Bay of Islands
Mrs. D. Blanchard
Miss Doreen Blanchard
Mrs. F. Blanchard

MERASHEEN P.B.
Mrs. Stan Ennis
Miss Marguerite Pittman
Mrs. Denis Walsh

MIDDLE BROOK Gambo
Mrs. B. Collins
Miss Victoria Collins
Mrs. Chesley Jerrett
Mrs. Curtis Jerrett
Mrs. Jesse Pritchett
Mrs. Paul Thoms

MIDDLE COVE St. John's East
Mrs. S. Power

MIDLAND Pasadena
Mrs. Tom Bishop

MILLER'S PASSAGE B.B.
Mrs. Richard Lambert

MILLERTOWN
Mrs. Ernest Boyde

MILTON T.B.
Mrs. Lawrence Blundon
Mrs. Raymond Blundon

MOBILE
Mrs. Philip Carew

MONKSTOWN P.B.
Mrs. C. Frampton

MORETON'S HARBOUR N.D.B.
Mrs. Stewart Taylor

MONROE T.B.
Mrs. Hedley Phillips
Mrs. Morley Stone
Miss Daisy Wiseman

MOORING COVE via Marystown
Mrs. Theresa Dober
Mrs. Helen Kelly

Mrs. Alice Nolan
Mrs. Lizzie Nolan

MORTIER, B.B. via Fox Cove
Mrs. Alphonsus Power

MOUCHBEGGAR, via Bonavista
Mrs. Gordon Mouland

MOUNT CARMEL via Salmonier
Mrs. Frank Nolan
Mrs. H. Nolan

MUSGRAVE HARBOUR Fogo
Mrs. R. C. Abbott
Mrs. Cecil Goodyear
Mrs. Melvin Goodyear
Mrs. Joyce Hicks
Mrs. Joseph West

MUSGRAVETOWN B.B.
Miss Denise Brown
Mrs. John Chaffey
Mrs. Kate Chaffey
Mrs. John Fitzgerald
Mrs. Eric Gulliford, Musgravetown East
Mrs. Ethelbert Greening
Mrs. Frank Greening
Mrs. Reginald Greening
Mrs. Rex Greening
Mrs. N. Greening
Mrs. Irving Matthews
Mrs. Barbara Saint
Mrs. Frank Skiffington
Mrs. William Skiffington
Mrs. Edwin Spurrell
Mrs. A. C. Stead

NEW BONAVENTURE T.B.
Mrs. John Ivany
Mrs. C. King
Miss Lorraine Locke
Mrs. Beatrice Miller

NEW CHELSEA T.B.
Mrs. Raymond Pynn

NEW HARBOUR T.B.
Mrs. Maxwell Cranford, Jr.
Mrs. E. Goosney
Mrs. Clyde Higdon
Mrs. Ethel Higdon
Mrs. Robert Higdon
Mrs. Viola Higdon
Mrs. M. Hillier
Mrs. Abram Thorne
Mrs. Adolphus Thorne
Mrs. Jacob Woodman
Mrs. Marilyn Woodman
Mrs. N. Woodman
Mrs. William Woodman

NEWMAN'S COVE via Bonavista
Mrs. Sidney Skiffington

NEW MELBOURNE T.B.
Mrs. Nancy Button
Miss Molly Clarke
Mrs. James Driscoll
Mrs. Robena Driscoll
Mrs. William Driscoll
Mrs. Allison Goodwin
Mrs. William Pynn

NEW PERLICAN T.B.
Mrs. Minnie Matthews
Mrs. L. Parrott
Mrs. Thomas White

NEWSTEAD N.D.B.
Mrs. Gordon Canning

NOGGIN COVE
Mrs. Curtis Gillingham
Mrs. Roland Gillingham
Mrs. Leslie Pennell
Mrs. George Snow
Mrs. Walter Snow

NORMAN'S COVE T.B.
Mrs. W. Martin
Mrs. Eric Piercey
Mrs. Martha Piercey

Mrs. Robert Piercey
Mrs. William F. Smith
Mrs. George Thorne
Mrs. Marion Thorne
Mrs. W. R. Wallace

NORRIS ARM N.D.B.
Mrs. J. Basha

NORRIS POINT Bonne B.
Mrs. James Humber

NORTHERN BAY C.B.
Mrs. Margaret Gear
Mrs. William Hogan
Mrs. William Johnson
Mrs. John March

NORTH HARBOUR P.B.
Mrs. Emily Dean
Mrs. Anna Power

NORTH RIVER C.B.
Mrs. Pat Morrissey
Mrs. James Snow
Mrs. Joyce Stevens, Clarke's Beach

NORTH SIDE Twillingate
Mrs. John Whitehorn

OCHRE PIT COVE C.B.
Mrs. James Gillingham

ODERIN P.B.
Miss Geraldine Conway
Mrs. Rosemary Lake

O'DONNELLS S.M.B.
Mrs. Agnes Hanlon
Mrs. John Hanlon

OLD BONAVENTURE T.B.
Mrs. Elizabeth Stone
Mrs. R. A. Stone

OLD PERLICAN T.B.
Miss Dorothy Green
Mrs. Reg Hopkins
Mrs. Nelson Howell
Mrs. Moses Squires
Mrs. Harry Strong

OLD SHOP T.B.
Mrs. Stanley Dawe
Mrs. Gilbert Janes

OUTER COVE St. John's East
Mrs. Martin Hickey
Mrs. Anne Houston

PACQUET W.B.
Mrs. George Gillingham
Mrs. W. A. Milley

PARADISE C.B.
Topsail Road, St. John's
Mrs. Rita Murphy

PENNY'S COVE via Carbonear
Mrs. Walter Galloway

PETERVIEW via Botwood
Mrs. Wilbert Seabright

PETTY HARBOUR, St. John's West
Mrs. Donald Chafe
Mrs. Edward Chafe
Mrs. E. E. Chafe
Mrs. Gardiner Chafe
Mrs. H. Chafe
Mrs. Henry Chafe
Mrs. John J. Chafe
Mrs. Jonathan Chafe
Mrs. Melvin Chafe
Mrs. Robena Chafe
Mrs. Viola Chafe
Mrs. Hugh Grieley
Mrs. Martin Hefferman
Mrs. Robert Howlett
Mrs. Frank Pack
Mrs. William Quinton
Mrs. William Barton Stack
Mrs. George Weir

Mrs. Harold Weir
Mrs. Harry Whitten

PILLEY'S ISLAND N.D.B.
Mrs. Nathan Ryan

PLACENTIA P.B.
Mrs. Molly Bittinger
Mrs. G. Clarke
Mrs. Michael Emberley
Mrs. Ann Kavanagh
Mrs. Annie Mooney
Mrs. A. Murphy
Mrs. Imelda Patterson
Mrs. Mary Patterson
Mrs. J. P. Williams

PETLEY T.B. Smith Sound
Mrs. Jane Rowsell

PLATE COVE WEST B.B.
Mrs. Joan Walsh

POINT CREWE Burin
Mrs. Donald Burton
Mrs. John H. Crewe

POINT LA HAYE S.M.B.
Mrs. James Kielly
Mrs. Edward Mandville

POINT LANCE P.B.
Mrs. Gerard Careen

POINT LEAMINGTON N.D.B.
Mrs. Frank Goulding
Mrs. Andrew Paul
Mrs. William White
Mrs. Mary Woodsworth

POINT VERDE P.B.
Mrs. Michael Greene

POOL'S COVE F.B.
Mrs. G. Williams
Mrs. Marion Williams

PORT ALBERT N.D.B.
Mrs. Sidney Mercer

PORT ANSON N.D.B.
Mrs. Fred Croucher

PORT AU BRAS Burin
Mrs. William A. Abbott

PORT AU PORT
Mrs. M. Harris

PORT AUX BASQUE
Mrs. Edward Marshall

PORT BLANFORD B.B.
Mrs. Eric Holloway
Mrs. Elsie Oldfield
Mrs. James Oldford
Mrs. W. Peddle

PORT DE GRAVE C.B.
Mrs. Walter Bussey
Mrs. Wilfred Bussey
Mrs. William Bussey
Mrs. Bert Christopher
Miss Alma Dawe
Mrs. Mona Dawe
Mrs. Greta Hussey
Mrs. Verna Lear
Mrs. Marion Morgan
Mrs. L. Ralph
Mrs. Florence Wells

PORT ELIZABETH P.B.
Mrs. Charles Bishop
Mrs. Fred Clarke
Mrs. Gerald Clarke
Mrs. Raymond Clarke
Mrs. Norman Collins
Mrs. Chesley Keeping
Miss Anna Loughlin
Mrs. Eric Moulton
Mrs. Annie Peddle
Mrs. Cecil Peddle

Mrs. F. Reeves
Mrs. Ernest Sheppard

PORTLAND B.B.
Mrs. John Curtis
Mrs. Harry Holloway
Mrs. Lenora Holloway
Mrs. Thomas Holloway
Mrs. Hilda White

PORT NELSON B.B.
Mrs. Cora White

PORT REXTON T.B.
Mrs. R. G. Adams
Mrs. Edward Ballett
Mrs. William Ploughman
Mrs. R. M. Rex

PORT ROYAL P.B.
Mrs. Gerard McFarlane
Mrs. Lawrence Walsh

PORT UNION T.B.
Mrs. James Bailey
Mrs. George Blackmore
Mrs. Mark Lodge, Sr.
Mrs. Victoria Lodge
Mrs. Reginald Mason
Mrs. J. R. Parsons
Mrs. Harold White

PORTUGAL COVE St. John's East
Mrs. F. Allen
Mrs. P. Andrews
Mrs. Jane Churchill
Mrs. Nellie Churchill
Mrs. Reginald Churchill
Mrs. Weston Churchill
Mrs. William Drukin
Mrs. Madeline Gibbons
Mrs. Patrick Gladney, Jr.
Mrs. Gordon Miller
Mrs. John Murphy
Mrs. D. H. Neary
Mrs. H. M. Peddle
Mrs. Albert Piercey
Mrs. Anne Piercey
Mrs. Edith Power
Mrs. Mary Somerton, Sr.
Mrs. Margaret Thorne

PORTUGAL COVE SOUTH St. John's East
Mrs. Ethel Molloy
Mrs. John W. Molloy
Mrs. Martin St. Croix

POUCH COVE, St. John's East
Mrs. David Connors
Mrs. Margaret Devereaux
Mrs. L. Gillett
Mrs. E. P. Hiscock
Mrs. Doris Hudson
Mrs. James Hudson
Mrs. Herbert Langmead
Mrs. Russell Langmead
Mrs. Jerry Murray
Mrs. M. Peyton
Mrs. Rennie Sullivan
Mrs. A. Williams
Mrs. Harris Williams

PRESQUE P.B.
Mrs. Selina Collins

PRINCETON B.B.
Mrs. J. L. Quinlon

PROTESTANT TOWN C.B.
via Portugal Cove
Mrs. Gordon Burry

PROWESTON P.B. via Davis Cove
Mrs. William Hynes

PUFFIN ISLAND B.B. via Greenspond
Mrs. Albert Wakeley
Mrs. Daniel Wakeley

PUSHTHROUGH Bay d'Espoir
Mrs. Jane Rowsell

QUEEN'S COVE T.B.
Mrs. Allan Goobie
Mrs. Robert Smith

RALEIGH W.B. North
Mrs. Bella Taylor

RAMEA
Miss A. Crewe
Mrs. S. Dominey
Miss Mildred Durnford
Mrs. Clyde Keeping
Mrs. Thomas Pink

RANDOM ISLAND T.B.
Mrs. Vernon March
Mrs. Linda Smith

REDCLIFF, St. John's
Mrs. Emma Croswait

RED COVE F.B.
Mrs. S. Strowbridge

RED HARBOUR P.B. via Port Elizabeth
Miss Ruth Hamilton

RED ISLAND P.B.
Mrs. Michael Counsel

REGINAVILLE S.M.B.
Mrs. Sebastian Power

RECONTRE WEST, Hermitage Bay
Mrs. Amelia Durnford
Miss Stella Symes

RENEWS
Mrs. Bertram Bailey
Mrs. James Conway
Mrs. Dennis Dinn
Miss Doris Keating
Mrs. Rita Larves
Mrs. Patrick McCarthy
Mrs. Peter Murphy
Mrs. Thomas Murphy
Mrs. Lawrence Rogers
Miss Catherine Squires
Mrs. N. Sullivan

RIVER HEAD C.B. via Harbour Grace
Mrs. James Barron
Mrs. Leonard Gushue
Mrs. Frank Ryan

RIVERHEAD S.M.B.
Mrs. Leo Corcoran
Mrs. Michael Corcoran
Mrs. Val Corcoran
Mrs. Pat Meaney

RIVERSIDE C.B. via Makinson's
Mrs. John Fisher

ROBERT'S ARM N.D.B.
Mrs. B. Anthony

ROCKY HARBOUR, Bonne Bay
Mrs. Fred Humber

RODERICKTON W.B.
Mrs. Anthony Carroll

SALMON COVE C.B. via Carbonear
Mrs. Naomi Case
Mrs. Jennie Parsons
Mrs. Elaine Penney
Mrs. Joseph Penney
Mrs. Olive Reynolds
Mrs. Freeman Slade

SALMONIER S.M.B.
Miss T. Dobbin

SALVAGE B.B.
Mrs. Ralph Brown
Miss Lorraine Dyke

SANDRINGHAM B.B.
Mrs. Kenneth Bradley

SANDY COVE B.B..
Mrs. Isabelle King

SANDY POINT, ST.G.B. via St. George's
Mrs. Maud McFatridge

SANDYVILLE
Miss D. Loveless

SEAL COVE C.B.
Mrs. Henry Butler
Mrs. Warrick Butler
Mrs. Eliazer Dawe
Mrs. Sadie Dawe
Mrs. Warren Dawe
Mrs. William Kennedy
Mrs. Charlotte Lear
Miss Norma Morgan
Mrs. Victor Morgan

SELDOM Fogo Dist.
Mrs. Norman Anthony
Mrs. Raymond Combden
Mrs. Norman Penney

SELDOM COME BY (Fogo)
Mrs. Gordon Roebotham

SHALLOWAY COVE B.B.
Mrs. Ignatius Furlong

SHEARSTOWN C.B. via Bay Roberts
Mrs. P. Badcock
Mrs. William Deering
Mrs. Harry Holmes

SHIP COVE C.B. via Port de Grave
Mrs. Greta Andrews
Mrs. Robert Andrews
Mrs. William Dawe
Mrs. Samuel Hurley

SHOAL BROOK, Bonne Bay
Mrs. Simon Parsons, Jr.

SHOAL HARBOUR T.B.
Mrs. Gordon Adams
Mrs. Ralph Bailey
Mrs. Jerry Barbour
Mrs. L. Barbour
Mrs. Nita Barbour
Mrs. C. L. Barnes
Mrs. Eleanor Butler
Mrs. Ruby Garnier
Mrs. R. Green
Mrs. S. Green
Mrs. James Greening
Mrs. Bert Hutchings
Mrs. Samuel Ivany
Mrs. Stanley Legge
Mrs. Charles Meadus
Mrs. Stewart Mills
Mrs. Barbara Ploughman
Mrs. Harold Stanley
Mrs. Cyril Wiseman
Mrs. Vernon Wiseman
Mrs. William Wiseman

SNOOKS HARBOUR, Random Is T.B.
Mrs. Colin Baker
Mrs. Walter Baker
Mrs. Lewis Hefford

SOUTH BROOK, Hall's Bay N.D.B.
Mrs. T. Head
Mrs. Meta James
Mrs. Walter Jones
Mrs. E. P. Wall (Pasadena)

SOUTH DILDO T.B.
Mrs. Victor Pretty

SOUTHPORT T.B.
Miss Nina Lambert

SOUTH RIVER C.B. via Clarke's Beach
Mrs. Christopher Boone, Sr.
Mrs. Frank Boone
Mrs. Lawton Boone
Mrs. Andrew Cummings
Mrs. Henry Ford
Mrs. Elmer Reid

SOUTH SHORE C.B.
Mrs. Harold Dawe

SOUTHERN BAY B.B.
Mrs. Harold Russell

SOUTHERN HARBOUR P.B.
Mrs. Dominic Best
Mr. Frank Benoit

SOUTHERN SHORE B.B.
Mrs. Harold Russell
Mrs. A. Swain (Calvert)
Mrs. Margaret Trainor

SPANIARD'S BAY C.B.
Mrs. James Dwyer
Mrs. Nellie Mercer
Mrs. Fanny Noseworthy
Mrs. Annie Sheppard (West)
Miss Ethel Sheppard
Mrs. G. Fred Smith
Mrs. G. Smith

SPENCER'S COVE P.B.
Mrs. Nita Barbour
Mrs. Thomas Boutcher
Mrs. Albert Hollett
Mrs. George Stacey

SPRINGDALE N.D.B.
Mrs. Margaret Clarke

SPRINGFIELD C.B. via Makinsons
Mrs. M. G. Pretty

SPIRIT COVE Str. Belle Isle via Port Saunders
Mrs. Alec Gould

ST. ALBAN'S, Bay d'Espoir
Mrs. Geraldine Snook

ST. ANDREWS, West Coast
Mrs. J. MacDonald

ST. ANTHONY, Hare Bay
Mrs. George Andrews (East Side)
Mrs. G. A. Cooper (East Side)
Mrs. M. Patey
Mrs. Uriah Patey

ST. ANTHONY BIGHT
Miss B. Simms
Mrs. Sandy Simms

ST. BRENDAN'S B.B.
Mrs. Gertrude Broderick
Mrs. John MacKay

ST. BRIDE'S P.B.
Mrs. Theresa Cochrane
Mrs. Agnes Conway
Mrs. Joseph Conway
Mrs. Anne Griffin
Mrs. Gerard Griffin

ST. GEORGE'S ST.G.B.
Mrs. J. E. Blanchard
Mrs. Ida Loder
Mrs. Iris Mills
Miss Isabelle Renouf, Steal Mountain Road

ST. JACQUES F.B.
Mrs. George Drake

ST. JOHN'S
Mrs. Cyril Abbott, Torbay Road
Mrs. Mollie Abbott, 4 Belvedere Street
Mrs. R. T. Abbott, 4 Belvedere Street
Mrs. E. Adams, 15 Morris Avenue
Mrs. E. B. Adams, 1 Pine Bud Avenue
Mrs. V. Adams, 19 Roache Road
Mrs. William Alcock, 13 Long's Hill
Mrs. William Allen, 63 Cochrane Street
Mrs. F. H. Allcorn, 205 Gower Street
Miss Margaret Allen, 17 Carnell Street
Mrs. A. Amminson, 553 South Side Road
Mrs. L. Andrews, 11 Monroe Street
Mrs. Rex Andrews, 13 Blackmarsh Road
Mrs. Sara Andrews, 202 Hamilton Avenue
Mrs. George Anstey, 30 Craigmillar Ave.
Mrs. Ruby Anstey, 141 St. Clare Avenue
Mrs. D. J. Anthony, 159 Forest Road
Mrs. H. Anthony, Anthony Street
Norma Anthony, c/o 199 LeMarchant Road

Mrs. Elsie Antle, 38 Franklyn Avenue
Mrs. F. Antle, 189 Pleasant Street
Mrs. Ernest Ash, 164 Topsail Road
Mrs. Flora Ash, 203 Elizabeth Avenue
Mrs. Hubert Ash, 45 Portugal Cove Road
Mrs. Myra Ayres, 18 Anderson Avenue

Mrs. Victoria Badcock, 1 Blackmarsh Road
Mrs. Mabel Baggs, 153 Empire Avenue
Mrs. Eileen Bailey, 143 Campbell Avenue
Mrs. Helen Balfour, King's Bridge Road
Mrs. H. A. Ball, 2 Thornburn Road
Mrs. Laura Ball, New Pennywell Road
Mrs. H. Ballam, 165 Military Road
Mrs. C. Bambrick, 191 Freshwater Road
Mrs. Richard Banfield, 27 Lake Avenue
Mrs. J. Barbour, 45 Cashin Avenue
Mrs. Marina Barbour, 229 Empire Avenue
Mrs. Bill Barnes, 19 Cashin Avenue
Mrs. Effie Barnes, 198 Elizabeth Avenue
Mrs. Margaret Barnes, 2 Kent Place
Mrs. W. J. Barnes, 23 Gower Street
Mrs. Henley Barrett, 126 Craigmillar Ave.
Mrs. Rita Barrett, 66 Monroe Street
Mrs. Lilla Barron, Torbay Road
Mrs. A. Barry, 296 LeMarchant Avenue
Mrs. Saul Barry, 11 Malta Street
Mrs. Florence Bartlett, 87 King's Road
Mrs. Raymond Bastow, Mundy Pond Road
Mrs. H. Batstone, 171 South Side Road
Mrs. Weston Batstone, 57 Beaumont St., W.
Mrs. H. Belbin, 4 Monchy Street
Mrs. Robert Belbin, 25 Warbury Street
Mrs. Bemister, 20 Colliers Lane
Mrs. Rex Bemister, 2 Lakeview Avenue
Mrs. William Benmore, 259 Hamilton Ave.
Mrs. Edward Bennett, 53 Sudbury Street
Mrs. Henley Bennett, 126 Craigmillar Ave.
Mrs. Mark Bennett, Box 52
Lady Beatrix Bennett, c/o Nfld. Hotel
Mrs. Fred Benson, c/o Oxen Pond Road
Mrs. Mona Berrigan, 39 Campbell Avenue
Mrs. Sarah Benson, 137 South Side Road
Mrs. L. Besso, Long Pond Road
Mrs. Victor Biddiscombe, Logy Bay Road
Mrs. Amy Bird, Box 1321, West End P.O.
Mrs. Bishop, 65 Cornwall Crescent
Mrs. B. Bishop, Box 2093
Mrs. Jack Bishop, 34 Hutchings Street
Mrs. Nellie Bishop, 155 Prowse Avenue
Mrs. Ralph Bishop, Mundy Pond Road
Mrs. Gerald Blackmore, 23 Dicks Square
Mrs. Phyllis L. Blackmore, 104 Freshwater Rd.
Mrs. Levi Blake, 8 Cookstown Road
Mrs. Blandford, 48 Cashin Avenue
Mrs. Helen Blundon, 14 Smith Avenue
Mrs. W. Blundon, Box 438 G.P.O.
Mrs. I. Bonia, 31 Laughlin Crescent
Mrs. Marie Bonia, 36 Kitchener Avenue
Mrs. Elizabeth Boone, Signal Hill Road
Mrs. W. Boone, Signal Hill Road
Mrs. Eric Bourdridge, 1 Aldershot Street
Mrs. B. Bowden, c/o Soper's, G.P.O. Box 74
Mrs. Avis Bradbury, 22 Robinson's Hill
Mrs. R. Bradbury, 72 Pennywell Road
Mrs. Ethel Brett, Box E5420
Mrs. S. M. Brennan, 12 Golf Avenue
Miss Thelma Brett, 7 Kirke Place
Mrs. T. Brewer, 145 Newtown Road
Mrs. Hilda Bridal, 8 Boncloddy Street
Mrs. W. Bridal, 8 Boncloddy Street
Mrs. Brown, 23 O'Neil Avenue
Mrs. C. T. Brown, 247 Empire Avenue
Mrs. Robert Brown, 142 Water Street
Mrs. H. Browne, 72 Carter's Hill
Mrs. Theresa Bruce, 67 South Side Road
Mrs. Clyde Budden, 23 Goodridge Street
Mrs. Margaret Budgell, 147 Circular Road
Mrs. R. Burgess, 56A Leslie Street
Mrs. A. J. Burke, 35 Craigmillar Avenue
Mrs. J. Burke, 18 Merrymeeting Road
Miss E. Burke, 47 Patrick Street
Mrs. Mary J. Burke, 55 Whiteway Street
Mrs. Thomas Burke, 32 Hamel Street
Mrs. W. Burry, 114 Campbell Avenue
Mrs. Arthur Burtsey, 18 Cathedral Street
Mrs. E. H. Burton, 40 Calver Street
Mrs. Max Bussey, 86 Campbell Avenue
Mrs. A. E. Butler, Box 8, Site 9
Mrs. C. A. Butler, Topsail Road, Box 530
Mrs. Florence Butler, 131 Hamilton Ave.
Mrs. J. Butler, Box 8, Site 9, Sub Service
Mrs. M. Butler, 30 Summer Street

Mrs. Nina Butler, 58 Lime Street
Mrs. Sophie Butler, 50 Tunis Court
Mrs. Stephen Butler, 120 Gower Street
Mrs. Ted Butler, Box 5, Site 9, Sub Service
Miss E. Butt, 136 Casey Street
Mrs. H. Butt, 68 Stamp's Lane
Mrs. Bert Butterworth, 31 Cornwall Crescent
Mrs. Gladys Byrne, Mundy Pond Road

Mrs. G. Cahill, 5 Barnes Place
Mrs. J. W. Cahill, 30 Hoyles Avenue
Mrs. H. Callahan, 137 A Gower Street
Mrs. Elizabeth Calver, 196 Duckworth St.
Mrs. Carberry, (A), Box 2078
Mrs. E. Carroll, 37 King's Bridge Road
Mrs. George Carville, 279 Blackmarsh Rd.
Mrs. Nellie Casey, 257 LeMarchant Road
Mrs. C. W. Cave, 20 Amherst Heights
Mrs. Russell Cave, 12 Penetanguishene
Mrs. Arthur Chafe, 10 Victoria Street
Mrs. Carol F. Chafe, Box E5337
Mrs. Ethel Chafe, 617 South Side Road West
Mrs. Jane Chafe, 67 LeMarchant Road
Mrs. John Chafe, 617 South Side Road West
Mrs. M. Chafe, 7 Masonic Terrace
Mrs. Rupert Chafe, 10 Victoria Street
Mrs. Walter Chafe, Blackmarsh Road West
Mrs. Ada Chaffet, 161 Patrick Street
Mrs. C. A. Chambers, 4 Summer Street
Mrs. William Chapman, 5 Graves Street
Mrs. B. Casey, 4 Joyce Avenue
Mrs. Norman Chaytor, 15 Guy Street
Mrs. William Chaytor, c/o 145 Gower St.
Mrs. William Chestney, 50 Monkstown Rd.
Mrs. V. Christopher, 129 New Cove Road
Mrs. Margaret Churchill, 49 Beaumont St.
Mrs. Max Churchill, 16 Linden Court
Mrs. Myrtle Churchill, c/o General Hosp.
Mrs. Mary Clark, Kenna's Hill, Apt. 12, Bldg. 4
Mrs. A. Clarke, 1 Grey Street
Miss A. M. Clarke, 21 Parade Street
Mrs. Carrie Clarke, 83 Newton Road
Mrs. Elizabeth Clarke, 54 Circular Road
Mrs. Robert Clarke, Plymouth Road
Mrs. Rose Clarke, Tor Bay, St. John's East
Mrs. Roy Clarke, 41 Golf Street
Mrs. William Clarke, Box E5001
Mrs. Gail Clouston, Box E5207
Mrs. Patrick Cochrane, 115 Circular Road
Mrs. A. T. Colburne, 161 Topsail Road
Mrs. Duncan Colburne, 25 Mullock Street
Mrs. G. Colburne, 34 Mullock Street
Mrs. E. P. Coleman, 148 Elizabeth Avenue
Mrs. Margaret Collier, 8 Berteau Avenue
Mrs. A. M. Collins, 21 Parade Street
Mrs. Gordon Collins, c/o West End P.O.
Mrs. Norman Collins, Black Head Rd. E.
Mrs. Rex Collins, P.O. Box 472, G.P.O.
Mrs. W. Collins, 52 Colonial Street
Mrs. Freeman Compton, 36 Graves Street
Mrs. John Congdon, 33 Linden Court
Mrs. Hilda Connolly, 64 New Cove Road
Mrs. Elizabeth Connors, 40 Power's Court
Mrs. Frank Cook, 34 Allandale Road
Mrs. H. W. Cook, Box E5270
Mrs. Walter Cooke, Golden Ridge Farm
Mrs. Gladys Coombs, 93 Campbell Ave.
Mrs. L. Coombs, 3 Vaughan Place
Mrs. S. Coombs, 22 Winter Avenue
Mrs. E. G. Cooper, 12 Calver Street
Mrs. Myrtle Cooper, Long's Hill
Mrs. Helen Corcoran, 117 Pennywell Road
Mrs. R. Corcoran, 219 Empire Avenue
Mrs. Kevin Costello, 3 Allandale Road
Mrs. Marjorie Coughlan, 121 Queen's Rd.
Mrs. W. Coughlan, 10 Gower Street
Mrs. Clara Coultas, 24 Downing Street
Mrs. Dorothy Coultas, 270 Greshwater Road
Mrs. R. B. Coupland, Kenna's Hill, Bldg. 1
Mrs. Doreen Courage, 47 Beaumont Street
Mrs. Betty Cousens, 323 A LeMarchant Road
Mrs. C. C. Cousens, 323 A LeMarchant Road
Mrs. C. Cox, 2 Shaw Street
Mrs. Hazel Cox, 10 Topsail Road
Mrs. Reginald Cox, 73 Lime Street
Mrs. D. Cramm, 35 Pine Bud Avenue
Mrs. Eldred Crane, 116 Circular Road
Mrs. V. Crane, Site 7, Box 9, Sub Service
Mrs. Elsie Craniford, 57 Quidi Vidi Road
Mrs. M. Crewe, 78 Goodridge Street
Mrs. Fred Crocker, 366 Duckworth Street
Mrs. J. Crocker, 9 Byron Street

Mrs. G. Crossman, 107 Pennywell Road
Mrs. Leo Crotty, 48 Boulevard Road
Miss Agnes Crowdell, 32 Henry Street
Mrs. Ralph Crummey, 35 Kitchener Avenue
Mrs. Marion Cuff, 175 Gower Street
Mrs. C. Cull, 60 Monroe Street
Mrs. Fremon Cull, 123 Merrymeeting Road
Mrs. Cull (L.), 49 Pennywell Road
Mrs. Leslie Culmore, 167 Pennywell Road
Mrs. R. B. Cunningham, Portugal Cove Rd.
Mrs. Robert Curnew, 16 Kitchener Avenue
Mrs. Anna Curran, 66 Mayor Avenue
Mrs. Carmel Curtis, 53 Craigmillar Avenue

Mrs. Margaret Dale, 723 Water Street
Mrs. Mary Daley, 145 Pleasant Street
Mrs. Grace Dalton, 723 Water Street
Mrs. Nora Dalton, 83 Hayward Avenue
Mrs. H. G. Darby, 134 Prowse Avenue
Mrs. Alfred Davis, 27 Cairo Street
Mrs. Jo Davis, 310 Hamilton Avenue
Mrs. Job Davis, 237 Empire Avenue
Mrs. M. Davis, 17 Westmount
Mrs. M. B. Davis, 310 Hamilton Ave.
Mrs. Jean M. Dawe, 6 Maple Street
Mrs. Ronald Dawe, Higgins Line
Mrs. Stephen Dawe, 402 Hamilton Avenue
Mrs. Laura Day, 48 Whiteway Street
Mrs. David Decker, 124 Bonaventure Ave.
Mrs. Mildred Decker, Marine Drive Box H 157
Mrs. Gordon Denny, 279 Freshwater Road
Mrs. T. Dewling, 168 Pennywell Road
Mrs. I. Dewling, 168 Pennywell Road
Mrs. J. Dicks, 42 King's Road
Mrs. Olive Dinn, 707 Water Street
Mrs. John Dinn, 560 South Side Road
Mrs. Pat Dinn, 439 South Side Road
Mrs. D. L. Doody, 26 Pennywell Road
Mrs. May Dooley, Waterford Bridge Road
Mrs. Mike Dooley, 16 Cook Street
Mrs. R. W. Downer, 2 Howlett Avenue
Mrs. Agnes M. Downey, 119 Gower Street
Mrs. C. Downton, 126 Empire Avenue
Mrs. C. Downton, 19 Carnell Street
Mrs. Don Downton, 55 St. Clare Avenue
Mrs. Muriel Downton, 47 Craigmillar Avenue
Mrs. Bennett Doyle, Box 19, Topsail Road
Mrs. Lillian Doyle, 129 Forest Road
Mrs. Robert Doyle, Signal Hill Road
Mrs. L. G. Driscoll, 75 Grenfell Avenue
Mrs. Graham Drover, 126 Craigmillar Ave.
Mrs. Betty Druken, St. John's East
Mrs. Mary Duff, 172 Campbell Avenue
Mrs. Robert Duffett, 23 Suez Street
Mrs. Edna Dunne, 67 Craigmillar Avenue
Mrs. Helen Dunne, 20 Coronation Street
Mrs. J. Dunne, 36 Gear Street
Mrs. Mary Dunne, 210 Freshwater Road
Mrs. Mary Dunne, Box 7, Site 9, Topsail Road
Miss Ann Dunphy, 207 Blackmarsh Road
Mrs. Moira Dunphy, 54 Rennies Mill Road
Mrs. E. Dyke, 94 Queens Road
Mrs. Rosalie Dyke, 187 Freshwater Road
Mrs. Kay Dwyer, 41 Craigmillar Avenue
Mrs. M. Dwyer, Box E5081

Mrs. Harry Eady, 181 Empire Avenue
Mrs. Alfred Eaves, 27 Cairo Street
Mrs. Allan Edwards, 1-A Howley Avenue
Mrs. Mary Ellis, 24 Goodridge Street
Mrs. G. Elton, 76 Shaw Street
Mrs. Charles Emberley, Blackmarsh Rd., W.
Mrs. Hazel Emberley, Torbay Road
Mrs. George Ennis, 375 Duckworth Street
Mrs. Kathleen Ennis, 375 Duckworth Street
Mrs. R. J. Ennis, 25 Goodridge Street
Mrs. James Escott, 66 Leslie Street
Mrs. Ruth Ethridge, 133 Empire Avenue
Mrs. C. G. Evans, Torbay Road
Mrs. Emmie Evans, 100 Bonaventure Avenue
Mrs. F. Evans, 246 Pennywell Road
Mrs. Vera Evans, 56 Flower Hill
Mrs. Vincent Evans, 44 Warbury Street
Mrs. W. J. Everett, R.C.A.F. Station, Torbay

Mrs. J. Fagan, 101 Bonaventure Avenue
Mrs. Pauline Fahey, 9 Long's Hill
Mrs. Ann M. Fanning, 80 Bonaventure Ave.
Mrs. Norman Farewell, Fort Amherst
Mrs. Allen Faushell, 229 South Side Road
Mrs. Ethel M. Fenerty, 100 Portugal Cove Rd.
Mrs. Alice B. Ferguson, 67 Waterford
Mrs. Angela Fifield, 55 Hoyles Avenue

Mrs. Fred Fisher, Portugal Cove Road
Mrs. L. Fisher, 96 Newton Road
Mrs. Carol Ann Fitzgerald, 27 Gear Street
Mrs. G. Fitzgerald, Tessier's Lane
Mrs. Margaret Fitzgerald, 285 Pennywell Rd.
Mrs. W. J. Fitzgerald, 69 Rennie's Mill Road
Mrs. F. Fleming, 140 Cashin Avenue
Mrs. Michael Fleming, 5 Knight Street
Mrs. Monica Fleming, 617 South Side Rd., W.
Mrs. R. Fleming, 2 Morris Avenue
Mrs. Rita Fleming, 36 Henry Street
Mrs. Cyril Flight, 166 St. Clare Avenue
Mrs. Pauline Flight, 7 Morris Avenue
Mrs. Stephen Flynn, 38 Craigmillar Avenue
Mrs. Irving Fogwill, 190 Topsail Road
Mrs. J. C. Follett, 134 Forest Road
Mrs. C. Forbes, 20 Smith Avenue
Mrs. Marion Ford, c/o Government House
Mrs. Ford, 51 Freshwater Road
Mrs. J. Foster, 15 Calver Street
Mrs. Elizabeth Fowler, 96 Casey Street
Mrs. Barbara Fowlow, 5 St. Michael's Ave.
Mrs. Vera Frampton, 9 Raleigh Street
Mrs. Shirley Fraize, 15 Mullock Street
Mrs. H. F. Francis, 13 Allandale Road
Miss Joan Francis, 23 Mount Royal Avenue
Mrs. Lillian Francis, 23 Mount Royal Ave.
Mrs. E. Freake, 90 Grenfell Avenue
Mrs. Garland Freake, Box 2107
Mrs. Charles Freeston, 4 First Avenue
Mrs. Ann French, 251 Empire Avenue
Mrs. D. J. French, 77 Waterford Bridge Road
Mrs. Lillian Froude, 105-A LeMarchant Road
Mrs. M. Furey, 50 Mullock Street
Mrs. Mary Furey, 34 McFarlane Street
Mrs. Rita Furey, 34 Mayor Avenue
Mrs. Evelyn Furlong, Torbay
Mrs. J. Fuzzard, 248 Pennywell Road

Mrs. Laura Gardner, 327 Hamilton Avenue
Miss B. Garland, 6 Dunford Street
Mrs. Hubert Garland, 217 Pennywell Road
Mrs. W. Gaulton, 157 Empire Avenue
Mrs. R. Geddes, 362 Duckworth Street
Mrs. B. George, 116 Prowse Avenue
Mrs. D. Giles, 34 Cashin Avenue
Mrs. W. H. Gillard, 70 Mayor Avenue
Mrs. Edna Gillingham, Bay Bulls Road
Mrs. L. Gillingham, 89 Barter's Hill
Mrs. Marilyn Gillis, 251 LeMarchant Road
Mrs. Gloria Gladden, 56-A Leslie Street
Mrs. Patrick Gladney, Jr., Portugal Cove Rd.
Mrs. H. Glynn, 14 Signal Hill Road
Mrs. Hilda Gollop, Major's Path
Mrs. Goodyear, 13 Goodridge Street
Mrs. R. E. Goodyear, Bldg. 1, Kenna's Hill
Mrs. J. Gosse, 78 Topsail Road
Mrs. Fred Gough, 24 Franklyn Avenue
Mrs. Nellie Gough, 3 Devon Row
Mrs. E. Grace, 217 Craigmillar Avenue
Mrs. Kathleen Grace, 98 Patrick Street
Mrs. M. Grant, Old Petty Harbour Road
Mrs. D. Greeley, 76 Monroe Street
Mrs. Enid Green, 22 William Street
Mrs. H. Green, 12 Franklyn Avenue
Mrs. L. Green, 188 Pennywell Road
Mrs. R. Green, 24 Allandale Road
Mrs. Sybil Green, 6 Carson Avenue
Mrs. D. Greene, 54 Golf Avenue
Mrs. B. Greening, 47 Freshwater Road
Mrs. Mabel Gregory, 12 Pearce Avenue
Mrs. William Gregory, 21 Pearce Avenue
Mrs. E. Guest, 351 South Side Road
Mrs. Fred Guest, 377 South Side Road
Mrs. Annie Gulliford, 320 LeMarchant Road
Mrs. H. W. Gulliford, 320 LeMarchant Road
Mrs. S. Guy, 5 Mount Royal Avenue
Mrs. Ruth Guzzwell, 18 Beaumont Street

Mrs. Harold Haas, 59-A LeMarchant Road
Mrs. G. E. Hadath, Bldg., 4, Kenna's Hill
Mrs. W. Hale, 187 Freshwater Road
Miss G. Haley, 73 Calvert Avenue
Miss Irene Halfyard, 7-A Robinson's Hill
Mrs. Jennie Halfyard, 20 Prescott Street
Miss Jessie Halfyard, 29 Henry Street
Mrs. Charles Hall, 164 Pennywell Road
Mrs. F. R. Hallett, 32 Cooke Street
Mrs. Mary Harley, 16 Gower Street
Mrs. A. C. Hamlyn, 28 Kitchener Avenue
Mrs. E. Hamlyn, 5 Smith Avenue
Mrs. J. Hamlyn, 238 Hamilton Avenue
Mrs. Hamlyn (Muriel), Site 11, Topsail Road

Mrs. Ralph Hamlyn, Thorburn Road
Mrs. Eric Hammond, 43 Portugal Cove Road
Mrs. Reginald C. Hammond, Box 481
Mrs. J. Hancock, 248 Pennywell Road
Mrs. M. Handrigan, 23 Coronation Street
Mrs. Janet Hanel, 9-A Kitchener Avenue
Mrs. Elizabeth Hannaford, 4 Topsail Road
Mrs. E. Hannon, Torbay Road
Mrs. Theresa Hannon, Torbay Road
Mrs. Mildred Hapgood, Newton Road Ext.
Mrs. Thomas Hapgood, Newton Road Ext.
Mrs. James F. Hardy, 306 Hamilton Avenue
Mrs. John Harnett, Empire Avenue West
Mrs. Nellie Harnett, 55 Pine Bud Avenue
Mrs. Albert Harris, 46 Charlton Street
Mrs. J. W. Hartshorn, 11 Atlantic Avenue
Mrs. Frank Harvey, 139 South Side
Mrs. J. H. Harvey, 113 Freshwater Road
Mrs. L. Hawe, Mason Road
Mrs. H. Hawkins, 52 Mullock Street
Mrs. W. Hawkins, Box H 125
Mrs. L Hayden, 6 Keat Place
Mrs. Margaret Hayes, 65 Allandale Road
Mrs. Pauline Hayes, New Pennywell Road
Mrs. William Hayes, 26 Buchanan Street
Miss Jessie Haynes, 109 Bonaventure Ave.
Mrs. Harvey Head, 90 Carter's Hill
Mrs. Catherine Heale, 7 Bond Street
Mrs. Alex Healey, 332 Freshwater Road
Mrs. Mary Healey, 45 Waterford Bridge Rd
Mrs. R. Healey, 5 Knight Street
Mrs. J. F. Hearn, 83 Pennywell Road
Miss Elsie Heater, 53 Brazil Street
Mrs. J. Heffernan, 6 Brine Street
Mrs. D. Helford, 24 Field Street
Mrs. Claire Hennebury, 101 King's Road
Mrs. James Hennessey, 23 Hoyles Avenue
Mrs. Joan Herder, 8 King's Bridge Road
Mrs. Annie Hickey, Nagle's Hill
Mrs. Laura Hickey, Blackhead Road
Mrs. John Hickey, Box E5048
Mrs. Mildred Hill, 75 Golf Avenue
Mrs. W. Hillyard, 162 Empire Avenue
Mrs. William Hillier, 11 Blackmarsh Road
Mrs. Brian Hiscock, 2 South Side Road East
Miss Daphne Hiscock, 2 Brazil Square
Mrs. E. G. Hiscock, 2 Brazil Square
Miss F. Hiscock, 3 Park Place
Mrs. Geraldine Hiscock, 301 Elizabeth Ave.
Mrs. Lester Hiscock, 2 South Side Road
Mrs. Frank Hodder, 45 Long Pond Road
Mrs. L. Hodder, 25 Cochrane Street
Mrs. Ray Hodder, 289 Pennywell Road
Mrs. Stephen Hodder, 1 Charlton Street
Mrs. James Hogan, Mundy Pond Road
Mrs. John T. Holden, Topsail Road, Site 4
Mrs. Peter Holden, Topsail Road, Site 4
Mrs. F. R. Hollett, 32 Cook Street
Mrs. George W. Hollett, c/o Mundy Pd. P.O.
Mrs. G. Hollett, Pennywell Road
Mrs. Robert Homles, 147 Empire Avenue
Mrs. Catherine Hommersen, 35 Cornwal Cr.
Mrs. M. Horan, South Side Road West
Mrs. Charles Horwood, 134 Campbell Ave.
Mrs. E. S. Hoskins, Site 1, Sub Sta., Box 30
Mrs. Robert Hounsell, 107 Strawberry M. Rd.
Mrs. Ronald House, Empire Avenue West
Mrs. Esther Howell, 157 Pleasant Street
Miss C. E. Howell, 15 Scott Street
Mrs. John G. Howell, 4 Summer Street
Mrs. R. Howell, 246 Pennywell Road
Mrs. Inez Hudson, 157 Pleasant Street
Mrs. L. Hudson, Box E5327
Mrs. Marguerite Hudson, 9 Albany Street
Mrs. Reg Hudson, 242 Freshwater Road
Mrs. V. Hudson, Box 848
Mrs. N. P. Hunt, 85 Bond Street
Mrs. A. J. Hurley, 19 Cochrane Street
Miss Judith Hussey, 9 Cornwall Crescent
Mrs. J. S. Hutchings, 14 Scott Street
Mrs. Marie Hutchings, 29 Downing Street
Mrs. Eleanor Hutton, 222 Water Street
Mrs. Ethel Hynes, 24 Goodridge Street
Mrs. Norah Hynes, Tessier's Lane
Mrs. William Hynes, 116 Forest Road

Mrs. B. Ivany, 17 Smith Avenue
Mrs. J. Ivany, 7 Downing Street
Mrs. Stirling Ivany, 243 Hamilton Avenue

Mrs. Elizabeth Jackman, 773 Water Street W.
Mrs. Nellie Jackman, 5 Brien Street
Mrs. Thomas James, Portugal Cove Road

Mrs. Alice Jamieson, 25 Cook Street
Mrs. Phyllis Jamieson, 25 Cook Street
Mrs. A. J. Janes, 10-A Linden Place
Mrs. Blanche Janes, 100 Prowse Avenue
Mrs. C. Janes, 206 Hamilton Avenue
Mrs. Frances Janes, 4 Hamilton Avenue
Mrs. Mary Jardine, 59 Long's Hill
Mrs. Audrey Jenkins, 52 Livingstone Street
Mrs. J. Jenkins, 20 Suez Street
Mrs. G. Jennings, 27 Prospect Street
Mrs. J. E. Jones, 63 Mayor Avenue
Mrs. Ena Johnson, 30 Pearce Avenue
Mrs. J. Johnson, 2-A Allandale Road
Mrs. Joan Johnson, 83 Pennywell Road
Mrs. Ruby Jolliffe, 12 Byron Street

Mrs. R. Kaltenbach, 33 Graves Street
Mrs. Mary Kane, 251 LeMarchant Road
Mrs. Frank Kean, 32 Summer Street
Mrs. Roland Kean, 11 Munroe Street
Mrs. Robert Keating, 5 Empire Avenue
Mrs. E. Kelland, 73 Pleasant Street
Mrs. Charles Kelloway, 60 Gower Street
Mrs. Herbert Kennedy, 320 Duckworth Street
Mrs. Mary Kennedy, 4 Murray Street
Mrs. Shirley Kelly, Torbay Road
Mrs. J. Keough, 11 Howlett Avenue
Mrs. Gertrude Kerwin, 20 Waldegrave St.
Mrs. Anne Kielly, 175 Gower Street
Mrs. Gladys Kielly 93 Brazil Street
Mrs. A. King, 51 Monkstown Road
Mrs. B. King, 1 Carson Avenue
Mrs. Eleanor King, 47 Pine Bud Avenue
Mrs. Elsie King, 27 Laughlin Crescent
Mrs. Fred King, 6 South Side Road
Mrs. George King, 27-A Cairo Street
Mrs. Helen King, 131 Prowse Avenue
Mrs. J. King, 13 Carson Avenue
Mrs. Jean L. King, 1 Carson Avenue
Mrs. S. King, 28 Freshwater Road
Mrs Sandy King, 28 Freshwater Road
Mrs. Andrew Kirkland, 76 Leslie Street
Mrs. George Kirkland, Kenmount Road
Mrs. Blanche Knee, 2 Bulger's Lane
Mrs. G. Knight, 18 Blackler Avenue

Mrs. J. F. Lacey, 163 LeMarchant Road
Mrs. H. Lane, 302 Pennywell Road
Mrs. Jean Lane, 35 Pleasant Street
Mrs. Leo G. Lannon, c/o West End P.O.
Mrs. Francis Lapie, 100 Prowse Avenue
Mrs. L. R. Larkin, 155 LeMarchant Road
Mrs. T. Laurentius, Box E5222
Mrs. Marie Lawes, 53 Cabot Street
Mrs. Harry Lawrence, 50 Flower Hill
Mrs. Miriam Lawrence, 50 Flower Hill
Mrs. Layman, 18 Carson Avenue
Miss Grace Layman, 18 Carson Avenue
Mrs. R. Leardon, 23 Summer Street
Mrs. Marilyn Leckie, General Hospital
Mrs. L. E. LeDrew, c/o R.C.M.P., Kenna's Hill
Mrs. Lucy M. Lee, 39 Monroe Steet
Mrs. Linda Legge, 11 Mayor Avenue
Mrs. T. Legge, 11 Mayor Avenue
Mrs. Edwin M. Legrow, 121 Campbell Ave.
Mrs. Herbert LeGrow, 167 Topsail Road
Mrs. Kenneth LeGrow, St. John's East
Mrs. Robert LeMessurier, 2 Carson Avenue
Mrs. Mary F. Leonard, 18 Queen Street
Mrs. Ada Leseman, 15 Kitchener Avenue
Mrs. H. Lipson, 10 Reeves Place
Mrs. Locke, 5 Froude Avenue
Mrs. Eric Lockyer, 10 Kitchener Avenue
Mrs. Gordon Long, 62 Hoyles Avenue
Mrs. M. Long, 11 Laughlin Crescent
Mrs. Herbert Long, 11 Gosling Street
Mrs. C. Loveless, 63 Brazil Street
Mrs. Sarah Ludlow, 78 Pennywell Road
Mrs. E. Luff, 67 Popular Avenue
Mrs. H. R. Luscombe, 344 Hamilton Avenue
Mrs. W. Lush, 324 Freshwater Road
Mrs. Robert Lynch, Box 183
Mrs. Allan Lyver, 123 Forest Road

Mrs. K. W. Mackey, 11 Kitchener Avenue
Mrs. D. W. MacPherson, 9 Allandale, Apts.
Mrs. Hartley MacWilliam, 36 Whiteway St.
Mrs. William Maddicks, 18 Prospect Street
Mrs. Cyril Maher, 39 New Cove Road
Mrs. Frank Maher, 3 Larch Place
Mrs. Olive Maher, 19 Goodridge Street
Mrs. John Mahoney, 263 Elizabeth Avenue
Mrs. T. G. Mahoney, 176 Freshwater Road

Mrs. R. Maidment, 320 Freshwater Road
Mrs. Estelle Malone, 38 Adelaide Street
Mrs. Blanche March, 109 Patrick Street
Mrs. Weston March, 109 Patrick Street
Mrs. Derek Marshall, 8 Linden Place
Mrs. G. F. Marshall, Portugal Cove Road
Mrs. Lloyd Marshall, 293 Pennywell Road
Mrs. Muriel Marshall, 293 Pennywell Road
Mrs. Clarence Martin, 103 Newton Road
Mrs. G. F. Martin, Sub Service, Box 41, Site 7
Mrs. Gerald Martin, Site 7 Sub Service
Mrs. Gordon Martin, King's Bridge Court
Mrs. G. R. Martin, 133 Newtown Road
Mrs. Mary Martin, 18 Holloway Street
Mrs. Mary Martin, 36 Fleming Street
Mrs. Nina Martin, Thornburn Road
Mrs. Amy E. Matthews, 127 St. Clare Avenue
Mrs. Gladys Matthews, 25 Shea Street
Mrs. Phyllis Matthews, 104 LeMarchant Road
Miss B. Maunder, 16 Forest Avenue
Mrs. B. Mawe, Portugal Cove Road
Mrs. John May, 228 Freshwater Road
Mrs. John McDonald, 218 LeMarchant Road
Mrs. B. McGrath, 40 Long Pond Road
Mrs. G. T. McGrath, 14 Mount Royal Avenue
Mrs. T. McGrath, 210 LeMarchant Road
Mrs. L. McIntyre, 14 Dartmouth Place
Mrs. Anne McKay, 131 South Side Road
Mrs. H. McLean, 47 Whiteway Street
Mrs. Austin McNamara, 33 York Street
Mrs. Frank McNamara, 127 LeMarchant Road
Mrs. Susan Mealey, 18 King's Bridge Road
Mrs. Colin Mercer, 34 Mullock Street
Mrs. Edith Mercer, Thorburn Road
Mrs. Edmond Mercer, 98 Newtown Road
Mrs. George Mercer, 46 St. Clare Avenue
Mrs. Herbert Mercer, 20 Richmond Street
Mrs. Lewis Mercer, 2 Elm Place
Mrs. Nada M. Mercer, 36 Amherst Heights
Mrs. Ruth Mercer, 63 Bennett Avenue
Mrs. R. C. B. Mercer, 7 Forest Avenue
Mrs. Jean Merrills, 53 Prince of Wales Street
Mrs. Douglas Mieley, 340 Pennywell Road
Mrs. I. Miller, 128 Pleasant Street
Mrs. Phyllis Miller, 120 Bonaventure Ave.
Mrs. Vincent Miller, South Side Road W.
Mrs. C. Mills, 76 Forest Road
Mrs. Ada Mitchell, 8 Raleigh Street
Mrs. Myrtle Mitchell, 42 St. Clare Avenue
Mrs. Ann Molloy, 57 Long's Hill
Mrs. B. Mongold, 53-B Stamp Lane
Mrs. C. Moore, 19 York Street
Mrs. Fred Moore, 36 Shaw Street
Mrs. Samuel Moore 5 Hayward Avenue
Mrs. B. Moores, 254 Freshwater Road
Mrs. Edna Moores, 103 Merrymeeting Road
Mrs. F. Moores, 101 Bonaventure Avenue
Mrs. Robert Moores, 13 Cashin Avenue
Mrs. Roy Moores, 18 Byron Street
Mrs. H. Mootrey, 160 St. Clare Avenue
Mrs. Robert Morey, 110 Campbell Avenue
Mrs. A. Morgan, 34-A Bannerman Street
Mrs. V. F. Morgan, 25 Newtown Road
Mrs. Andrew Moriarity, Topsail Road
Mrs. Edgar Morris, 8 Boulevard
Mrs. Gordon Morris, 17 Calver Street
Miss Mary Morris, 9 Military Road
Mrs. R. Morris, Canada Experimental Farm
Mrs. Bertha Morrissey, Portugal Cove Road
Mrs. Edith Moulton, 126 Quidi Vidi Road
Mrs. H. Moulton, 104 Queen's Road
Mrs. Maud Moulton, 16 Cornwall Heights
Mrs. James Mugford, 10 Franklyn Avenue
Mrs. May Mugford, 15 McDougall Street
Mrs. Madeline Murie, Fir Dale Drive
Mrs. Frank Mullett, 242-A Pennywell Road
Mrs. Blanche Murphy, 68 Carter's Hill
Mrs. Helen Murphy, 18 Holloway Street
Miss J. Murphy, 163 Waterford Bridge Road
Mrs. Jessie Murphy, 13 Adelaide Street
Mrs. L. Murphy, 26 William Street
Mrs. Leo Murphy, Portugal Cove Road
Mrs. Mary Murphy, 20 Warbury Street
Mrs. N. W. Murphy, 8 Bond Street
Mrs. Jean Murray, 31 York Street

Mrs. William Neal, 99 Rennies Mill Road
Mrs. William Neal, 100 Waterford Bridge Rd.
Mrs. Anne Neary, Portugal Cove Road
Mrs. H. Neil, 50 Hoyles Avenue
Mrs. Max Nelder, 6 Fraude Avenue
Mrs. Caroline A. Nelson, 31 Shaw Street
Mrs. Jennie C. Netten, 47 Bond Street

Mrs. G. Newbury, 125 Cabot Street
Mrs. William Newbury, 7-A Robinson's Hill
Mrs. Nancy Newport, 17 Long Street
Mrs. Douglas Noel, 2 Morris Avenue
Mrs. Eric Noel, Penetanguishene
Mrs. Marion Noftall, 8 Cathedral Street
Mrs. Alice Norman, Site 1, Cowan Avenue
Mrs. Frank Norman, 93 Campbell Avenue
Mrs. Pearl Norris, 132 Elizabeth Avenue
Miss Marjorie Northcott, 22 Dick's Square
Mrs. Cynthia Noseworthy, 43 Craigmillar
Mrs. D. G. Noseworthy, 79 Monroe Street
Mrs. Helen Noseworthy, 9 O'Neil Avenue
Mrs. Joyce Noseworthy, 41 Cornwall Cr.
Mrs. J. R. Noseworthy, 218 Freshwater Rd.
Mrs. William Noseworthy, 9 O'Neil Ave.
Mrs. William Noseworthy, 32 Gear Street

Mrs. Harry Oake, 47 William Street
Mrs. J. T. O'Brien, 118 Military Road
Mrs. M. O'Brien, 21 Beaumont Street
Mrs. M. O'Keefe, 71 King's Road
Mrs. Bride O'Leary, 23 Central Street
Mrs. Mary O'Leary, 56 Cashin Avenue
Mrs. Muriel O'Leary, 49 Beaumont Street
Miss Muriel O'Leary, 53 Cabot Street
Mrs. Leo A. O'Mara, 62 Pine Bud Avenue
Mrs. William O'Neill, 34 Scott Street
Mrs. M. O'Reilly, 94 Casey Street
Mrs. C. O'Rourke ,23 Osbourne Street
Mrs. Gertie O'Rourke, 61 Cabot Street
Mrs. Kathryn M. O'Rourke, 23 Osbourne St.
Mrs. Augusta Osmond, 76 Topsail Road
Mrs. C. Osmond, 38 Blackmarsh Road
Mrs. Frank Osmond, 59 Golf Avenue
Mrs. George Osmond, 136 Empire Avenue
Mrs. J. Osmond, 88 Blackmarsh Road
Mrs. Peter Osmond, 2 British Square
Mrs. Rose Oxmond, 134 Craigmillar Ave.
Mrs. Vivian Ozark, Box 399 G.P.O.

Miss Linda Packer, 10 Strawberry Marsh Rd.
Miss Rhonda Packer, 10 Strawberry Marsh Rd.
Mrs. H. Parmiter, 367 South Side Road
Mrs. Albert Parsons, Topsail Road
Mrs. E. Parsons, 36 Shaw Street
Miss Janet Parsons, 6 Blatch Avenue
Mrs. Jean Parsons, 202 LeMarchant Road
Mrs. Kathleen Parsons, 3 Devon Row
Mrs. M. Parsons, 36 Victoria Street
Mrs. M. Parsons, South Side Road West
Mrs. M. Parsons, 47 Bennett Avenue
Mrs. Myra Parsons, 29 Tunis Court
Mrs. Sadie Parsons, Donovan's, Topsail Rd.
Mrs. T. Parsons, 118 Topsail Road
Mrs. F. Palmer, 7 Popular Avenue
Mrs. E. Patey, 125 Pennywell Road
Mrs. Leander Peach, Box E5305
Mrs. Marie Pear, 15 Monroe Street
Mrs. R. Pear, 151 Pleasant Street
Mrs. Charles Pearce, 204 Hamilton Ave.
Mrs. C. Pearcey, 204 Hamilton Avenue
Mrs. Brendan Peddigrew, Mount Scio Road
Mrs. Muriel Peddle, 11 Vaughan Place
Mrs. Max Pellett, 94 Prowse Avenue
Mrs. Joseph Pelley, 152 St. Clare Avenue
Miss S. Pelley (no address)
Mrs. Timothy Penney, 22 Mayor Avenue
Mrs. A. G. Percy, 95 Portugal Cove Road
Mrs. Arthur Perry, 16 Byron Street
Mrs. James Perry, 53 Cabot Street
Mrs. T. R. Perry, Kenmount Road, Box 994
Mrs. Picketts, 42-A McFarlane Street
Mrs. E. R. Piercey, 158 Pleasant Street
Mrs. Victor Piercey, 33 St. Clare Avenue
Mrs. G. Pike, 21 McDougal Street
Mrs. George Pike, 723 Water Street
Mrs. Juanita Pike, 412 Hamilton Avenue
Mrs. Vera Pike, 47 Cornwall Avenue
Mrs. L. R. Pilgrim, Buckmaster's Field
Miss Dorothy A. Pinsent, 31 Long Pond Road
Mrs. J. E. Pinsent, 31 Long Pond Road
Mrs. Charles Pitcher, 598 South Side Road W
Mrs. G. Pitcher, 2 Gill Place
Mrs. R. Pitcher, 118 Topsail Road
Mrs. K. Pittman, 54 Alexander Street
Mrs. Lillian Pittman, 413 Elizabeth Avenue
Mrs. Ralph Ploughman, Empire Avenue West
Mrs. D. B. Powell, 91 Gower Street
Mrs. Edward Power, 240 Duckworth Street
Mrs. Edith Power, Portugal Cove Road
Mrs. Leo Power, Fort Amherst Lighthouse
Mrs. M. Power, 8 Cabot Street

Mrs. Rita Power, 5 Salisbury Street
Mrs. Marie Power, Kenna's Hill
Mrs. Tom Power, 326 Freshwater Road
Mrs. Isabel Pretty, 3 Monroe Street
Mrs. F. Preston, 46 Barnes Road
Mrs. Pridham, 134 Cashin Avenue
Mrs. Alice Prim, 34 Shaw Street
Mrs. Matthew Prim, 34 Shaw Street
Mrs. J. Probert, 75 Gower Street
Mrs. H. G. Puddester, Allandale Apts.
Mrs. J. M. Puddester, 11 Scott Street
Mrs. Muriel Purchase, 69 Monkstown Road
Mrs. Eleanor Pynn, 664 South Side Road
Mrs. Mary Punn, 615 South Side Road W.

Mrs. Margaret Quinlan, 41 Freshwater Rd.

Mrs. Gertie Regular, 54 Hayward Avenue
Mrs. M. Rae, Box E5302
Mrs. John V. Ralph, 30 Linden Court
Mrs. R. Randall, 31 Boncloddy Street
Mrs. V. L. Randell, 124 Freshwater Road
Mrs. Bride Reddy, 11 Holloway Street
Mrs. F. Reddy, 11 Holloway Street
Mrs. H. Redmond, 124 Military Road
Mrs. M. Redmond, 7 Angel Place
Mrs. Peter Redmond, 12 Macklin Place
Mrs. Muriel Rees, 134 Circular Road
Mrs. Maude Regular, 80 Circular Road
Mrs. B. Reid, 111 St. Clare Avenue
Mrs. C. Reid, 15 Long's Hill
Mrs. F. W. Reid, 11 Scott Street
Mrs. G. Reid, 11 Scott Street
Mrs. P. B. Rendell, 3 Riverview Avenue
Mrs. Kathleen Richards, 15 Mayor Avenue
Mrs. Boyd Riche, 2 O'Neill Avenue
Mrs. Robert Riche, Outer Battery
Miss Lillian Rideout, 19 Circular Road
Miss Helen Roache, St. John's East, Torbay
Mrs. Bernice Robbins, 150 Empire Avenue
Mrs. Eric Roberts, 102 Cabot Street
Mrs. Geraldine Roberts, 13 Darling Street
Mrs. H. D. Roberts, 112 Military Road
Mrs. J. Roberts, 70 Edinburgh Street
Miss Rita Roberts, 6 Lake View Avenue
Mrs. Stephen Roberts, 59 Flower Hill
Mrs. W. Roberts, 11 Calver Street
Mrs. C. Robinson, Jr., Box 96, G.P.O.
Mrs. W. Robson, 20 Suez Street
Mrs. Dianne Rogers, Kenmount Road
Mrs. H. Rogers, Outer Battery
Mrs. Irene Rolls, 24 Atlantic Avenue
Mrs. C. A. Ronayne, 39 Victoria Street
Mrs. Cecil Rose, Pouch Cove, St. John's East
Mrs. Dorothy Rose, 13 Cashin Avenue
Mrs. Laura Rose, 405 South Side Road
Mrs. J. A. Rowe, 6 Atlantic Avenue
Miss Joyce Rowe, 1 Charlton Street
Mrs. Frances Rowsell, 258 Empire Avenue
Mrs. Ann Rumsey, 108 Lime Street
Mrs. Daphne Russell, 26-A Brazil Street
Mrs. Dora Russell, 1 Stoneyhouse Street
Mrs. May Russell, 70 Cashin Avenue Ext.
Mrs. L. Ryan, 21 Boncloddy Street
Mrs. Mary Ryan, Box 29, Site 7, Sub Station
Mrs. Mary Ryan, Logy Bay Road
Mrs Mary B. Ryan, 51 Harvey Road
Mrs. William Ryan, St. John's West, Goulds

Mrs. Chesley Samson, 35 Cashin Avenue
Mrs. Merle Sandland, 119 Cabot Street
Mrs. John Saturley, 36 Leslie Street
Mrs. E. R. Scammell, 135 Elizabeth Avenue
Mrs. Mary Scammell, 43 Cochrane Street
Mrs. Gordon Scaplen, 33 Freshwater Road
Mrs. Sceviour, 111 Campbell Avenue
Mrs. I. Scott, 22 Queen's Road
Mrs. E. Seaward, 117 Springdale Street
Mrs. Reginald Sellars, 13 Barter's Hill
Mrs. Ina Sheaves, 18 Waldegrave Street
Mrs. C. Sheppard, 19 Circular Road
Mrs. Eugene Sheppard, Logy Bay Road
Mrs. J. Sheppard, 75 Berteau Avenue
Mrs. Lilla Sheppard, 75 Berteau Avenue
Mrs. Margaret Sheppard, 132 Circular Rd.
Mrs. Susan Sheppard, 105 Quidi Vidi Road
Mrs. Olive Shields, 308 Pennywell Road
Mrs. M. E. Shiers, 143 Pleasant Street
Mrs. J. Short, 43 Pine Bud Avenue
Mrs. John Short, South Side West
Mrs. Vida Shuglo, 37 Topsail Road
Mrs. Doris Simmons, 20 Freshwater Road
Mrs. M. Simms, 132 Craigmillar Avenue

Mrs. Irene Simon, 30 Linden Court
Mrs. E. P. Simoneaux, 32 Sudbury Street
Miss Andrea Siennott, 117 Freshwater Road
Miss Angela Sirnott, 9-A Freshwater Road
Miss Annie Skinner, 10 Gill Place
Mrs. H. C. Small, 4 Maple Street
Mrs. Mary Smallwood, Box H238
Mrs. Fred W. Smeaton, 29 Sudbury Street
Mrs. Betty Smith, 16 Erie Street
Mrs. Cecil Smith, 35 Bennett Avenue
Mrs. Chesley M. Smith, 41 Spencer Street
Mrs. D. Smith, 20 Shea Street
Mrs. Lionel Smith, 68 Merrymeeting Road
Mrs. Mona Smith, 35 Bennett Avenue
Mrs. Philip Smith, 53 Flower Hill
Mrs. R. J. Smith, 62 New Portugal Cove Road
Mrs. Sam Smith, 27 Prospect Street
Mrs. W. Smith, 7 Masonic Terrace
Mrs. R. Smyth, 2 Stoneyhouse Street
Mrs. Robert Smoat, 212 Pennywell Road
Miss Edith Snelgrove, 33 Stephen Street
Miss Barbara Snow, Torbay Road
Mrs. Douglas Snow, 25 Cornwall Crescent
Mrs. Hugh Snow, 25 Howley Avenue
Miss Margaret Snow, 26 Prescott Street
Mrs. Nornam Snow, 135 Cabot Street
Mrs. T. Snow, 252 Duckworth Street
Mrs. Ida Snook, 42 Cookstown Road
Mrs. Marie Somerton, 2 Cook's Hill
Mrs. Roland Sooley, Murphy's Avenue
Mrs. S. Sooley, 55 Stamp Lane
Mrs. F. Soper, 264 Hamilton Avenue
Mrs. Thomas Soper, Box 74
Mrs. Florence Sparkes, 7 Albany Street
Mrs. H. Sparkes, 7 Albany Street
Mrs. R. F. Sparkes, 10 Prince William Place
Mrs. Robert Sparrow, 123 Prowse Avenue
Mrs. Hilda Spracklin, 177 Topsail Road
Mrs. Mildred Spurrell, Thorburn Road P.O.
Mrs. E. Squires. c/o Mundy Pond P.O.
Mrs. Geraldine Squires, 67 Sprindgale Street
Mrs. Herbert Squires, 34 Fleming Street
Mrs. James E. Squires, Box H114
Mrs. Mona Squires, Box H114
Mrs. Mary Stamp, St. Ann's Park
Mrs. William Stanford, Top Battery Road
Mrs. B. M. Stanley, c/o West End P.O.
Mrs. Mary St. Croix, 23 Central Street
Mrs. Douglas Steele, 71 Calver Avenue
Mrs. Cecelia Stennett, 11 Parade Street
Mrs. E. Stevens, 43 Leslie Street
Mrs. Fred Stevens, 10 O'Neil Avenue
Mrs. James Stevens, 45 Pine Bud Avenue
Mrs. B. Stirling, 15 Monroe Street
Mrs. Florence Stirling, 9 Rankin Street
Mrs. Stockley, 17 Goodridge Street
Mrs. Joan Strang, 19 Newtown Road
Mrs. H Sullivan, 37 Cochrane Street
Mrs. Mary Sullivan, 29 Graves Street
Mrs. Robert Sutherby, 100 Pleasant Street
Mrs. Irene Sutton, 10 Blackler Avenue
Mrs. Jessie Sweetapple, 53 Hoyles Avenue
Mrs. John Symonds, 308 Hamilton Avenue

Mrs. F. Tavenor, 18 Raleigh Street
Mrs. Anne Taylor, 93 Campbell Avenue
Mrs. Frank Taylor, 21 Albany Place
Mrs. Fred Taylor, 212 Pennywell Road
Mrs. Fred Taylor, 57-B Carpasian Road
Mrs. G. F. Taylor, 28 Raleigh Street
Mrs. G. M. Taylor, 1 Clouston Avenue
Mrs. Phyllis Taylor, 224 Freshwater Road
Mrs. M. Tessier, 19 Power Street
Mrs. B. Thistle, 3 Chapel Street
Mrs. David Thistle, 12 Scott Street
Mrs. H. Thistle, 313 Blackmarsh Road
Mrs. A. Thomas, 28 Suez Street
Mrs. Bessie Thomas, 64 Bonaventure Ave.
Mrs. Rose Thomas, 10 Barnes Road
Mrs. Sara Thomas, Box E5351
Mrs. A. G. Thorburn, Site 4, Topsail Road
Mrs. Hugh Thorne, Main Road, Torbay
Mrs. John Thorne, 6 Forest Avenue
Mrs. C. Tibbs, 308 Freshwater Road
Mrs. E. L. Tilley, 30 Morris Avenue
Mrs. Hannah Tilley, 40 Golf Avenue
Mrs. John Tilley, 98 Prowse Avenue
Mrs. John Tilley, 158 Forest Road
Mrs. Joseph Tilley, 15 Boncloddy Street
Mrs. S. D. Tilley, 18 Pierce Avenue
Mrs. Eric Tippett, 78 Cochrane Street
Mrs. W. B. Titford, 84 Barnes Road
Mrs. B. Tomlinson, Site 9, Box 15, Sub Service

Mrs. Max Toope, 84 Carter's Hill
Mrs. Jane Torraville, 47 William Street
Mrs. Edith Tricco, Donovan's, Topsail Road
Mrs. J. K. Trickett, 111 Allandale Road
Mrs. Ruth Trickett, 111 Allandale Toad
Mrs. Chesley Tucker, Thorburn Road
Mrs. Elsie Tucker, 114 Prowse Avenue
Mrs. Hubert Tucker, 11 Calver Avenue
Mrs. Mary Tucker, 36 Mayor Avenue
Mrs. Reg Tucker, 51 Golf Avenue
Mrs. Roy Tucker, Blackmarsh Road
Mrs. Mary Tulk, 202 LeMarchant Road
Mrs. E. Tuttle, 28 Livingstone Street

Mrs. Florence Udle, 97 Quidi Vidi Road
Mrs. Ann Underhay, 572 South Side Road
Mrs. D. Underhay, Site 11, Topsail Road
Mrs. Jean Underhay, Site 11, Topsail Road

Mrs. George Vaughan, 25 First Avenue
Mrs. B. Verbree, Box E5325
Mrs. Beatrice Vey, 49 Whiteway Street
Mrs. F. G. Vivian, Bonaventure Avenue
Mrs. F. G. Vivian, 3 Merrymeeting Road
Mrs. Roy Vivian, 97 Campbell Avenue
Mrs. Victoria Vokey, 38 Sulva Street
Mrs. M. Voorhoeve, 75 Portugal Cove Road

Mrs. Louise Wakelin, 56 Long Pond Road
Mrs. John F. Wall, Torbay Road,
Mrs. Alice Walsh, 103 Pennywell Road
Mrs. D. Walsh, 26 Cook Street
Mrs. I. Walsh, 27 Queens Road
Mrs. Gertrude Walsh, 238 Blackmarsh Road
Mrs. Gregory Walsh, 238 Blackmarsh Road
Mrs. Mercedes Walsh, 230 Hamilton Avenue
Mrs. V. S. Walsh, Bannerman Road
Mrs. Rosalind Walsh, 56 Pennywell Road
Mrs .Gilbert Walters, 89 Grenfell Avenue
Mrs. W. Warford, 137 Empire Avenue
Mrs. Jennie Warren, 12 Cashin Avenue
Mrs. Alice Way, 7 Fitzpatrick Avenue
Mrs. Arthur Way, 46 St. Clare Avenue
Mrs. Eugene Way, 199 LeMarchant Road
Mrs. Mary Way, 81 Golf Avenue
Mrs. Thomas J. Weeks, Pepperell A.F.B.
Mrs. Augusta Wellon, 3 Carson Avenue
Mrs. Isabel Wellon, 3 Carson Avenue
Mrs. Jeanette Wells, 100 Circular Road
Mrs. Mabel Wells, 9 Mayor Avenue
Mrs. Ray Wells, 100 Circular Road
Mrs. M. Westcott, 41 Alexander Street
Miss Margaret Westcott, 289 Pennywell Rd.
Mrs. M. Whalen, 13 Westmount Avenue
Mrs. Mary Whalen, 112 Craigmillar Avenue
Mrs. Agnes Wheeler, 30 Forest Road
Miss M. Wheeler, 19 Circular Road
Mrs. John Whelan, 36 Spencer Street
Mrs. Stella Whelan, 40 Bonaventure Avenue
Mrs. W. B. Whelan, Cornwall Avenue
Mrs. Annie Whiffen, 10 Avalon Street
Mrs. Sandra White, 84 Bonaventure Ave.
Mrs. W. White, 94 LeMarchant Road
Miss Alma Whiteaway, 339 Hamilton Ave.
Miss I. Whiteaway, 13 Dunford Street
Miss Ina Whiteaway, 339 Hamilton Avenue
Miss L. Whiteaway, 153 LeMarchant Road
Mrs. Joan Whitten, 33 Liverpool Avenue
Mrs. R. Wicks, 17 Westmont
Mrs. A. N. Wight, 27 Power Street
Mrs. George Wight, 151 Pleasant Street
Mrs. Len Wight, 64 Blackmarsh Road
Mrs. M. Willar, 13 Smith Avenue
Mrs. F. Williams, 106 Whiteway Street
Mrs. Madeline Williams, 471 South Side Rd.
Mrs. Richard Williams, 13 Spencer Street
Mrs. Abel Windsor, 16 Clifford Street
Mrs. C. Winsor, 328 Hamilton Avenue
Miss Edna Winsor, 24 Barnes Road
Mrs. Melinda Winsor, 40 Calver Avenue
Mrs. R. Woodfine, 74 Hayward Avenue
Mrs. A. Woodland, 297 Pennywell Road
Mrs. Mary Wordron, 37 Kitchener Avenue
Mrs. Mabel Wornell, 228 LeMarchant Road
Mrs. D. E. Worsley, 6 Dartmouth Place
Mrs. W. H. Wright, 43 Cashin Avenue
Mrs. H. K. Wyatt, 154 Pennywell Road
Mrs. G. Wylie, Mount Scio Road

Mrs. George Yarn, 18 Hamel Street
Mrs. A. Yetman, 7 Beaumont Street
Mrs. Arthur Young, East End P.O.
Mrs. Jim Young, 195 Gower Street

Mrs. John Young, 195 Gower Street
Mrs. W. R. Young, 119 Bond Street
Mrs. G. Youden, 29-A Rankin Street

ST. JONES WITHIN T.B.
Mrs. Isaac Holloway

ST. JOSEPH'S S.M.B.
Mrs. Charles Furey
Mrs. Kathleen Ryan

ST. JOSEPH'S COVE Bay d'Espoir
Mrs. Vincent Dolliment
Mrs. Jeremiah Sutton

ST. LAURENCE P.B.
Mrs. Harry Downs
Mrs. S. Cusick
Mrs. Emma Fowler
Mrs. Alfred Giovannini
Mrs. Michael Etchegary
Mrs. Greg Handrigan
Mrs. Rupert Kelly
Mrs. E. Paul
Mrs. Kevin Pike
Mrs. Dennis Power
Mrs. T. Molloy
Mrs. L. Slaney
Mrs. Alex Tarrant
Mrs. Gus Tarrant

ST. MARY'S S.M.B.
Miss Joan Ann Dillon
Miss Mona Dillon
Mrs. Michael Dillon
Miss Sadie Dillon
Mrs. John Hogan
Mrs. Betty Lee
Mrs. Owen Lee
Mrs. Michael Power
Mrs. Anne Quinlon
Mrs. Catherine Ryan
Mrs. Patrick Vail
Mrs. Winnie Walsh
Mrs. Jerry Yetman
Mrs. Matt Yetman

ST. PHILLIP'S C.B.
Mrs. Gladys Clark
Mrs. Lillian Coswell

ST. PHILLIP'S HILL C.B.
Mrs. Jennie Tucker
Mrs. Randall Tucker

ST. SHOTT'S Trepassey
Mrs. Minnie Finlay

ST. VINCENT'S S.M.B.
Mrs. Michael Gibbons
Mrs. Paul Halleran
Mrs. James Moriarity
Mrs. Theresa Moriarity

STEPHENVILLE ST.G.B.
Mrs. Millie Dallard, Box 33
Mrs. James Gale
Mrs. Joy Hillier, Box 490
Mrs. George Ogden, Box 378
Mrs. Alice Piercey, Box 182
Mrs. Oscar Yates

STOCK COVE B.B. South
Mrs. Gregory Aylward

SUMMERFORD N.D.B.
Mrs. Donald Earle
Mrs. Hilda Earle
Mrs. Sidney Wheeler

SUMMERVILLE B.B.
Mrs. Mary Ducey
Mrs. John Frye
Mrs. Bridget Hollohan
Mrs. James Humby, Jr.
Mrs. Marine Quinton

SUNNYSIDE T.B.
Mrs. George Drover
Mrs. Llewellyn Foote
Mrs. Chesley Mercer
Mrs. Willis Penney
Mrs. Douglas Smith

SWIFT CURRENT P.B.
Mrs. Lewis Eddy
Mrs. Eugene Stacey
Mrs. George Vaters
Mrs. W. Stacey

TERRA NOVA
Mrs. M. Batten
Mrs. O. Colbourne
Mrs. Allan Freeman
Mrs. Eldon Penney
Mrs. Leonard Sweetapple

THORNLEA T.B.
Mrs. Edward Smith

TICKLE COVE B.B.
Miss M. Kelly

TILT COVE N.D.B.
Mrs. Irene Winsor

TILTING Fogo Dist
Mrs. Pierce Broaders
Mrs. James Greene

TIZZARD'S HARBOUR N.D.B.
Mrs. E. Boyd

TOPSAIL C.B.
Mrs. Douglas Allen
Mrs. Henry Baird
Mrs. J. Baird
Mrs. Arthur Barnes
Mrs. Cecil Barnes
Mrs. Charles Barnes, Sr., Spruce Hill Road
Mrs. Weston Barnes
Mrs. Gerald Boggan
Mrs. A. Boland
Mrs. Emily Carter
Mrs. Pat Geehan
Mrs. Donald Hall
Mrs. Wilbur Herrett
Mrs. Helen Kearley
Mrs. Ralph Kearley
Mrs. William Kearley
Mrs. Annie McCarthy
Mrs. Ed. Meaney
Mrs. Maud Mercer
Mrs. William Myles
Mrs. Derek Perchard
Mrs. E. G. Perchard
Mrs. Margaret Perry
Mrs. H. W. Pike
Mrs. R. N. Robertson
Miss Eleanor Somerton
Mrs. Ethel Somerton
Miss Hilda Somerton
Mrs. Austin Tipple
Mrs. Gordon Tippett
Mrs. Mabel Verge

TORBAY St. Johns East
Mrs. Ethel Byrne
Mrs. Gerald Casey
Mrs. Cyril Coady
Mrs. James Coady
Mrs. C. G. Evans
Mrs. Alfred Field
Mrs. Martha Field
Mrs. Marie Gosse
Mrs. John Gosse, Indian Meal Road
Mrs. Ann Manning, (Bauline)
Mrs. Andrew Roche
Mrs. Ronald Tapper
Miss Gertrude Thorne
Mrs. Margaret Whitty (Main Road)

TOR'S COVE Ferryland Dist.
Mrs. Michael Gatherall
Mrs. John G. Power

TOWNSIDE P.B.
Mrs. Ann Kavanagh

TRAYTOWN Alexander Bay
Mrs. Dorothy Arnold
Mrs. Beatrice Gulleksen
Mrs. Loretta Ralph

TREPASSEY S.S.
Mrs. John Curtis
Mrs. Michael Curtis
Mrs. Monica Curtis
Mrs. Ellen Finlay

Mrs. Patrick Halleran
Mrs. E. Hewett
Mrs. Margaret Molloy
Mrs. Patrick Pennell
Mrs. I. Waddleton

TRINITY B.B.
Mrs. Patrick Brown
Mrs. Frances Connolly

TRINITY T.B.
Mrs. Percy Barbour
Mrs. Mabel Coleridge
Mrs. Nellie Haytor
Mrs. James Ivany
Mrs. Edna M. Jones
Mrs. Charles Kelly
Mrs. Lucy King
Mrs. William McGrath
Mrs. Edmund Spurrell
Mrs. Arthur White, Jr.
Mrs. Arthur White, Sr.
Mrs. Nelson Warren

TRITON N.D.B.
Mrs. Robert Winsor

TROUTY T.B.
Mrs. Henry Johnson
Mrs. John Johnson
Mrs. Maxwell King
Mrs. John Miller
Mrs. Raymond Morris
Mrs. George Pearce

TURK'S COVE T.B.
Mrs. James George
Mrs. Agnes Harty

TWILLINGATE N.D.B.
Mrs. E. Crewe
Mrs. Hardy Lambert, Box 4
Miss Betty Raymond
Mrs. Irene Raymond
Mrs. Elmo Stockley
Mrs. George Strickland
Mrs. John Whitehorne (Northside)

UPPER GULLIES C.B.
Mrs. Effie Andrews
Mrs. Leslie Anthony
Mrs. Adeline Bussey
Mrs. Graham Coates
Mrs. L. Dawe
Mrs. Malcolm Dawe
Mrs. Phyllis Haines
Mrs. Marion Morgan
Mrs. Leah Rideout
Mrs. Prudence Rideout
Mrs. Mae Rowe
Mrs. Marion Warford
Miss Shirley Warford

UPPER ISLAND COVE C.B.
Mrs. Harold Barrett
Mrs. William Barrett
Mrs. John Coombs
Mrs. Maxwell Jones
Mrs. Thomas Mercer
Mrs. William Newman
Mrs. Bertha Young
Mrs. Enid Young

VALLEYFIELD B.B.
Mrs. Clifton Hoyles

VICTORIA C.B.
Mrs. H. Clarke
Mrs. Harold Cole
Mrs. Ruby Feltham
Mrs. E. Hiscock
Mrs. Thomas Penney
Mrs. Job Snow
Mrs. George Vaters
Mrs. Max Waters, Carbonear Power House

VICTORIA Gander Bay
Mrs. D. Ludlow
Mrs. O. Torraville
Mrs. Rex Torraville

VICTORIA COVE Fogo Dist.
Mrs. Phyllis Gillingham
Mrs. F. Torraville

WAREHAM B.B.
Mrs. Miriam Rogers

WESLEYVILLE B.B.
Miss Shirley Andrews
Mrs. M. Mullett
Mrs. Raymond Parsons
Mrs. George Windsor

WEST BAY CENTRE Port au Port Penin
Mrs. Gordon Hynes
Miss Helen LePrieur
Mrs. Carl McIsaac

WESTERN ARM W.B.
Mrs. Sadie Baldwin
Mrs. W. Rice

WESTERN BAY C.B.
Mrs. Florence Crummey
Mrs. Jordan Kennedy
Mrs. Myrtle Sellars, (B.D.V. Dist.)

WEYBRIDGE T.B. Random Island
Mrs. William Adey
Mrs. Mark Fifield
Mrs. James George
Miss Barbara Reid
Mrs. Charles Reid
Mrs. Dot Reid
Mrs. Ellis Reid

WHITBOURNE
Mrs. S. Cooper
Mrs. Ethel Evans
Mrs. H. Gordon
Mrs. Arthur Gosse
Mrs. Chesley Gosse
Mrs. Charles Gosse
Mrs. Cyril Gosse
Mrs. Frank Gosse,
Mrs. Harold Gosse
Mrs. Hettie Gosse
Mrs. John Gosse
Mrs. Harold Hicks
Mrs. A. M. Hutchings, Jr.
Mrs. Baxter Hutchings
Mrs. Ernest Morgan
Mrs. H. G. Noseworthy
Mrs. Gerald Parsons
Mrs. B. Stead
Mrs. Julia Wicks
Mrs. D. M. Williams
Mrs. William Williams

WHITEAWAY T.B.
Mrs. Frank Drover
Mrs. Walter Drover
Mrs. Violet Hefford
Mrs. Elsie Legge
Mrs. Wilfred Rowe

WINDSOR
Mrs. Alma Curtis, 8 First Ave.
Mrs. Ray Etheridge, Box 405
Mrs. Clyde Hunter, Main Street East
Mrs. Jarvis Hunter, Main Street
Mrs. Stanley King
Mrs. Colin Morris ,Masters Lane
Mrs. Helen Moss, 39 Coronation Ave.
Miss Mary Moss, 39 Coronation Ave.
Mrs. James O'Dee, 13th Avenue
Mrs. Hayward Pretty
Mrs. Harry Pynn, Main Street East
Mrs. Agnes Raymond
Mrs. Earl Street

WINTER BROOK B.B.
Mrs. Walter Bowen
Mrs. Ella Russell
Mrs. John Russell
Mrs. Margaret Russell

WINTERTON T.B.
Mrs. Harold Downey
Mrs. Harold Downing
Mrs. Marcus French
Miss Agnes Green
Mrs. Joshua Hiscock
Mrs. Raymond Hindy
Mrs. Valetta Piercey
Mrs. Henry Pitcher
Mrs. Bramwell Thorne
Mrs. Thomas Tucker

WITLESS BAY S.S.
Miss Betty Carey
Mrs. Jane Carey
Mrs. Mary Carter
Mrs. Edward Harrigan
Mrs. Frank Maloney
Mrs. Isabel Maloney
Mrs. Essie Morris
Mrs. Bride Murphy
Mrs. John Murphy
Mrs. Leonard Norris
Mrs. Rita Smith
Mrs. Betty Tobin
Mrs. Pierce Tobin
Mrs. Peter Vickers
Mrs. Thomas Walsh

WOOD'S ISLAND Bay of Islands
Miss Doris Duffy

WOODVILLE via Codroy
Mrs. Isaac Fiander
Miss Marie Fiander

WOODY ISLAND P.B.
Mrs. Cambridge Allen
Mrs. Ivy Jean Allen
Mrs. James Allen
Mrs. Alfred Eastman
Mrs. Alice Smith
Mrs. Bert Williams
Mrs. E. Williams

WOODY POINT Bonne Bay
Mrs. Herman Pike

WRECK COVE F.B.
Mrs. Charlie Cox

OUT OF PROVINCE—(Change of Address Notices received) (Not listed under original address)
Miss Janet Brill, New York, N.Y.
Mrs. George Broadbent, New Bedford, Mass.
Mrs. Clarence Cline, New York, N.Y.
Mrs. Charlie Collett, Summerside, P.E.I.
Mrs. William Cullen, Cape Breton, N.S.
Mrs. Penney, Montreal, P.Q.
Mrs. Maud Peterson, Westmount P.Q.
Mrs. Liselotte Keddy, New York, N.Y.
Mrs. D. A. Scofield, New York, N.Y.
Mrs. R. Smoot, Chesapeake, Ohio
Mrs. V. G. Sundstrom, Winnipeg 9, Man.
Mrs. James Vokey, Montreal, P.Q.

To all who contributed recipes without including their names, the publishers would also like to say
"THANK YOU"

The publishers wish to thank the officers and members of the Newfoundland Home Economics Association for helping to select and test the recipes in this book and for compiling the information relating to Newfoundland history and customs.

We also thank radio station CJON, St. John's, whose unstinting efforts generated widespread interest in this project and thus helped to ensure the excellent quality of the recipes received.

On behalf of the publishers,

Sally West

EDITOR

Sally West
Homemakers' Consultant
Maple Leaf Milling Company Limited, Newfoundland

Since joining the Maple Leaf Milling Company, Newfoundland as Home-makers' Consultant in August of 1957 Sally West has been winning a secure place for herself in the hearts of Newfoundland homemakers.

Each day she brings to her radio listeners in her cheery down-to-earth way helpful information, recipes, neighbourly news bulletins, household hints, anything to make the homemaker's job a bit easier, more pleasant and more satisfying. Her radio programme, "What's Cooking" has become almost part of the day's routine with thousands of Newfoundlanders.

Sally finds lots of inspiration for her talks right in her own home, where she is kept busy looking after the needs of husband Reg and daughter Betty.

If you do not hear Sally West regularly, perhaps you would like to make her acquaintance. You can hear "What's Cooking" five times a day over radio station CJON, St. John's.

INGREDIENT MEASUREMENT EQUIVALENTS
(Some measures are rounded off for ease of use)

Ingredient Equivalents
1 teaspoon = 5 ml
1 tablespoon = 15 ml
1 cup = 250 ml
½ cup = 125 ml
¼ cup = 60 ml
4 cups =1 litre
1 pound = 450 gm

Oven Temperature Equivalents	
Fahrenheit	Celsius
300°	145°
325°	160°
350°	175°
375°	190°
400°	200°
450°	230°

Pan Size Equivalents
8 inch x 8 inch = 20 cm x 20 cm
9 inch x 9 inch = 23 cm x 23 cm
9 inch x 11 inch = 23 cm x 32 cm
4 inch x 8 inch = 10 cm x 20 cm
5 inch x 9 inch = 13 cm x 23 cm